D1575243

To Jason Epstein—my gratitude for this book,
but far more in honor of the fidelity and intelligence
by which he has served so many other authors

Sight-Readings

AMERICAN FICTIONS

Elizabeth Hardwick

RANDOM HOUSE

NEW YORK

Copyright © 1998 by Elizabeth Hardwick

All rights reserved under International and Pan-American Copyright
Conventions. Published in the United States by Random
House, Inc., New York, and simultaneously in Canada by
Random House of Canada Limited, Toronto.

Owing to limitations of space, acknowledgments of permission to quote
from previously published sources will be found on page 285.

All the essays that appear in this work have been previously published.

Library of Congress Cataloging-in-Publication Data
Hardwick, Elizabeth.
Sight-readings : American fictions / Elizabeth Hardwick.
p.   cm.
ISBN 0-375-50127-4
1. American literature—History and criticism.   2. Authors,
American—Biography.   3. United States—Civilization.   I. Title.
PS121.H24   1998   810.9—dc21   97-38412

Random House website address: www.randomhouse.com
Printed in the United States of America on acid-free paper
Book design by J. K. Lambert
2 4 6 8 9 7 5 3
First Edition

Sight-Readings

Author's Note

Minor changes have been made in most of these essays and in some instances more substantial alterations have been done. The essay on Edmund Wilson is an expanded version of one published in *The New Yorker*. "The Fate of the Gifted" appeared in *The London Times Literary Supplement*. The article on Joan Givner's biography of Katherine Anne Porter appeared in *The New York Times Book Review*. "Gertrude Stein" appeared in *The Threepenny Review*. "On Washington Square" served as an introduction to the Library of America paperback edition of the novel. The review of Elizabeth Bishop's prose appeared in *The New Republic*. The article on Mary McCarthy's *Intellectual Memoirs* was written as the introduction to the edition published by Harcourt Brace Jovanovich. The remaining essays were published in *The New York Review of Books*. I am grateful to the editors for asking me to write, publishing what I wrote, and giving permission for the reprinting.

Contents

Old New York

thumb in the dike of Manhattan was one of her themes as a novelist. It might be said of this theme what Henry James wrote of Nathaniel Hawthorne: "It is only in a country where newness and change and brevity of tenure are the common substance of life, that the fact of one's ancestors having lived for a hundred and seventy years in a single spot would become an element of one's morality."

Being from New York, rather than from Salem, Massachusetts, Edith Wharton was not a Yankee and not a lingering Puritan conscience inhabited by ghosts and provincial scruples. She grew up a cosmopolitan from the first, early traveling abroad with her parents; she married after the usual biographical unsteadiness in the matter of broken engagements and again traveled abroad, then settled on Park Avenue and in Newport and, much later, built herself a grand house in Lenox, Massachusetts, kept traveling, finally sold the house, divorced her husband, Edward Wharton—"cerebrally compromised Teddy," as Henry James called him, summing up this wild manic-depressive who gave her a lot of trouble. Along the way, she had a three-year affair with the romantically overextended seducer Morton Fullerton. And then in 1913, after the divorce, she settled permanently in France. Yet there was more to it than that.

Edith Wharton was twenty-nine when her first short story was published and thirty-seven when her first collection appeared in 1899. Two years before, *The Decoration of Houses,* written with the architect Ogden Codman, had been published. Even though starting late, Edith Wharton quickly became a professional writer in the best sense of the phrase. She wrote steadily, novel after novel, made money, and spent money with a forthright and standard-bearing loyalty to those twins of domestic economy, taste and comfort.

She liked expensive motorcars and once told Henry James that the last of these had been purchased with the proceeds from *The Valley of Decision,* a two-volume mistake about eighteenth-century Italy with characters named Odo and the Duke of Monte Alloro that showed Italy can be as dangerous for certain English-language novelists as the vapors from the undrained marshes. (To the point:

Hawthorne's *The Marble Faun,* a weary and unsuitable surrender to the moist murk a gloomy eye might discover in the beautiful country. Hawthorne himself did not make the common surrender to Italy and complained of "discomfort and miseries," found the Roman winter an unadvertised blast of chills, and could not countenance nudity in sculptures.)

Henry James, looking at Mrs. Wharton's motorcar purchased by the assault on Italy, and referring to *The Wings of the Dove,* is reported to have said, "With the proceeds of my last novel, I purchased a small go-cart, or wheel-barrow, on which my guests' luggage is wheeled from the station to my house. It needs a coat of paint. With the proceeds of my next novel I shall have it painted."

There is a tradesman's shrewdness in Edith Wharton's work. She knows how to order the stock and dispose the goods in the window. She was a popular author, or, to be more just, her books were popular, not always the same thing. (Even in her day there were writers, many of them women susceptible to sentiment, who trafficked in novels in the present-day manner—more soybeans on the commodities market.) Edith Wharton is free of lush sentiments and moralizing tears. In *The House of Mirth,* her triumph, she is not always clear what the moral might be and thereby creates a stunning tragedy in which the best and the richest society of New York reveals an inner coarseness like pimps cruising in Cadillacs.

Nevertheless, she is often caught up in contrivance as a furtherance of product. And she likes the ruffled cuff and transcontinental glamour, interesting enough in itself but speeding to pointlessness. The novel is viewed as a frank transaction between elements, elements to be laid out and pasted down like tiles in a frame. A "situation" is of course the necessity of fiction. Yet what of the cracks, the anxiety we sense in greater novelists about the very intention of the careful arabesques so purposefully designed and all of a sudden baked hard as rock?

In a story by Chekhov called "Terror," a young man has been flirting with the wife of his good friend, and she has been sighing in the Russian manner for him. Somehow, he at last takes her to his room, which the husband enters to get his cap left there earlier, set up, we would say, by the dramatist's art. At the end, the young man wonders: "Why has it turned out like this and not differently? To whom and for what was it necessary that she should love me in earnest and that he should come to my room to fetch his cap? What had the cap to do with it?"

Neatness of plotting; balancing of the elements by a handy coincidence beyond necessity: That is the way it often goes with this prodigious worker, busy at the morning's pages. She tends to lay hold with some of the gregarious insistence she displayed as the sort of hostess who organizes trips after lunch. Too many caps to be retrieved at the bedside of indiscretion, too much of a gloss. It's the last slap of the polishing cloth and then forge ahead in a majorful fashion.

The Reef, for instance: The young man is hoping to marry the recently widowed woman he has long loved. She puts him off with family affairs in her mother-in-law's château in France and with problems relating to her young child and to her stepson. All are Americans, but the château somehow appears as naturally as if it were a deed to a woodlot. In a fit of chagrin, the young man has an affair in a cheap Paris railroad hotel with a penniless American girl trying her hand at this and that abroad. This manifestation of impatience over and done with, the widow and the young man recombine, so to speak. And soon the girl from the railroad hotel turns up and will become engaged to the stepson, heir to the château and all the rest. The plot is suspenseful and executed with considerable gallantry and many Jamesian pauses in articulation— questions that are not quite asked, answers that hang in the air, the cues in the matter of a dialogue to a moral dilemma. The convenience of the young girl's turning up to be promptly fallen in love with by the heir is too brilliant, too tidy.

The Mother's Recompense: A mother has abandoned her husband and daughter, and New York society has erased the blot of her existence as if she were a smudge to be washed off a window. She lives abroad rather shabbily unanchored but has for a time the pleasant anguish of an affair with a younger man, who proves to be the great love of her life. When the old members of the New York family die, the daughter brings her mother back. It's a lottery ticket for the bolter: everything forgiven, luxury, and social reestablishment. Soon, the young man drops down on the scene; the daughter falls in love and means to marry him. You turn a corner, or rather a page, and there he is, or there she is. Moments of social comedy set out as deftly as the knives and forks; dramatic encounters in the splendid old arks of the Hudson Valley or in the mansions moving upward on Fifth Avenue.

Edith Wharton is a challenging figure just now. In her finesse and talent, her glamour and worldliness, she shares in some of the renewed affection for the threatened New York City architecture of the Beaux Arts period. Even her snobbishness and spendthrift ways are not remote from the activities of the haute couture ladies that daily fill the pages of the city's newspapers. With Edith Wharton, it was always an "approach up a red carpet," as the English man of letters Percy Lubbock says in his courteous but sly memoir of their friendship. She was, in most of her writing life, not one to loiter with curiosity about the crude crunch of New York, and she cannot even be claimed as an old-stock patriot since she fled the frontier and the American presence with its "vainglory, crassness and total ignorance."

In line with the contemporary appetite for tawdry revelation, the grande dame received a boost in her literary ratings thanks to R.W.B. Lewis's biography and the publication of a very knowing fragment of pornography found among her papers. She composed, yes, a father-daughter scene, a frankly hot exercise in appreciative specification not unlike Auden's "The Platonic Blow":

Letting herself downward along the divan till her head was in a line with his middle she flung herself upon the swelling member, and began to caress it insinuatingly with her tongue. It was the first time she had ever seen it actually exposed to her eyes, and her heart swelled excitedly: to have her touch confirmed by sight enriched the sensation that was communicating itself through her ardent twisting tongue. With panting breath she wound her caress deeper and deeper into the thick firm folds, till at length the member, thrusting her lips open, held her gasping, as if at its mercy.

The House of Mirth was written while Edith Wharton was still living in New York in 1905—or partly living in New York on Park Avenue when not at the new house in Lenox or in Newport or abroad. The tragic force of this ambitious early novel—early in her career at least—has to do with the broadness of conception, the immediacy of the strokes and scenes, rather than, as was so often later the case, a concentration upon details of manners, such as divorce for a woman. (It is interesting that in this novel one woman who seems to be invited everywhere has been divorced twice.)

It is a society novel of city mansions and great country houses, expensive bridge games, Paris clothes, and lavish weddings. Into this, the author has placed a perfect center, Lily Bart, a spectacularly resonant creation, trying to keep afloat after a very realistic collapse of the foundation of the part she was designed to play. Lily is spoiled, pleasure-loving, and has one of those society mothers who are as improvident as a tornado. The father comes home one day from "downtown," and while Lily is chattering about the need every day for fresh flowers in the house at twelve dollars a dozen, the weary man replies: "Oh, certainly my dear—give him an order for twelve hundred." There is a sardonic stress to his reply, and the father is asked if he is ill. "Ill—No, I'm ruined," he says.

Quite soon both parents are dead and Lily is sent to live with an aunt, an old goose in good society and well-heeled but dull and stingy in everything except an allowance for clothes. At the opening Lily is twenty-nine, beautiful, clever, an adornment for dinners and weekends that demand expenditures, at the bridge table for one, which she cannot afford and for which she is secretly in debt. It is clearly time for her to marry, after having foolishly turned down respectable offers. Marriage to a rich man is her aim, and early in the book she has her chance with a plodding, timid young heir, but certain acts of impetuosity and the news of her gambling debts frighten him away.

That is the way it goes. Every move Lily makes, whether innocent or calculating, leads to disaster and compromise. Her efforts go on very much in the manner of a continental farce. Although she is chaste, she tends again and again to be discovered in a sort of rumpled state. Men, married and otherwise, pursue her and, when rejected, blackmail her. Each scene is interesting, and if observers are always on hand to find her walking in the park when she'd rather not be seen or coming out of a house at the wrong hour, no unfortunate arrangement of circumstances is altogether without credibility.

The brilliance of the characterization lies in Lily's self-knowledge. She is never unaware of her own motives, and when her manipulations fail she does not impugn the self-interest of others working against her own. As one who has been on the town too long and who is poorer than anyone knows, Lily quite understands self-interest. She loses every gamble, and each opportunity snaps back like a trap. Her acquaintance with luxury is a fatal habituation. "Of luxury, the fruit is luxury," as Thoreau phrased it. At last, disinherited by her aunt because of "gossip," she sinks into irreversible poverty, an urban slide something like that of a luckless courtesan, although Lily Bart is only a New York society girl without means and without connections except of the kind that issue invitations. In the end, she takes an overdose of sleeping medicine.

Surrounding this personal debacle is a large society, not a representation of the city so much as a society that twists and turns upon itself, within the list, the mostly rich and sometimes dull and overfed. The predatory sexuality, the heartlessness, and the coarseness are quite startling when viewed against the more mildly rebuked, nostalgic renderings of the old guard in the later works.

For instance, Gus Trenor, whose credentials we cannot doubt since "with all his faults, Trenor had the safeguard of his traditions, and was less likely to overstep them because they were so purely instinctive." Of course, the "instinctive" graces are often out to lunch when life, here and elsewhere, scratches with its small and large irritations. Still, the rather glum and fumbling needs of poor Gus bring to mind instincts of the old urgency.

His wife is Lily's best friend, with all the relevant modifications of both words, and gives parties and weekends on Long Island, or is it up the Hudson? Mr. Trenor has appeared harmless enough but is insufficiently attended to. On one of the occasions, social, at Bellomont, his estate, he hears of Lily's desperate situation and offers to invest her last thousand dollars. Not long after, he presents her with ten thousand dollars, supposedly profit from a tip. Having gone to this trouble, Trenor turns as ornery as a ward boss. He gossips about the money and insinuates that there was no market tip; there was only his generosity, for which he wants womanly attentions of the usual concreteness. He sends her a telegram in his wife's name, summoning her late in the evening to his mansion on Fifth Avenue. Of course, the telegram is a trick of the most benighted asininity and Trenor is alone. He makes a clumsy effort to seduce Lily, but clumsy or not the intention is altogether realistic. Edith Wharton is bold about sex, even something of a nudging procuress when the plot allows. "Hang it, the man who pays for the dinner is generally allowed a seat at the table," the overheated man growls when he is rebuffed. (Lily's last act before committing suicide is to return, in the manner of Socrates before the hemlock, the profit from Trenor's "investment" on her behalf.) But where are the gentle manners, the agreeable repressions attendant upon civility learned at the tables set with the "du Lac Sèvres" and the "van der Luyden Lowestoft" and the "Dagonet Crown Derby"?

The House of Mirth in its flashlighting around New York casts its beam upon a Mr. Sim Rosedale. In the practice of the period, Rosedale is referred to as a "little Jew" and weighted down, as if by an overcoat in summer, with a thickness of objectionable moral and physical attributes—each readily at hand for the confident satirist. The fellow has made a lot of money downtown, and thus his path crosses that of the more or less well-bred Wall Street New Yorkers, who find him useful since their own capacities, with the help of spendthrift wives, are thinning like the hair on their heads.

Rosedale is ferociously set upon entering the society described in the novel; he has the money and is determined to have the dance. It must be said he comes upon the scene as free of family, traditions, religious or otherwise, as bereft of community as a scout on the plains. Rosedale is no slithering continental sybarite like August Belmont, but instead a shrewd, if uncouth, trader, and from history it might be doubted that he would be so quick to wish this particular dilution of himself and his fortune. The author understands it is fate and probity that lead the dull, rich Mr. Gryce to pass over Lily Bart and to unite his pile with that of the dull, rich Evie Van Osburgh. Edith Wharton would not, however, have known of Rosedale's possible familiar life, and so his muscular push into smart society must be taken as, well, natural.

In any case, the advancing Sim Rosedale is an important figure in this plot of threatening circumstance. Since Lily is beautiful, unmarried, and as fashionable as satin, Rosedale has settled upon her as the mate to show his accumulations to advantage. She refuses him, with "repugnance." But as her opportunities wither and her desperation augments, she decides to take the florid Rosedale and his millions after all. In a powerfully executed scene, Lily faces up and says, "I am ready to marry you whenever you wish." The crafty usurper turns her down. Her rotten luck, those scandal-mongering observers of her trek here and there on the stairs of a bachelor-filled apartment house and on a yacht in the Mediterranean and the compromising reportage they have engendered, are a fund of disadvantage. She is no longer a good investment.

Lily Bart is a flawed, self-absorbed, and, oh, yet decent beauty of the kind that tests the novelist's art. Sympathy is aroused by the honesty of her impulses, and she has an emotional clarity that makes even an occasional charity believable. Emotional clarity—honesty, in fact—is less efficient in society than garrulous self-justification. With Lily, this clarity is like a pinch of arthritis in her manipulating hand.

Her helplessness in poverty may be laid to society's withholding from the clotheshorse beauty the proper training for independence as a woman, independence being knowing how to work and forgo the dressmaker. There is a suggestion of the sadness of laboring incapacity in the exposition Edith Wharton has supplied. Certainly, Lily Bart is not a pioneering candidate for Radcliffe College; indeed, she cannot trim a hat, one of the occupations girls fallen from prosperity attempt in this as in other novels. Yet the author knows the lamentable inadequacy of "the modelling of her little ear, the crisp upward wave of her hair" as a preparation for a paycheck. And, above all, what she stresses is the blight of a conditioning for luxury without the means.

Lily Bart knows what she knows, coquetry for the most part, and to have been prepared otherwise would have been another novel. At one point, Lily explains that people think one can live *on* the rich, when the fact is that it takes money to live *with* the rich. To be without sufficient money is like diving into the concrete of a drained swimming pool. This novel is Edith Wharton's finest achievement because money is the subject, of greater significance than the crippling, if amusing and charming details of convention in a small, historically perhaps attractive but insignificant stockade. That at least was true of Manhattan even when it was "old."

2.

New York: No novelist in his or her volumes has set out to be the social historian of the actual city, this restless monster of possibility and liability. It is not easy to imagine a voraciousness to consume the remarkable, shapeless scope or, even in a practical condensation, to imagine a Zola tramping through the warehouses of meat at dawn or trailing the garment workers home to some godforsaken borough in the evening. The city itself has never been a whole as the other great cities were until recently, when New York's peculiar instability and visionary tribalism became a worldwide condition: Turks in Berlin, Arabs in Paris, colonials in London. New York literature is the literature of the precinct, whether it be the Mafia, Hell's Kitchen in Crane's *Maggie: A Girl of the Streets,* or Salinger's Glass family on Central Park West. A great claim is usually made for Edith Wharton as a social historian, although how that can be confirmed by so intensely hermetic an imagination is a puzzle.

The gorgeous innuendo of Henry James's New York pages in *The American Scene,* the lilting metaphors of distress and dispossession: It was 1904 when the chagrined pedestrian made his way through the fatally designed "streets intersecting with a pettifogging consistency." He spent some hours on Ellis Island, the utopian gateway, and cautioned the unwary against doing the same. To witness the "inconceivable alien" in their herded numbers was to have "eaten of the tree of knowledge and the taste will be forever in his mouth." But the effulgent language of James's wounded curiosity can be said to redeem the space of his withdrawal, to honor the gross elaboration and "untempered monotony" of the Waldorf Astoria and to fix in a glance the very topography of the city lying in its rivers and "looking at the sky in the manner of some gigantic hair-comb turned upward."

New York, with its statistical sensationalism, is a shallow vessel for memory since it lives in a continuous present, making it difficult to recall the shape of the loss deplored, whether it be the gray tin of the newsstand or the narrow closet for the neighborhood's dry cleaning, there and gone over a vacation. As for people, the rapid obsolescence of deities makes its point each season; or, if surviving the gleeful erasure of fame, the penalties pursuing society's accommodation can be severe, or so it is often asserted by the fatigued famous.

In my time, the preservationists say, men got up when a woman entered the room. When poor Blanche DuBois, passing the louts at the poker table, says, "Don't get up, I'm only passing through," how is that to be understood without "tradition"? There's a bit of that in Edith Wharton.

The Custom of the Country (1913) was for the most part written in France. It is a curiosity of a hybrid kind. Here we have a fierce scold not of the alien from Odessa or Sicily but of the natives undertaking an interior migration from Apex City to Manhattan. Their landing, ready for absorption, is a twofold pain: Their pockets are lined with cash, and they don't know when to get up and when to sit down. The mode of the composition is split in the middle: one half a description of the invaders in a satiric accent, the other a whirlwind of folly and destruction on an international scale.

So we open to the Spragg family from Apex. Spragg, wanting to transpose itself to Sprague or something, but efficient, perhaps in suggesting many backcountry impediments and wonders of maladaptation not unlike those of Ring Lardner's hicks in *The Big Town,* or his Mrs. Gullible finally achieving her wish to meet Mrs. Potter Palmer, doing so in a hotel corridor, and being asked to bring more towels.

Mr. and Mrs. Spragg are woebegone pilgrims, and the old father with his "lymphatic patience" brightened only by the Masonic emblem on his waistcoat is as unlikely a trader on Wall Street as the man behind the pickle barrel in the corner grocery. But he has made money in some way and the hajj to Mecca is, you might say, made on the roller skates of his daughter, Undine, who for a good while has been dreaming about Fifth Avenue in her Apex backyard. The choice of this family to bear the history of new money in the metropolis carries more of the tone of parody than of a serious imaginative decision.

William Dean Howells created similar migratory birds in *A Hazard of New Fortunes.* His Dryfoos tribe hits town with a fortune made from natural gas in Northern Ohio and Indiana. Natural gas would seem to be a very happy source for American finance, but the boomtown alteration of fortune does not decorate the newly rich man's psyche. In New York, old Dryfoos wails, "I ain't got any horses, I ain't got any cows. I ain't got any chickens, I ain't got anything to do from sun-up to sun-down." Dryfoos and his strike have, like the Spraggs, been transported by ravening daughters who want to bust into New York society.

It is no doubt prudent to have daughters if one would display in fiction the barbarities of social climbing and portray in all its anxious athleticism a passion for shopping. Of course, consumption and insatiability are the overhanging atmosphere of the city itself, gathering all classes, top to bottom, in its dreamy, poetic smother.

Undine Spragg arrives on the scene with youth, natural, and beauty, extraordinary, and every moral and practical liability a golden girl from the heart of the country can fold in her trunks. She is an infection, a glassy, little, germ-filled protagonist. We meet her set up with her family in the Hotel Stentorian, in rooms that go by the name of the Looey Suite, to be furnished with a good deal of oversized mahogany and gilt and laughable hangings on wall and window. Undine gets "round" right off and meets, without giving him notice, a young man, Ralph Marvell. Soon, she receives from his sister an invitation, which she throws in a basket, but which is rescued by a Mrs. Heeney, masseuse and manicurist, who cries out, Marvell! His mother is a *Dagonet,* and they live with old Urban Dagonet down on Washington Sqaure!

Mrs. Spragg chews on this: "Why do they live with somebody else? Haven't they got the means to have a home of their own?" Undine, perplexed and suspicious, questions why a sister should have written and why the invitation should ask the mother's permission when it is Undine who is asked to dine and why dine instead of have dinner and why write the note on plain white paper when pigeon-blood red is all the rage?—that kind of thing. *Go steady, Undine,* Mrs. Heeney advises.

Not long after, Undine is married to Ralph Marvell, and the plot advances to the lamentable results of this—for him. The Marvells are old New York, impeccable in birth and manners, not rich, living in their comfortably shabby houses on Washington Square, three generations within. Ralph is bookish and perhaps will himself write books; he is quiet, charming, has been to Harvard and Oxford, tried law but didn't have a flair for it, and now does nothing apart from reading and living according to his nature.

The European wedding journey is the first foreign experience for Undine, and it proves to be an experience foreign to Ralph Marvell's previous life. Undine despises Siena, altogether too slow and too hot. When asked if the summer wasn't hot in Apex, she replies that she didn't marry to go back to Apex. In Paris, the Comédie is "stuffy," and the husband attends alone while she is busy and, surreptitiously, having the family rings reset and buying a lot of clothes without the money. In fact, the couple doesn't have money for the passage home, and there are turns of plot attendant upon that. Undine is piling up the wreckage, flooding the banks of the river, and leaving the Marvell heritage and finances tumbled down in the mud.

Ralph Marvell is a creation of the novelist's art, and his attractiveness is evident on the page. His marriage to Undine is, however, a sort of haystack of implausibility stuck in the middle of urban life. She is given only one quality and that is great beauty. Beauty will always be an assertion the reader is compelled to accept but cannot keep his mind fixed upon. The hair—was it red?—and the "glow" when some diversion pleases the beauty are not exactly traits to be probed so much as color floating and drifting without a trace.

Undine, the character, is a witch of ignorance, insensitivity, vanity, and manipulation. She is mean to her parents, indifferent to the child she finally bears, and impossible to imagine as anything other than tedious. Whatever negotiable assets she has are practical only to certain vulgar sensualists, of which there are quite a few on the scene. She divorces Ralph Marvell without asking his permission and imagines after making herself fully available that she will cause Van Degen, a rich and decadent member of the Marvell set, also to get a divorce and to marry her. But the canny Van Degen thinks better of it and does not come forth.

Along the way, a most fantastical marriage for Undine does come about. She unites with the Comte Raymond de Chelles, a handsome young nobleman with ancient credentials, a house in the Faubourg, a château in Burgundy, little money to combine with Undine's less, since old Spragg has not prospered on Wall Street for all the reasons sufficient from the beginning.

Why must Edith Wharton and, in a different manner, Henry James decorate their pages with ancient titles to confound the romantic history of their Americans? Undine inflicts appalling indignities upon the poor Comte, but she is strangely imagined to be fidgeting about in the cold halls of a turreted castle. What is so interesting about Gilbert Osmond, the fortune hunter in *The Portrait of a Lady,* is that he acts like a prince of the realm but is indeed quite recognizable as an insufferable American expatriate, long resident in Florence. Prince Amerigo, in *The Golden Bowl,* fortunately does not flourish the papal title, and he is mostly seen maneuvering about London offering his fate to Americans, too many of them as it turns out.

But how peculiar it is to have the delightful, candid Christopher Newman in *The American* set off in pursuit of the daughter of the noble De Bellegarde family. The ancient Europeans will be cut from the cloth, stamped out one after another without distinguishing shapes, a bit like the weird American manufactures from which Newman made his finally unsuitable millions. The titled Europ⸴ represent mystery, inflexible pride, hidden motive, insⸯ manners, melodrama, and unreality: trappings, fuss, aˑ that must stand in the place of the author's having ⸴ or observed experience of the character and inⱦ peans so high.

Howells in *A Hazard of New Fortunes* ᴴ foos shopping, primping daughters ⸴

European bog. Christine Dryfoos meets her fate in the person of a French nobleman "full of present debts and of duels in the past." It is added that the father and his natural-gas dollars can manage the debts, but the duelist had better watch out for Christine, "unless he's practised with a panther."

The international novels are in fact novels of traveling Americans meeting each other abroad with a few natives thrown in. In *The Golden Bowl,* the Ververs cast their immense fortune at the foot of a prince, but the prince is a passenger, and the motors of the action are in the hands of the Ververs and the American, Charlotte Stant. Mme. Merle, so mysterious, is finally just another American, like the radical-chic Princess Casamassima, another visitor like the Touchetts, whose gifts will buy for Isabel Archer a fantasy of native blood, Gilbert Osmond, decorated with impecunious winters abroad, a little collection of things, and the hauteur of his meaningless displacement.

Undine at last finds a perch on Fifth Avenue as the wife of Elmer Moffat of Apex, an old pal to whom she had been briefly married as a girl. The discovery of her concealment of this fact is a contingent reason for Ralph Marvell's suicide. So Undine will travel from the picket fence to Fifth Avenue on the back of Apex Elmer, loud and red-faced as a fire truck. Elmer is now a railroad magnate, like— can it be?—Commodore Vanderbilt. The much-used bride is to be largely rewarded, and when the dispenser is Edith Wharton the loot will be lavish and banal. Undine is to have "a necklace and tiara of pigeon-blood rubies belonging to Queen Marie Antoinette, a million dollar cheque ... a new home, 5009 Fifth Avenue, which is an exact copy of the Pitti Palace, Florence."

As a social historian, Edith Wharton does not pause to get it just ight, on the dot. She proceeds from a very generalized memory d an often commonplace fund of attitudes. *The Custom of the Coun-* has placed its points at extremities that undermine the evolu- ry rush of the actual city. The invading Visigoths with their nstruments of fortune, like Spragg's marketing of a hair-waver from which comes Undine's name and his later having a worthless parcel of land upon which Apex was to build its water system, are not the usual transfers to Manhattan. The middle-sized towns of the Middle West would be more likely to claim the powers of Spragg and to contain the gossip-column ambitions of dressing-up Undine. The old Spraggs' rustic souls are fashioned out of impermeable materials, and the city casts its stones of enlightenment their way without making a dent.

New York City is a frame in these novels, not a landscape: 5009 Fifth Avenue? Even less well foretold is the failure to understand the magical progression of taste, so hasty, in the newly rich of the city. For what is easier than the acquisition of acceptable responses? Culture, as society finds it, is not saturation but an acquaintance with the labels of things valued, be it the Parthenon or white walls. The culture of consumption is infinitely accommodating, and the terms of cultural dissemblance are an available cosmetic, another pot of rouge. Very few Undines would scorn Siena or the Comédie Française, scorn out loud. Quickly, the proper patience appears, no matter how deep the stab of boredom in an actual confrontation.

The Marvell house on Washington Square, the seat of the genteel opposition, is one thing, but in New York "divided space" is preeminent, and the hotel and apartment living the hick Spraggs embrace cannot be thought of as retrograde. Was there in old New York an aristocratic style, an intimate weave of obscure inherited practice and value? Perhaps, but the style as it has come down to us was always drowning in the city's hyperbolic congestion of effects, the glare of the futuristic, the fantastical democratizing compulsion of Manhattan's eternal newness.

When Henry James set up his house in *Washington Square*, he did not force the historical inappropriateness of the terms found in the novels of Edith Wharton. He placed in his house, a memory dear to him from his youth, a member of the professional upper classes, with no worrisome tics about who might be a Dagonet, who a Van der Luyden. Dr. Sloper is an intelligent, hard-nosed, serious practitioner in a useful arena of knowledge, a possible New Yorker. True, the doctor is said to have married into one of the "best" families, but this has no dizzying command over the rather surgical common sense with which he approaches family affairs. What has its woeful effect upon him is that his wife has died and left him an improbable daughter. This chagrin is not unreasonable, or unthinkable perhaps, for a metropolitan gentleman. Catherine is dear, awkward, unfashionable, and indeed would seem to have many qualities of a Boston girl transplanted carelessly to New York. In Boston, among the Yankees, Catherine's modesty and the plainness and wish to please would not be impediments in a girl of good family.

In New York, Catherine is a perturbation. When the selfish, false idler, Morris Townsend, begins to court her, the doctor's intervention is cruel and practical. He is shrewd about Townsend and with his oily, ironic efficiency is not mindful of the fruits of his shrewdness in the broken heart of his daughter. The novel is a perfectly faceted diamond, clear in its icy progression. The drama sits on its corner downtown as confidently as the house Dr. Sloper built for himself. Social habits, conventions, prohibitions of the group have no part in the dilemma. Dr. Sloper knows his objections to Townsend as frankly as if the young man had come begging with a tin cup. Townsend does not care for Catherine, wishes only to marry her money, and while the sophisticated doctor can no doubt understand both, he sees that the conditions promise to be baneful down the road.

Wharton's *Age of Innocence* has great appeal because of the charm of the two figures, Ellen Olenska and Newland Archer. If it has a definition, an engine, it is divorce as a social stigma, a disability not to be incurred by a woman. She must, no matter what provocation, hang on legally, even if at a distance. She must not for a mere wish to be free of it all act on her own behalf. Ellen Olenska, a Mingott connection, has married a titled swine of a Pole. She has left him and returned to New York; he will take her back, but there is no thought of his swaying from whatever disgusts have been his pleasure. If she divorces, there will be scandal, and she will lose her money brought to the marriage and what is spoken of as "everything else."

The scandal of the intriguing Countess, with her irregular escape from her husband, combined with the powerful Mingott clan's displaying her in the family opera box, bring forth the beginning gasps of curiosity and social dismay. It is not a very weighty casualty, and yet Edith Wharton must find something to give reality to the deputed social standards. Good manners and the family plate are not sufficient for drama. Hindrance and exclusion are needed to give the old dominion coherence, to act as a sort of velvet rope in a museum protecting the plunder. Of course, there is great provincialism afoot here, since we know from Proust that a great French aristocrat can drop his Croix de Guerre on the floor of a male brothel without diminishing his prestige.

A good deal of the plot is concerned with who will come to a dinner in honor of the Countess, who will visit her, and so on. The loyalties of the old families are tested, and the best, the oldest, the most valued come forth bravely to smile over the canvasback ducks and to shame the timid, the complacent, and the insecure.

Ellen Olenska is glamorous and in tribute to her cosmopolitan life a bit exotic, a bit of a bohemian in her "little house" on an unfashionable New York street. She reads Paul Bourget, Huysmans, and the Goncourt Brothers. Newland Archer, conventionally reared by doting, placid women, a cousin to everyone who is anyone, has just married an unimaginative, nice young woman of his own set. Archer and Ellen Olenska fall in love, and it is a flaming passion that almost sends the lovers to a hotel room. The consummation is withheld, the Countess Olenska, divorced, returns to Europe, and Archer grows into a husband and father with bittersweet memories, recorded in one of those codas that span the years and might well have been forgone.

Edith Wharton suffered throughout her marriage to the Boston bon vivant, Teddy, as he was called. Teddy was worldly, liked the pleasures of dog and stream and wine cellar. He had no interest in scholarship, high or low, but took over a good deal of the management of houses and practical affairs and that went well, until it didn't. The two seem to have been a poor sexual match. Edith had her three-year affair with Fullerton, her strong affections for Henry James and others, especially for Walter Berry—a New York Van Rensselaer, an expert in international law and widely considered a snob, in her own vein. She was buried by his side, in Versailles.

Morton Fullerton, Harvard, son of a minister in Waltham, Massachusetts, became a political and cultural journalist, at one time the correspondent from France for the London *Times*. Fullerton seems to have been an attractive, perhaps we could say a lovable, young man. In his love life, he is something like a telephone, always engaged, and even then with several on hold. Whether he wished so many rings on his line is hard to tell; perhaps he was one of those who would always, always answer. In any case, among his callers were, in youth, Ronald Gower, a homosexual and friend of Oscar Wilde; Margaret Brooke, the Ranee of Sarawak; his cousin, Katherine Fullerton Gerould; Victoria Chambert, whom he married and with whom he had a child while living with a Mme. Mirecourt— and Edith Wharton.

When you have decided that Fuller likes older women—the Ranee and Mme. Mirecourt—he takes up with those younger, his cousin and Victoria Chambert. At the time of his affair with Mrs. Wharton there was a balance with no special signification: she was forty-five and he was forty-two. The Fullerton women tracked down thus far by academic prurience seem to have been of a forgiving nature and remained friendly to him throughout the years. Mme. Mirecourt clung like a burr and, as an expression of her enduring affection, was quite troublesome.

Teddy Wharton fell into the care of psychiatrists and into mood-swing follies, even going so far as to set himself up with a girl in a Boston apartment. He ran through his wife's money, and his increasing instability led to divorce. Twenty-eight years they had together, and, insofar as one can know, most of them were useful if not "satisfying" in the current sense. But then how satisfying could the dear love of the ambivalent Walter Berry have been? Edith Wharton appears to have been a type found in abundance on the contemporary scene: surprisingly sexy when the availabilities allowed, but owing to a dominant attraction to stylish amusements, happily surrounded by homosexuals, always, of course, of the right sort.

Once the deed was done, the divorce signed, she seemed to settle with a forward-looking fortitude. Even in her day, divorce was common in the best society, and it might be thought she held on to the prohibition mostly as a literary device to serve as a dramatic expression of the old manners—a necessary addition to the appointments of the house and the seating at the table. She used divorce again and again in her fiction, even sometimes seeming to entertain a certain moral nostalgia for its rigors. There is no doubt it was a handy circumstance for exile and for "cutting." The bald fact was that there were not many other stands to be taken in her created world, where the virtues were birth, the grand style, if suitable, with the rich Van der Luydens; good taste and modesty of pretension, the old bourgeois style, with the Marvells.

Edith Wharton had never been "modern" as a writer and had few theoretical questionings about the shape of the novel. "I certainly don't think Edith often read," Percy Lubbock wrote. Visiting her, he sometimes felt "a book had a scared look as she carried it off, as though it knew what it was in for." Yet she was a celebrated novelist, bore many honors, and experienced the threat of displacement in the clamorous, avant-garde elation of the 1920s. *The Waste Land* did not receive her favor, and *Ulysses* was to be named "school boy drivel." Living in upholstered exile, in the manner of Mrs. Wharton and Bernard Berenson, may have the gloomy effect of attaching one to intransigence in the arts, against the uprooted impertinence of modernism.

Mrs. Wharton had her turf, that almost forgotten sepia New York, to be turned over and over again, like setting the plow to the family farm every spring. A group of four short novels, under the title *Old New York* and boxed together, appeared in 1924. At the time of writing them, she was living in her final grand house, Pavillon Colombe, in Saint Brie, France, not far from Paris.

False Dawn, subtitled *The 'Forties*, proposes the adventures of a young man sent out on the civilizing Grand Tour and deputed to bring back works of art for his father's collection: Guido Reni, Carlo Dolci, and the like. Instead, spurred on by the development of a friendship with a young Englishman, who, we are asked to believe, is John Ruskin, he purchases Carpaccio, Fra Angelico, Giotto, and Piero della Francesca. The choices lead to his being disinherited by his father and scorned by old New York. Complacency and backward taste appear to be the indictment. "Carpatcher, you say this fellow's called.... Something to do with those new European steam-cars, I suppose, eh?" the outraged father cries out. Satiric dialogue, engaging enough in conversation, is a crash of dissonance on the Wharton page. And she likes to preen a little, to glide up on Ruskin and sneak up on the unlikely Piero purchase as if they were two cups of tea at Doney's.

In *The Spark*, a crusty old New Yorker claims to have learned human wisdom from a talkative fellow while being nursed in a Washington hospital after Bull Run. It is the dear bard Whitman himself. *The Old Maid*, another of the novellas, is a skillful melodrama set in the 1850s and telling of the sadness of an unwed mother's having to pretend to be a devoted aunt as she watches her child grow up, a condition as common in the villages as in the city.

The *Old New York* volumes are anecdotal fictions. There is not much air in them. Throughout Edith Wharton's work the society is small and its themes repetitive. The reader will become a sort of cousin of the blood as the defining names appear again and again. Memory has been emptied out by the long years abroad, and a certain perfunctoriness and staleness hang over the scene. Christine Nilsson will be singing *Faust* at the Academy of Music; the carriage will give way to the coupé. Characters go to balls and dinners and stop by to drink tea. They scarcely set foot on more than a few predictable blocks and on the way do not pass restaurants or saloons or thieves or workmen going home. Manhattan is a "set" but with no sense of crowds.

An early story, "Bunner Sisters," was rejected by an editor and put aside for many years before being offered in a collection. It is one of the author's most interesting works and an extraordinary wandering from the enclave. The sisters make trimmings and sew on ribbons in their dismal tenement; they meet a dreary opium addict, a wreck of a German who fixes clocks and who devastates their miserable struggle. The details of existence are vivid; the author knew at one time that people took streetcars, bought a few pennies worth of food with fierce concentration upon the cost, made pitiful journeys to the wastes of New Jersey. Gradually, the feel and the spell of the city were lost and only interiors remained, the stuffs of definition.

Ethan Frome is a village tragedy, and the tale is cut to the measure of rural New England as a strong popular image. The village is named Starkfield; Ethan is a melancholy, silent, and longing country man, ruined by the slow agony of life with his complaining, "sickly" wife, the kind whose neurosis is colored by a run on patent medicines. His hope for redemptive love by way of the young servant girl, Mattie, is thwarted, and their attempt to commit suicide by sledding down a dangerous hill on a splendid snowy night produces not death but a crippled, altered Mattie to be taken in by the now triumphant wife, and the three to be left to their eternal rural isolation and misery. There is less experience of life in this story than in "Bunner Sisters." Short as *Ethan Frome* is, it is heavily designed and shows the difficulties encountered in the telling, the structure. It is operatic, *opera verismo*, with the power to retain its grip on the memory, as the long popularity of the work indicates.

Dreiser's *Sister Carrie* was written in 1900, five years before *The House of Mirth* and twenty years before *The Age of Innocence*. Dreiser, from the Middle West, went over the city on foot, as it were, striking out from the first ring of the city's chimes, the trainman's call of "Grand Central Station!" The first flat is on Seventy-eighth and Amsterdam, and soon Nassau Street is mentioned. The horns of the ferryboats sound in the fog; there is Broadway to give its lessons, and the glaring celebrity of Delmonico's, and Sherry's, too; serge skirts at Lord and Taylor, lights on Plaza Square, and dinner for $1.50, rooms set apart for poker, casinos, barbershops, advertisement billboards, Wooster Street, a half pound of liver and bacon for fifteen cents, chorus girls, soldiers on the street, a strike, significant in the plot. And, of course, the Bowery and Potter's Field for Hurstwood. Carrie at the end will rock in her chair in the Waldorf, the golden monument of the period, and try to read *Père Goriot*, urged upon her by an ever-upward Ralph Marvell sort.

The plebeian "tinsel and shine" of Carrie's destiny and the bankrupt disaster of Hurstwood are not Edith Wharton's world, nor must it have been so. Still, she works with her own tinsel and is a recorder of dreams much less true to the city, as history, than those of Sister Carrie. Density of experience is lacking and not, we gather, lamented. In her novels, Manhattan is nameless, bare as a field, stripped of its byways, its fanciful, fabricated, overwhelming reality, its hugely imposing and unalterable alienation from the rest of the country—the glitter of its beginning and enduring modernity as a world city.

(*1988*)

On Washington Square

The James family came from New York State, the father having been born in Albany. Whether they are New Yorkers in the sense of the city is not altogether certain since they fled it early and did not like it much when they came back from time to time. Still the city, its streets, its fluid, inconstant, nerve-wrung landscape, had a claim upon Henry's imagination, even if the neglectful civic powers did not properly return the claim.

In any case, Henry James was born in New York City in 1843, in a house on 21 Washington Place, a street adjacent to Washington Square, itself a small park announcing the end of lower Fifth Avenue and adorned by an ambitious bit of architecture that James would describe as "the lamentable little Arch of Triumph which bestrides these beginnings of Washington-Square—lamentable because of its poor and lonely and unsupported and unaffiliated state." That was in 1904, when the sixty-one-year-old author returned from abroad to write *The American Scene*, his prodigious impressions of his homeland from New England to Palm Beach, impressions fresh, he hoped, as those of a curious stranger but still "as acute as an initiated native."

He would, of course, return to Fifth Avenue and to Washington Place. There, he found what he called a "snub." The birthplace of 21 Washington Place had been "ruthlessly suppressed" in one of those early convulsive seizures of destruction New York City to this day does not see as a defect in the municipal nervous system so much as an explosive, rather pagan, celebration of the gods of engineering and speculation. James, viewing the "amputation" of the birthplace, is led to confess that he had somehow imagined on Washington Place "a commemorative mural tablet—one of those frontal records of birth, sojourn, or death, under a celebrated name." This is an affecting aside of family and personal pride, a controlled twitch of chagrin, from which he retreats by observing the supreme invisibility of a plaque, acknowledging some long-gone worthy, placed on an apartment door in a fifty-story building, one of the "divided spaces" that were to be the principal habitations in the city.

—

The novel *Washington Square,* published in 1880, when James was thirty-seven years old, is an early work, at least early in style and in the untroubled presentation of its strong and thoroughly lucid plot. The novel is not strikingly under the domination of its place-name, but we note that the author allows himself a moment of autobiographical diversion, an insertion more or less of his private relation to the title:

> I know not whether it is owing to the tenderness of early asso-
> ciation, but this portion of New York appears to many persons
> the most delectable. It has a kind of established repose which is
> not of frequent occurrence in other quarters of the long, shrill
> city; it has a riper, richer, more honorable look ... the look of
> having had something of a social history ... It was here that

your grandmother lived, in venerable solitude ... It was here that you took your first walks abroad, following the nursery-maid with unequal step and sniffing up the strange odour of the ailantus-tree which at that time formed the principal umbrage of the square.

In the opening pages of the novel, Dr. Sloper has set himself up in a new house on Washington Square. The doctor is a credible, highly interesting man of the professional class who has achieved the status accruing to the serious practice of medicine. He is busy, successful, intelligent, witty—an engaging figure on the city scene, and while learned in the medical arts he is not "uncomfortable," by which it is meant that Dr. Sloper is one of those popular physicians whose personal attractiveness will somehow soothe the tortures of treatment. He has a well-to-do clientele and is passed by referral from one "good family" to another in the way that was usual before the age of intense specialization.

The doctor has moved to Washington Square from a house near City Hall, a part of the city being turned into offices and other structures of business. In moving uptown, he is following the direction of residential preference in the early 1880s—one of the details of metropolitan dynamics that interested "old New Yorkers" such as James and Edith Wharton. With a rather vagrant historicism, these authors like to follow, in a mood of amusement, the displacements of fashion as they try to place their characters on the city map. Thus, we are told that the doctor's dead wife had been "one of the pretty girls of the small but promising capital which clustered around the Battery and overlooked the Bay, and of which the uppermost boundary was indicated by the grassy waysides of Canal Street." The doctor has now made his own move uptown, but his drama is not residential; it is familial, an intense battle, almost military, of strategy, retreat, and attack, fought with his daughter, Catherine Sloper.

The doctor is in his fifties, and, while not a man to offer futile protests against the devastations of fate, he has endured two painful wounds, or perhaps we should say three. He lost a treasured son at the age of three and then lost a much-loved wife—a beautiful woman with a fortune, social standing, and every domestic charm—lost her at the birth of a second child, "an infant of a sex which rendered the poor child, to the doctor's sense, an inadequate substitute for his lamented first-born, of whom he had promised himself to make an admirable man."

His was a genuine grief, with the added gall of a professional frustration in having been unable to ensure the survival of his family. But there is the surviving daughter, Catherine, now grown into a robust, rosily—rather too rosily—healthy young woman. Facing this last, lone Sloper, the doctor can assure himself that "such as she was, he at least need have no fear of losing her." The "such as she was" is the plot of *Washington Square:* the destiny of the daughter and the father's tone in his relations with her.

The beginning pages are written in a comedy-of-manners style, and each turn is amusing, calmly and confidently expert. Such a style will command, with its measured cadences and fine tuning, a bit of benign condescension toward the cast and toward the friendly modesty of the New York social landscape in the first half of the nineteenth century. Thus, it is said of the doctor, "He was what you call a scholarly doctor, and yet there was nothing abstract in his remedies—he always ordered you to take something."

Washington Square was written after James made his literary and social "Conquest of London," as Leon Edel phrases it in the title of the second volume of his James biography. The author had breakfasted with Turgenev, met Tennyson, Browning and Gladstone, visited the great country houses, and indeed, as a cosmopolitan, wrote most of *Washington Square* in Paris. It is a perfect novel of immense refinement and interest, and one feels the execution gave James little trouble—that is, if one keeps in mind the breathless deliberations of the fictions that were to follow. Of course, the moral and psychological insinuations of this early work are not finally so self-evident as they appear to be on the lucid pages.

At the time James was devoting himself to the portrait of Catherine Sloper leading her life in her father's "modern, wide-fronted" house on lower Fifth Avenue, he was already thinking of the more challenging American girl, Isabel Archer, and the complex duplicities of *The Portrait of a Lady*, published soon after. In any case, when he was gathering the New York edition of his novels, which began to appear in 1907, he unaccountably excluded *Washington Square*. Perhaps it seemed to him a small, provincial tale after he had sent heiresses to Europe to test themselves and their American dollars on the ferocious competitions of the international scene. The American girls in the "large" novels are weighted with nuance and with the fictional responsibility to live up to their rather inchoate but grand attributions. Catherine, housebound in New York and incurious about the great world beyond, may have appeared a sort of vacation, one that allowed James a wonderfully relaxed compositional tone when compared with that of *The Wings of the Dove* or *The Golden Bowl*.

Catherine Sloper is an heiress but not a beguiling "heiress of the ages"; she is heir only to money. Indeed, the early descriptions of Catherine are composed with such a boldly discounting eye, such intrepid divestment, that the reader feels a wince of discomfort. Catherine is large and homely, but, at the beginning, a contented, virtuous girl of her class. She is guileless, affectionate, docile, and obedient. She has a "plain, dull, gentle countenance," and, although drastically without coquetry, she wishes to please, most of all to please her father. "She was not quick with her book, nor, indeed, with anything else." Along the way of depiction, James himself seems to draw back from the distance imposed by the manner of composition. If he does not quite retreat, we can say he takes a short little step to the side before persevering to write, "though it is an awkward confession to make about one's heroine, I must add that she was something of a glutton."

And there are woeful brush strokes ahead: Catherine's clothes, her "lively taste for dress." This "taste" causes her father to "fairly grimace, in private, to think that a child of his should be both ugly and overdressed." There is to be the merciless comedy of the "red satin gown trimmed with gold fringe" into which Catherine will more or less pour herself for an evening party at which her cousin's engagement is to be announced. There, in the awful red dress she will meet her fate, the fortune hunter Morris Townsend, meet that fate in the company of her other fate, her adored, "ironical" father.

So Catherine will meet Morris Townsend—extraordinarily handsome, "beautiful," she calls him—a New Yorker who has been knocking about the world rather than staying at home to sell bonds or to enter the law. In his knocking, he has spent his small inheritance and seems to have spent his friends and made himself unwelcome. Back in his native city, he claims to be looking about for something to do; meanwhile, he is staying with his sister—in fact living on his sister, who is in very reduced circumstances as a widow with five children. A sordid record with a few travel stickers from European hotels. Townsend is a distant connection of the young man Catherine's cousin is to marry. At the party, he goes for Catherine's attention with the watchful concentration of a sportsman waiting for the game to fly in the range of the gun.

Catherine, surprised by joy, as it were, is overwhelmed, hard hit with the rustic fluster of her inexperience. She will be joined by the tirelessly articulating duenna, Mrs. Penniman, Dr. Sloper's widowed sister, who lives in the motherless house and acts as a sort of chaperone and companion for the girl. Mrs. Penniman completes the quartet of the action, her addition to the stage being a fluff-filled swoon of sentimentality and a very intrusive meddling. In the support of Townsend's dubious campaign, Aunt Penniman will show herself as insistent, canny, and devious, as if she were await-ing a broker's fee.

With the unexpected courtship of Catherine, the tone changes; we are not, after all, to witness a deft seduction in the Restoration mode but a tangle of coldness, calculation, and conflicting motive, all at Catherine's expense. If the result is not quite a tragedy, it is a conclusion of most serious and lasting heartbreak. Perhaps in terms of fictional art, James was wise to give Catherine the works: her dis-maying vital statistics, her dumpiness, and her baffled maneuvering will set her up like one of those dolls at the country fair, ready to be idly knocked down for a prize. Still, she, all unstylish blushes and innocent gratitude, will profoundly solicit the sympathy of the reader as a heroine from real life, one not so remote from readers of both sexes, each of whom will have some defects in the lot-tery of romance. (I would not go as far as Leon Edel and claim that Catherine is "the image of himself [James] as victim of his brother's—and America's—failure to understand his feelings." The sibling rivalry Edel greatly favors as the psychological burden and ultimate creative spur of Henry's triumphant life—the wound and the bow—will even find William James lurking in the shadow of Dr. Sloper.)

Dr. Sloper, the most interesting and complicated character in the novel, is perhaps villainous in his genial, confident presence in the family and his also genial, confident intrusions into the love affair. He is a father who will ask when Catherine appears in the di-sastrous red satin dress, "Is it possible that this magnificent person is my child?" Told of Townsend's pursuit, he will puff on a cigar and reply, "He is in love with this regal creature, then?" Because the doctor is smart and observant himself, we are not surprised to learn that he thinks Catherine "as intelligent as a bundle of shawls." The "ironical" accent in the doctor's intercourse with his daughter is flamboyant, if lightly tossed about. One feels he enjoys the exercise of this established mode of communication; by it, he has turned a flaw of character, the absence of paternal propriety, into a manner, or a mannerism.

The plot of *Washington Square* is simple in its framing. Time is running out for Morris Townsend, and he must find someplace to land. Before meeting Catherine, he has obviously known of her inheritance from her mother, some ten thousand a year, and can figure out for himself her expectations upon the death of her father. So he makes his way to the side of the pleasant, wallflowerish Catherine. And, doing so, he picks up the admiration, if merely as an exciting diversion, of Aunt Penniman. The widowed chaperone's conspiracy on his behalf is immediate, like the burglar charming the housemaid over the fence and coming away with the key to the kitchen door. Visits to the house on Washington Square take place, and Catherine quickly falls into a kind of alarmed love.

Townsend means to marry Catherine, but he is quick to sense the impediment of Dr. Sloper, whom he is not foolish enough to imagine an easy conquest. And Sloper is, as feared, not in the least attracted to Townsend. The doctor says, "He is not what I call a gentleman. He has not the soul of one. He is extremely insinuating; but it's a vulgar nature. I saw through it in a minute. He is altogether too familiar—I hate familiarity."

Townsend will naturally decide that the doctor finds him unsuitable only on the ground of his poverty. He understands the doctor's power but not the fact that this particular father is the last person to imagine an adventurer like Townsend captivated by the unqualified Catherine. Shallowness, idleness, and insincerity, not poverty, are the grounds of Dr. Sloper's contempt:

> The fact that Morris Townsend was poor—was not of necessity against him; the doctor had never made up his mind that his daughter should marry a rich man. The fortune she would inherit struck him as a very sufficient provision for two reasonable persons, and if a penniless swain who could give a good account

of himself should enter the lists, he should be judged quite upon his personal merits.

The doctor wishes Catherine to be loved for her moral worth—he gives her that virtue, if not much else. Dr. Sloper's caustic, teasing banter with his daughter offends but does not amount to inattention; after Catherine has announced her engagement, he can be said to be very much on the case. He will make his way over to Second Avenue to call upon Mrs. Montgomery, the sister with whom the suitor is living. This, the most brilliant scene in the novel, provides a formal advancement of the plot and an advancement of the subtleties in the disposition of James's New York City physician. He has married a rich woman, and we gather he himself is of a respectable if not glittering family, but he is self-created and not a snob.

He goes downtown on Second Avenue, a swerve to the east, an unpromising direction at that time. Basil Ransom in *The Bostonians* lived as an impecunious young lawyer from the defeated South on that outré avenue, lived in close acquaintance with the "fantastic skeleton of the Elevated Railway, overhanging the transverse longitudinal street, which it darkened and smothered with the immeasurable spinal column and myriad clutching paws of an antediluvian monster." Excursions into the slushy, unreclaimed portions of Manhattan had for James the fearful, if beckoning, aspect of an assignation. In the New York City sections of *The American Scene*, we experience alarm for his palpitating heart as he goes— portly, sensitive, alert gentleman with a walking stick—into the immigrant's New Jerusalem, into Little Italy, and visits the portentous hordes with their bundles pouring forth from Ellis Island. In *Washington Square*, Mrs. Penniman, heavily veiled, embarks upon a perilous journey to an "oyster saloon in the Seventh Avenue, kept by a negro," in order to consummate another of her fatuous, capriciously encouraging interviews with Morris Townsend. But then that lady has had some experience of the outside of things, since we have been told that she accepted her brother's invitation to live in Washington Square with "the alacrity of a woman who had spent ten years of her married life in the town of Poughkeepsie."

So the doctor will venture downtown to Second Avenue, where he will observe with approval Mrs. Montgomery's neat little house of red brick and, inside, the tidy, if pitiable, efforts at decoration—"desultory foliage of tissue paper, with clusters of glass drops," and so on. He notes the cast-iron stove "smelling strongly of varnish" and finds the widowed lady to be "a brave little person," to whom he gave "his esteem as soon as he had looked at her."

The visit is crucial in every sense. The doctor states, without qualification, that Catherine will have her ten thousand a year, but if she marries Townsend, "I shall leave every penny of my own fortune, earned in the laborious exercise of my profession, to public institutions." The visit, in a guarded way, also reveals that Mrs. Montgomery has been giving money, of which she has little, to her brother, who takes it since he has none. In the end, the poor sister, having in the conversation formed an idea of the good nature and vulnerability of Catherine, says, "Don't let her marry him!"

Catherine, incurably smitten, would marry without her father's consent, painful as the possibility might be. This immovable passion and defiance are most interesting to the doctor. " 'By Jove,' he said to himself, 'I believe she will stick—I believe she will stick!' " And so she does, even after a year abroad, the old family deprogramming hope, a year of misery and intellectual waste since she "failed to gather animation from the mountains of Switzerland or the mountains of Italy." She does not relent, and Townsend is waiting, having, with the hospitality of Mrs. Penniman, made himself at home in the house on Washington Square, smoking the doctor's cigars, sitting by the fire, and listening to the aunt's prediction that Catherine will in the end get her father's fortune.

When she returns, Townsend is still idly trying to discount the possibility of disinheritance; thus, a remarkable dialogue between the two young people takes place, beginning with Catherine:

> "We must ask no favours of him—we must ask nothing more. He won't relent, and nothing good will come of it. I know it now—I have a very good reason."
> "And pray what is your reason?"
> She hesitated to bring it out, but at last it came.
> "He is not very fond of me!"
> "Oh, bother!" cried Morris, angrily.

Townsend ungraciously, surreptitiously, takes his leave, and that is the story.

The plot, among the novels of James, is an open one of a simple heart ruthlessly manipulated, of trust and goodwill dishonored. The central drama is between Catherine and her father, a drama of serious moral questions beyond the struggle of their opposing wills. There is not much questioning to be done on behalf of Morris Townsend, a young man of every conceivable vanity, a natural squanderer of money, friendships, family, anything at hand.

One of the footnotes James has placed in the seduction of Catherine's money is that Townsend, although destitute, puts a remarkably high value upon himself. When Catherine announces she will defy her father and is ready to flee the house with her "lover," she can rightly wonder why her ten thousand should not be sufficient. The repudiation of this income because it will not be augmented at her father's death is an insult of the most severe kind—and another folly committed by the conceited squanderer who imagines he can do better, whether by some vague plans for business or by way of a woman with a greater fortune.

Money in exchange for love is the dilemma of many of the heroines in James's novels. And a most curious way he has with it. Isabel Archer in *The Portrait of a Lady* is, by a tangled and not altogether credible route, willed seventy thousand pounds. She is given the money so that she can be free, so that she can achieve her best self, which, as it turns out, is to make her the object of fortune hunters, just as the rich Milly Theale in *The Wings of the Dove* will be. Love, or the appearance of it, is to be paid for by American money, paid in cash in a transcontinental intrigue that is dark and vastly complicated.

Catherine has been denied beauty, gaiety, all the romantic mystery and glamour of the heiresses abroad. James took the dare of the negative. Catherine is as alone as an animal in a field. No Lord Warburton is seeking her hand as she decides to choose another; no lively young female friend attends her wandering; and if her response is reckless, as it is, the recklessness comes not from her own gift for desperate decision but from credulity and isolation.

The troubling aspect of the doctor's destruction of Catherine's romance lies in the fact that he intrigues with more brio than we can countenance. On the other hand, does the reader wish Catherine to succeed in marrying Townsend? The best that can be said for the match is that the contract of life should guarantee the right to make one's own mistakes. James had thought deeply about the need to "experience," to take the dare, to live, and to him, sedentary as a monument, to live meant personal experience, to risk love. Catherine does "stick," as her father discovers with astonishment.

She meets "The Beast in the Jungle":

> To have to meet, to face, to see suddenly break out in my life; possibly destroying all further consciousness, possibly annihilating me; ... striking at the root of all my world and leaving me to the consequences, however they shape themselves.

We are not sure how greatly Catherine understands consequence at the time of her defiance, but she comes to understand humiliation and heartbreak. When a shabby, shopworn Townsend returns years later to ask for friendship, her answer is no. "You treated me too badly. I felt it very much; I felt it for years."

Washington Square is a perfectly balanced novel, narrow in its focus, rather claustrophobic, yet moving along with a speed suitable to the importunate demands of Morris Townsend in the matter of "settling" himself. In *The Notebooks,* James records the novel's origin in a story he heard from his friend the actress Mrs. Fanny Kemble. She told of her own handsome, penniless, selfish brother's pursuit of a "dull, plain, common-place girl, only daughter of the Master of King's Coll., Cambridge, who had a handsome private fortune (£4000 a year)." She was of that "slow, sober, dutiful nature that an impression once made upon her, was made for life." Her father disapproved of the engagement and vowed she would not get a penny of his money if she married. The young man, like Townsend, for a time thought the father could be brought around, but when it was clear there was to be no remission of the disinheritance, the suitor made a rapid retreat, leaving the girl desolated and never to marry. We note that here, too, there is a Mrs. Montgomery in the wings and that, when asked for advice by the unfortunately enamored young woman, she "advised the young girl by *no means* to marry her brother."

It was all there, the structure, the actors to be set down in New York on Washington Square. But James, assembling the bricks and mortar of the action, gradually found Catherine Sloper deeply entrenched on the inside, rather than the witty outside, of his imagination. Magically, he paces through each pause in her articulation, each artless question, each accumulation of baffled emotion, and thus Catherine comes to attract, profoundly. Her painful yet original dimensions come through to us slowly, as if in a haze, in contrast, for instance, to Isabel Archer's claims, rich and brilliant as they are, which begin by assertion: "You wished a while ago to see my idea of an interesting woman. There it is!"

Catherine is just raw feeling itself and literalness. Humbly, she tries to make her way through a crushing thicket of casual remarks, hoping to discover a literalness equal to her own and important to her understanding of her situation. "Did *he* say that?" she will ask Mrs. Penniman, who is busily reporting some putative exchange with Townsend. And, "Did *he* tell you to say these things to me?" By the force of her singular concentration in the midst of the off-hand and careless, she achieves a sort of personal, moral independence and certainly the dignity of the stubbornness and fidelity of her feelings.

And James was to take the father, merely a presence, an instrument, in the anecdote from which the plot derived, and create Dr. Sloper, a grand perplexity, a puzzle of disappointment and self-assurance. He is accustomed to control and boldly exercises it, but he dashes against a daunting sheet of rock: Catherine's feelings. The doctor is perhaps finally to be seen as Catherine's personal protector against certain disaster, but he is a protector of such provoking lapses and gaps that we cannot wish him victory. In the end, his victory, if that is what it is, does not rescue Catherine. Only Morris Townsend's abandonment can accomplish her salvation, if that is what is accomplished.

In any case, Catherine has lived, has known the assault of love. And when she says of her father, "He is not very fond of me," she has bitten of the fruit of knowledge, experienced the classical recognition moment and the power of enlightenment. Perhaps we can say that Catherine will become as clever as her father and can inflict upon him the fiercest vexation, which will amount to his genuine and lasting distress. Long after the romance with Townsend has been devastated beyond renewal, her father will still wish her to promise that she will not, at his death, marry the young man. Her answer: "I cannot promise that, Father."

The matter of the promise beyond the grave reveals Dr. Sloper's utter failure to understand where his daughter has been and where she is. As a final stroke of perverse underestimation, he reduces her portion in his will and writes: "She is amply provided for from her mother's side;... her fortune is already more than sufficient to attract those unscrupulous adventurers whom she has given me reason to believe that she persists in regarding as an interesting class." Catherine's comment about the punitive last testament is: "I like it very much. Only I wish it had been expressed a little differently." A proper burial for the interesting, ironical New York City physician.

(1990)

Americans
Abroad

~

The Genius
of Margaret Fuller

＄o passed away the loftiest, bravest soul that has yet irradiated the form of an American woman: Thus wrote the editor Horace Greeley. Yet before this noble soul, Margaret Fuller, passed away, many would have forgone *irradiated* in preference for *irritated*. She was brave and lofty, and she did irradiate and also irritate, irritate herself especially with strained nerves, fantastical exertions, discomforts large and small.

Margaret Fuller, a New England creation, commemorated in Mount Auburn Cemetery in Cambridge in impressive blocks of stone, was born in the wrong place, the place thought to be the only right one for an American intellectual in the nineteenth century. That is, she was born in Cambridgeport, Massachusetts, around Harvard, Boston, Concord, and all the rest. She sprang out of the head of all the Zeuses about: her father Timothy Fuller, Emerson, Goethe. The head being the protesting organ it is, she suffered life-long from migraine headaches, and even as a young girl left on the scene more than a bit of the fatigue and sense of pounding insistence thought to be the dispensation of a learned woman. There were many enlightened and cultivated women about, but she was the only seriously learned one in her circle, perhaps in the country.

As a life, a biography, hers is the most dramatic, the most adventuring of all the "flowerings." Her life was strikingly split into two parts by experience and ended by tragedy. Staying at home in Concord and Boston, she might have ended as comedy.

She was born into an incestuous air, this world that provided as a wife the sister of one's best friend, as a husband, the son of a family connection. Hawthorne married Sophia Peabody; Emerson married Ellen Tucker; Henry Adams married Marian Hooper, the daughter of Dr. Hooper and a Sturgis on the maternal side. This sexual handiness, as it were, the prudent over-the-fence alliances, narrowed experience in Margaret Fuller's circle but seemed to produce around Boston and Concord a domestic placidity that encouraged the high notes of Transcendentalism, a local philosophical blending, an indefinable idealism of the divinity within humanity, union with nature, the "eternal One." Henry Adams, thinking of Emerson and pondering his own non-Boston experience of the nation as a whole, thought all this *naif*.

(It is almost elevating to learn from a discreet footnote here and there that Clarence King, the distinguished geologist and Adams's great friend in *The Education of Henry Adams,* was the common-law husband of a New York black woman and the father of a son by her. King himself was from Newport, Rhode Island, and a graduate of Yale rather than Harvard; perhaps this climate slightly to the south had an effect upon this far-flinging, if that is what it was. Allowing for the condescension of "common-law," King apparently wished to do right and to honor the union. Upon his death, Mrs. King brought a lawsuit to secure for her son the trust fund assured her in King's letters. She lost, defeated by the WASPs and their mastery of *per stirpes*.)

Margaret Fuller did not attract the passion for neighborly unions. Indeed, one might say her only true American lover was

Professor Perry Miller of Harvard, born more than a century later. Margaret Fuller herself was born in 1810 and was thus seven years younger than Emerson. She was the daughter of Timothy Fuller, a scholarly man, graduate of Harvard, representative in Congress from Massachusetts, and later a practicing lawyer. His education of his daughter began early. Like John Stuart Mill, she was put in the stocks, and one of her finest pieces of writing has to do with the memory of her father's wish to make her "heir to all he knew."

> Thus I had tasks given me, as many and various as the hours would allow, and on subjects beyond my age; with the disadvantage of reciting to him in the evening, after he returned from his office.... I was often kept up till very late; and as he was a severe teacher, both from his habits of mind and his ambition for me, my feelings were kept on the stretch till the recitations were over. Thus frequently, I was sent to bed several hours too late, with nerves unnaturally stimulated. The consequence was a premature development of the brain, that made me a "youthful prodigy" by day, and by night a victim of spectral illusions, nightmare and somnambulism, which at the time prevented the harmonious development of my bodily powers and checked my growth, while, later, they induced continual headaches, weakness, and nervous affections, of all kinds. As these again reacted on the brain, giving undue force to every thought and every feeling, there was finally produced a state of being both too active and too intense, which wasted my constitution, and will bring me,—even although I have learned to understand and regulate my now morbid temperament,—to a premature grave.

Overwork, as she names it. Hysteria and the nightmares, whatever torments remembered, the result was a storehouse of knowledge and certainly an identity, even a vanity. Long after her father subsided as a tutor, she spent her youth in frantic application, reading, as Emerson wrote, "at a rate like Gibbon's." Thomas Wentworth Higginson's biography has her, at the age of fifteen, up at five, with the hours laid out: one for the piano, one for Sismondi's *European Literature* in French; then Brown's philosophy, then a lesson in Greek; in the evening, two hours reading in Italian, a bit of walking, more piano, and retiring at eleven to write in her diary.

Thus, we have the forced bud continually self-forced, nerve-wrung, eccentric, and, as we might expect, proud of her learning, aggressive in conversation, tremendously eager for friends, given to crushes, and yet with it all a devoted daughter. Timothy Fuller died suddenly, leaving the family in a bad way. At this moment, Margaret had planned to accompany the Farrar family to Europe. But she gave it up and remained at home to help in the support of her brothers and sisters. This meant teaching. First, a spell at the Temple School, Bronson Alcott's leafy squirrel house of learning; and then a real position for two years in Providence, whence in a letter to Emerson she made one of her many confident pronouncements that were to be long remembered and to decorate her memory in the manner of a bit of local scandal: "I see no divine person; I myself am more divine than any I see—I think that is enough to say about them." After two years, she returned to Boston to make her way as a writer, beginning with a translation of Eckermann's *Conversations with Goethe*.

From the first, she was a figure, a star, a somewhat blinding one, constantly talked about as a sight to be taken in, like Bronson Alcott's unworldliness and Thoreau's recalcitrance. Conversation was her love and even if some were fearful in approach because of the intrepid "truthfulness" of her social exchanges ("Stand from under!" Emerson cautioned himself), she had the trait of all conversationalists; an immense availability. She liked to visit and sometimes stayed too long. One of the saddest periods of her youth came after her father's decision to retire from the Boston scene and to take his family to the smaller village of Groton, thus removing his daughter from the company of the young men and professors around Harvard with their spiritual and intellectual interests.*

Her mission was self-culture, as one memorialist phrased it. And always the wish to uplift others, friends, anyone. She practiced a kind of hot Transcendentalism alongside Emerson's cooler sort. She could be found holding an arm, gazing into eyes, insisting upon inspiration, sublimity, and *grow, grow, grow.*

She was very noticeable to the men around Harvard, some of whom she had known earlier at a private academy where she, although a female, was allowed at fifteen to go for special study in Greek recitation. There was her mind to startle and also her appearance, her black cloak, and many odd features of the head, not always easy to describe.

The Transcendentalist Frederic Hedge, her friend from his Harvard days: "No pretension to beauty then or at any time, her face was one that attracted, that awakened a lively interest."

Emerson: "nothing prepossessing. Her extreme plainness—a trick of incessantly opening and shutting her eyelids—the nasal tone of her voice—all repelled; and I said to myself, we shall never get far."

Poe worried about her upper lip, which, "as if impelled by the action of involuntary muscles, habitually uplifts itself, conveying the impression of a sneer."

William Henry Channing on the matter of her neck found its curve "swan-like when she was sweet and thoughtful, but when she was scornful or indignant it contracted, and made swift turns, like a bird of prey."

J. R. Lowell: "a pythoness."

Oliver Wendell Holmes: "ophidian."

---

*It was from Bell Gale Chevigny's book, *Margaret Fuller: The Woman and the Myth,* with its masterly organization of many then-unpublished letters, along with the comments of contemporaries, that I came first to understand the complexity of Margaret Fuller and her situation.

The concentration upon appearance is somewhat overwrought among those who took beauty if it arrived on the doorstep and did without if a fine and useful character prevailed. Emerson's first wife, Ellen Tucker, has been described as a "remarkable beauty"; Ellen Fuller, Margaret's younger sister, was a romantic charmer who married the romantic, quite unsteady, charmer Ellery Channing. Henry Adams, writing about his engagement to "Clover" Hooper, said, "She is certainly not handsome; nor would she be quite called plain, I think."

So, Margaret Fuller was homely, even distracting in mannerisms, but she charmed by an overwhelming responsiveness and curiosity and had many women friends from whom she received confidences and to whom she gladly gave advice. Emerson, in his essay after her death, wrote that she wore her friends "like a necklace of diamonds around her neck" and that "her friendships, as a girl with girls, as a woman with women, were not unmingled with passion, and had passages of romantic sacrifice and ecstatic fusion."

Be that as it may, it was her habit throughout her years in America to presume on male friendships, pushing them to intentions that were not forthcoming, with a result very distressing to her spirits. She is so often not quite in touch, confused perhaps by the dramas of friendship, a sort of insufficiency in nuance, missing signals. Soul mates appeared—or so it seemed—but her "soul" was too soon declarative and consuming.

First, her cousin George Davis is said to have "thwarted her." Then a true falling in love with a member of her circle and a close friend, Samuel Ward: "No, I do not distrust you, so lately have you spoken the words of friendship. You would not be so irreverent as to dare to tamper with a nature like mine, you could not treat so generous a person with levity ... if you love me as I deserve to be loved, you cannot dispense with seeing me ... J'attendrai." Still, the nest-like scene, and it turned out that Samuel Ward, a close friend, was going to marry another close friend of his and also a close friend of

Margaret Fuller's—Anna Barker. Later in New York she was to experience the painful debacle of her "romantic" connection with a man named James Nathan.

Emerson and Margaret Fuller formed a complicated alliance and one of the most interesting friendships between a man and a woman in American literature. Before their meeting and while Emerson was still a clergyman, she was somewhat doubtful of fame in the pulpit. "It is so easy for a cultivated mind to excite itself with that tone." On the other hand, she was eager to show him her translation of Goethe's drama *Tasso*. They met in 1835, and she first visited Emerson in Concord in 1836. "His influence has been more beneficial to me than that of any American, and from him I first learned what is meant by an inward light."

Emerson found her, at the age of twenty-six, well read in French, Italian, and German literature but needy in the matter of English literature. He pressed upon her the works of Chaucer, Ben Jonson, Herbert, Sir Thomas Browne, and others. The absence of English fiction represents Emerson's indifference to the form as perhaps too much shackled to event and casual life. Of Dickens he wrote: "London tracts ... local and temporary in his tints and style, and local in his aims."

Margaret Fuller "adored" Mme. de Staël and was often called the "American Corinne" because of her dramatic and romantic presentation of herself. She came to forgive George Sand for the laxness of her life and greatly admired her and her work. But what would she have thought of the refined obscenities of *Clarissa?* Of *Tom Jones* or *Tristram Shandy?* The mixed and complex English fictional tradition cannot be what Emerson meant when, in "The American Scholar," he called for "the meal in the firkin; the milk in the pan; the ballad in the street; the news of the boat; the glance of the eye; the form and gait of the body," but where was one to find the expression of "the common and the low" if not in English fiction? It is the development of Margaret Fuller's style—not to be laid at the door of Emerson—that suffered from an absence of dogs and cats and rude particulars and the humorous. She did not have Emerson's wit, his rapid concentration of an image, a quick short sentence. She told him that he used too many aphorisms, and he said that if he used too many, she used too few.

Her letters are a heat of energy, warmth of friendship, family love, and family duty, a blazing need to communicate, no matter the aching head and midnight coming on. In the New England period, there is also a wrenching struggle with nature, the woods, sunsets, moonlights. "The incommunicable trees begin to persuade us to live with them, and quit our life of solemn trifles." Emerson: "What is a farm but a mute gospel?"

The sweetness of the Massachusetts countryside, the little villages, the fields and woods and streams. This is what they had—literary genius in a sort of retirement; rustication, snowy nights and early flowers. The great writer Thoreau redeemed the nature-writing workshop in Concord with his daunting struggle in letters and notebooks to catch the kiss of a moonbeam and honor the hoot of a barn owl. It was Thoreau's genius to carry landscape and weather as far as they could go.

Hawthorne in his notebooks fought with the whortleberry bush and the gleam from the lighthouse at Marblehead. "And its light looked very singularly, mingling with the growing daylight. It was not light, the moonshine, brightening as the evening twilight deepens; for now it threw its radiance over the landscape, the green and other tints of which were displayed by daylight, whereas at evening all those tints are obscured." And so on, with here and there a hit: the neighbor's ox who looked very much like Daniel Webster.

Margaret Fuller attempted, early, a composition on the passion-flower and would sometimes advise one to see a certain sunset at *exactly a quarter to six.* A great deal of moonlight occupies her pen. Emerson, in his memoir, is rather contemptuous of her naturing, even though he himself may be said to have led the charge for these confrontations.

Margaret's love of beauty made her, of course, a votary of nature, but rather for pleasurable excitement than with a deep poetic feeling. Her imperfect vision and her bad health were serious impediments to intimacy with woods and rivers. She never paid— and it is a little remarkable—any attention to natural sciences. She neither botanized, nor geologized, nor dissected.

What was not known then, and certainly not known to herself, was that her nature was profoundly urban and her talent, in the end, was for sightseeing, meeting people, for issues; her gifts as a writer were for a superior journalism. Everything that happened, in her head, in her reading, in her travels, was there to be used. In 1843, she made a journey to the western part of the country, and the next year her first original book was published, *Summer on the Lakes.* She sees a lot, thinks about the Indians, the settlers, Chicago, immigrants, and forswears a descriptive account of Niagara Falls. "Yet I, like others, have little to say, where the spectacle is for once great enough to fill the whole life and supersede thought, giving us only its presence.... We have been here eight days, and I am quite willing to depart. So great a sight soon satisfies, making us content with itself, and with what is less than itself."

In Concord, visiting the Emerson house, the second Mrs. Emerson—not a beauty like Ellen, who died young of tuberculosis—experiences the discomforts arising from the presence of a husband-adorer and disciple in the house, waiting for him to be free to inspire, to read his poems aloud, to take a nature walk. Hurt feelings, tears; Mrs. E. asks Margaret to take a walk with her one evening and M. answers that she cannot because she is going to walk with Mr. E. That sort of thing.

And the inevitable "friendship" discussions with Emerson, heavy with feeling on Margaret Fuller's side. She wants some sort of exclusiveness, recognition: "I am like some poor traveller of the desert, who saw, at early morning, a distant palm, and toiled all day to reach it"—followed by a transparent Persian fable, which Emerson pretends not to understand. And, another letter,

> I have felt the impossibility of meeting far more than you; so much, that if you ever know me well, you will feel that the fact of my abiding by you thus far, affords a strong proof that we are to be much to one another.... How often have I left you despairing and forlorn. This light will never understand my fire.

Emerson in his memoir does not avoid analysis of this disconcerting appeal for more, more.

> Our moods were very different; and I remember, that, at the very time when I, slow and cold, had come fully to admire her genius, and was congratulating myself on the solid good understanding that subsisted between us, I was surprised at hearing it taxed by her with superficiality and halfness. She stigmatised our friendship as commercial. It seems her magnanimity was not met.

Together they began *The Dial* in 1840, with Margaret Fuller as the editor for two years. It was a Transcendentalist forum, "to lift men to a higher platform." Criticism, it was felt, would be most useful to the soul of the country, and, not to be forgotten, criticism is what the group was able to compose and thus to celebrate Genius and the Transcendental calling.

Fuller offered an essay on Goethe, the supreme genius, a defense against accusations of immortality and egotism. Her essay is intense and rather more parochial than it need be, except for being addressed to an audience alarmed and distrustful. "Pardon him, World, that he was too worldly. Do not wonder, Heart, that he was so heartless. Believe, Soul, that one so true, as far as he went, must yet be initiated into the deeper mysteries of Soul."

Emerson thought the Goethe essay her best, and Professor Perry Miller views it as a moment in history. Here Margaret brashly defends *Werther* against the prevailing American opinion that it was a foul corrupter of youth; and she praises *The Elective Affinities,* which American men regarded as the nadir of sensual depravity. Viewed in this perspective, Margaret's essay is a basic document in the history of intellectual freedom in the United States.

The work on *The Dial* exhausted her, and Emerson assumed the editing for the next two of the magazine's four years. "I remember, after she had been compelled to relinquish the journal into my hands, my grateful wonder at the facility with which she assumed the preparation of laborious articles that might have daunted the most practised scribe."

———

Conversations. The famous gatherings in Boston in which Margaret Fuller led and instructed a number of well-bred women began in the rooms of Miss Elizabeth Peabody on West Street. The object was "to pass in review the departments of thought and knowledge, and endeavor to place them in due relation to one another in our mind." Since eloquence was the leader's gift, she had to do a good deal of orating to pinch the minds of her fellow explorers into speech. The account of one conversation that survives is a comedy, and perhaps that is why it survives. The topic was "What Is Life?" Pushed and prodded, a Miss C. replied, "It is to laugh, or cry, according to our organization."

"Good," said Fuller, "but not grave enough."

Another reply by Mrs. E., perhaps the second Mrs. Emerson, who was an attendant, " 'We live by the will of God, and the object of life is to submit,' and went on into Calvinism."

When pressed to give her own idea of what life is, M.F. began with "God as Spirit, Life, so full as to create and love eternally, and yet capable of pause."

The conversations were said to spread her fame about town. She

dressed for them and assumed a sibylline manner quite extraordinary. Some thought she got the idea from Bronson Alcott's ever-
lasting questioning and his Orphic Sayings. But what seems more
likely is that the conversations were a sort of reduced, miniature,
and homebound wish for a platform, and a platform such as Emerson had in his lectures in this hall and that, in little towns and cities.
She, too, could speak on the great subjects, but Miss Peabody's parlor, excitable as it was in the hour before noon, with the wives of the
great men, Mrs. Bancroft, Mrs. Child, Mrs. Parker, and various
Misses looking on, was the only lyceum available.

The second part of Margaret Fuller's life was to last only six
years, from 1844 until her death in 1850. Act 2 was overcrowded
with incident after the pastoral, repetitive Act 1, which was book
after book, the same friends, much talk, letters, reviews, and the
management of *The Dial*. In spirit, it was a sort of treadmill of en-
thusiasms for Goethe, Beethoven, Michelangelo, Raphael, Mythol-
ogy, the Classics, French socialism—all written down, somewhere.
"Her pen was a non-conductor" merely signified her flat failure as
a poet, which of course she had struggled with also. Emerson continued to think of her as a talker, a parlor orator, or even as a monologist "who seldom admitted others upon an equal ground with
herself." She could also gossip, which frightened him. "The crack-
ling of thorns under the pot."

In *The Dial*, she published "The Great Lawsuit—Man versus Men;
Woman versus Women." The article was much expanded and elabo-
rated into *Woman in the Nineteenth Century*, published in 1845. And
then she left Boston for New York, thought at the time to be an out-
post in the intellectual life. "The high priestess of Transcendentalism
cut her ties with the provincial homeland," Perry Miller wrote.

"Let them [women] be sea-captains if they like." This offhand swat
to seafaring Massachusetts, the China trade, the widow's walk at the
top of the house, the codfish cake for breakfast, remains the best-
known statement in Margaret Fuller's long, prolix defense of women.
The work was completed in less than two months, during a vacation

in a Hudson River town, and probably written without a library, except for the one in her head. It is a compendium of custom relating to women, ancient and modern opinion buried in poetry, literary allusion, and common observation. The index lists Elizabeth Barrett Browning, Dante, Desdemona, Petrarch, Plato, Spinoza, Swedenborg, Xenophon, and many others. The author herself appears in the disguise of a certain Miranda, well educated, taught honorable self-reliance from the cradle, privileged in learning and preparation for independence of thought; and not hindered by beauty from the development of talents and sense of self. "She was fortunate in a total absence of those charms which might have drawn to her bewildering flatteries, and in a strong electric nature, which repelled those who did not belong to her, and attracted those who did."

It is a bookish book, a fundamental document in the history of feminist thought. An intense, pleading tone, elevated, careful not to give offense, but determined. The strong and dignified women of literature and history—Iphigenia, Antigone, Britomart, the French Revolution's Madame Roland ("O Liberty, what crimes have been committed in thy name!")—appeal to her more than the powerful, devious Queen Elizabeth, "without magnanimity of any kind."

Margaret Fuller certainly knew Mary Wollstonecraft's *Vindication of the Rights of Women*. Here, she makes an unaccountable mistake, seeing Mary Wollstonecraft's marriage to the prodigious nitwit William Godwin as her best claim upon our attention: "a woman whose existence better proved the need for some new interpretation of woman's rights, than anything she wrote."

Mary Wollstonecraft's work is much more homely and practical, less rhetorical and less respectful—and more cynical about the world. She despises women brought together in boarding schools; too much giggling and lounging about in dirty undergarments. "Parental affection is, perhaps, the blindest modification of perverse self-love," and she asserts that the habit of overlooking the faults of one's parents inclines the child to overlook his own. "The two sexes mutually corrupt and improve each other."

Mary Wollstonecraft's worldliness may have offended Margaret Fuller. She does not mention the *Vindication*, but points instead to Godwin's book in support of his wife. The omission indicates a distaste, just as distaste, conscious or not, might explain why Emerson in his cramped and complicated essay on Fuller, thought by some to be patronizing but in fact the most alive and brilliant words written about her, never mentions *Woman in the Nineteenth Century*, the work that established her fame in America and abroad.

In Fuller's book, we notice again and again the belief in the "electrical" and "magnetic" element in women's nature. "Women who combine this organization with genius are very commonly unhappy at the present time." What makes *Woman in the Nineteenth Century* affecting beyond its arguments for education, independence, and so on, is the pathos of autobiography lurking in the text. Even the often lamented diversions into higher learning and allusion show the will to transcendence. She herself, in the wide sweep of her being, is the best American woman the nineteenth century had to offer; and she is, for all that, merely a phenomenon, an abandoned orphan. That is part of what the book means to say.

Emerson on Margaret Fuller: "A complacency that seemed the most assured since the days of Scaliger." Also, "the presence of a rather mountainous ME." Who can doubt it? But what the whole span of her life shows is that she got it all from being around Boston at the transfiguring moment and would have lost it all had she not escaped. She was a sort of stepchild, formed and deformed by Concord, by the universalism and the provincialism. Emerson notes this so-willing adaptation to the best of the intellectual landscape, as well as its gradual unsuitability, not only to the fact that she was a woman who had to earn her living, but to her nature. Among other things, she was not a solitary, not a gardener.

I think most of her friends will remember to have felt, at one time or another, some uneasiness, as if this athletic soul craved a larger atmosphere than it found; as if she were ill-timed and mis-mated, and felt in herself a tide of life, which compared with the slow circulation of others as a torrent with a rill.

She was altogether too familiar in the minds of New Englanders. They loved her—the word is not too strong even for Emerson's feelings. Noble, truthful, faithful, brave, honest: The words appear again and again in what was written and said about her. Yet it is the fate of an eccentric to be repetitive in the hometown. There is no intermission. Each appears in his hat and coat and tics day after day. The first thing to be noticed as she moves to New York and then to Europe is that she is no longer quite so noticeable, so fixed and peculiar, perhaps because being one of many, even if Poe, a New York acquaintance, divided the world into men, women, and Margaret Fuller. Above all, Transcendentalism—"going to heaven in a swing" as one mocker put it—nearly turned her into a fool.

She moved to New York in December 1844, invited by Horace Greeley to be a professional book reviewer for the *New York Tribune* and also to contribute general articles; and invited by Mrs. Greeley to stay with them in their house in the Turtle Bay section of the city. For the paper she wrote reviews and "pieces" on just about everything: the theater, concerts, prisons, asylums, poor women, institutions. Her reviews were, for the most part, short and quickly written. She gives too much space to the novels of Charles Brockden Brown and too little to James Fenimore Cooper and the stories of Hawthorne, although she is generally favoring in her glances. She made a striking attack on Longfellow as "artificial and imitative." As a critic, she does not have the mind for the details of a work but rather for its general effect, and so there is a sameness in the language and a tendency, strong, to moral description of literature. "The atmosphere of his verse refreshes," and again, "a lively though almost sensuous delight in the beautiful," "the richness and freshness of his materials," and so on. She has little notion of the power of William Prescott's *Conquest of Mexico*.

The most interesting of the critical pieces in the *Tribune* is a cool and sly rebuke to Emerson's *Essays: Second Series*. A maddening part of the review is taken up with a description of a populace too busy and too shallow to grasp the fineness in its midst. This is followed by an interesting, but again generalized and exhorting, picture of Emerson on the platform. "One who could see man in his original grandeur ... raising to the heavens the brow and the eyes of a poet." Yes, Emerson is a father of the country. But then in an indirection, as if some disembodied critic and not herself were speaking: "The essays have also been obnoxious to many charges.... The human heart complains of inadequacy, either in the nature or experience of the writer, to represent its full vocation and its deeper needs.... These essays, it has been justly said, tire like a string of mosaics or a house built of medals." A string of mosaics or a house built of medals—one of her best prose moments. At the expense of the master and still a friend to whom she wrote letters up to the end.

Then the entrance in 1845 of James Nathan, when they were both about thirty-five years old, he being six months or so younger, both unmarried, but he certainly more *experienced*. Nathan was born in Holstein, Germany, came to New York as a young man, worked in the "commission business," but, in common with many another, liked to wonder if he had not sold the soul of a poet for, well, what?—"commissions" perhaps. He had blue eyes, played the guitar, and after a meeting at the Greeleys', took her to see a plaster model of the city of Jerusalem.

Alas, she is quite soon set off, on the road again. A large group of letters begins, because the Greeleys didn't much like Nathan and the two had to meet here and there, missing each other at planned meetings; and as a writer, she has the natural inclination, highly developed, to put every turn of feeling on paper.

When they went to see the model of Jerusalem, she learned that Nathan was a Jew, and although at times Fuller had shown the inclination of the period to Jewish stereotyping, she takes a quick leap. "I have long had a presentiment, that I should meet— nearly—one of your race, who would show me how the sun of today shines on the ancient Temple—but I did not expect so gentle and civilized an apparition and with blue eyes!"

A lot is to be discovered. Nathan was in the process of rehabilitating a "maiden" and when the maiden turns out to be his mistress, so far as we can tell from M.F.'s letters, his explanation, too, has to be taken in. "I only wished to be satisfied, and when you told me how you viewed the incident I really was so. Do not think of it ever again."

Then Nathan makes an "assault upon her person," as it was spoken of at the time. She rebuffs him, but here it is possible to think of more complication of feeling, during and after, than most commentators might find evident. She writes to him, of course, and quickly about this "sadder day than I had in all my life." She had been exposed to "what was to every worthy and womanly feeling so humiliating." And,

> I know you could not help it. But why had fate drawn me so near you? ... You have said that there is in yourself both a lower and a higher being than I was aware of. Since you said this, I suppose I have seen the lower! ... Will you not come with me before God and promise me severe truth, and patient tenderness, that will never, if it can be avoided, misinterpret the impulses of my soul?

Nathan sends her a little dog, a burdensome gift for one moving here and there in the city and working day and night and writing to him day and night. The letters become quite frenzied with that pitiful wonder of the injured person of what she might have done wrong. Nathan is given to confessions of weakness that interest her, being new, no doubt. "Your hand removes at last the veil from my eyes. It is indeed myself who have caused all ill." What is unbalancing in this episode is that she is still writing in the transcendental mode of friendship and beauty and perfect trust in which the "assault"—unthinkable in Boston among familiars—was confusing but quite a new circumstance to think about.

But the weighty letters, the difficulty of reading them to say nothing of responding, this made its mark, and Nathan took flight to Europe, with the "maiden" along and promising to return. She wrote and received no answer. Did the letter arrive? Had his letter gone astray? When he does write, it is to ask for a favor, and then months pass without a word.

In 1846, she left the *Tribune* and sailed at last for Europe, where she still hoped to unite once more with Nathan. In Edinburgh, he wrote that he was being married, but he refused to return her letters, refused even a second request, saying, "I shall do nothing with them but what is right, manly, and honorable." He promised to destroy the letters but did not do so. His son tried to sell them. In the end, Nathan left a stipulation in his will that they should be published. And published they were, in 1903, a half century after Margaret Fuller's death, as *The Love Letters of Margaret Fuller,* with a fatuous, unnecessary introduction by Julia Ward Howe and a swinish "reminiscence" by Nathan, written in 1873 and apparently left with the letters for posterity.

> I cannot suffer their [the letters'] exquisite naturalness and sweetness to sink into the grave.... I can wreathe no fresher laurels around the cherished memory of Margaret than by showing, through these letters, that great and gifted as she was as a writer, she was no less so in the soft and tender emotions of a true woman's heart.

"Had I only come ten years earlier! Now my life must be a failure, so much strength has been wasted on abstractions, which only came because I grew not in the right soil," Margaret Fuller wrote to Emerson, from Italy. She went first to England and Scotland, with letters from Emerson to Carlyle and others; useful, but she was herself known. *Woman* had been published in England, *The Dial* was admired, and her reviews in the *Tribune*—along with the fact that she was, in the same journal, to support herself abroad by interviews with "personalities" and descriptions of the scene—did not hinder any more then than now.

She met everyone, even the aged Wordsworth at Grasmere and De Quincey, and picked up gossip. "It seems the cause of Coleridge's separation from his family was wholly with himself; because his opium and his indolence prevented his making any exertions to support them."

The most important meetings of her later life were with two vivid, spectacular, radical intellectuals: Giuseppe Mazzini, fabulous throughout Europe, and Adam Mickiewicz, the great Polish poet and patriot. And another meeting with a young Italian, the Marchese Giovanni Angelo Ossoli, by whom she had, at the age of thirty-eight, a son out of wedlock and whom she later married or did not marry.

Most of the admiring commentaries on Margaret Fuller are eager for her to "find herself as a woman" and also to become a radical in social reform. It is not possible to know if she found herself as a woman, but she did love and was loved by Ossoli, although she was careful not to claim apotheosis.

She became a radical by way of her passionate response to the European unheavals of 1848. (Emerson was in Europe in 1848, and she wrote him from Rome: "Why did you not try to be in Paris at the opening of the Assembly? There were elements worth scanning.") There was social reform and then some around Concord, but as an aesthete she was bored by Brook Farm, and the Boston Abolitionists were "so tedious, often so narrow, always so rabid and exaggerated in their tone." Her thoughts about political agitation changed when she began to connect the antislavery movement with the liberation of Italy, for which she hoped in her *Tribune* dispatches to arouse American sympathies.

It was at the Carlyles' that she met Mazzini.* He was in exile,

---

*I am indebted for much about the European period of Margaret Fuller's life to Joseph J. Deiss, *The Roman Years of Margaret Fuller.*

raising money for Italian refugees, planning a campaign of return, writing in all the leading English journals not only on politics but on art and literature, and charming almost everyone in the nation with his great personal beauty and the purity of his idealism and self-sacrifice. "The most beautiful man I ever saw," was the comment of men and women alike. The cause of Italian liberation and the character of Mazzini, and later that of Garibaldi, electrified the English literary imagination and found its way into countless poems, novels, and plays. In 1879, almost thirty years after Margaret Fuller's death, there appeared an imaginary conversation in verse, written by the radical journalist W. J. Linton. The title was "Mazzini and the Countess Ossoli." At the end of this curious bit of versifying, Mazzini has left the stage and "the Countess, alone, prays for him."*

The friendship with Mazzini was genuine in England and grew even closer in Rome. They held many important things in common, Mazzini wrote to his mother, whom Margaret Fuller visited when her boat landed in Genoa. Before leaving England for Paris, there had been a plan to smuggle Mazzini into Italy in disguise and with a false American passport. More than one thing went wrong and just as well.

In Paris, Fuller met Mickiewicz at George Sand's apartment. Their encounter, he said, was one which "consoles and fortifies." She was "a true person" and "the only woman to whom it has been given to touch what is decisive in the present world and to have a presentiment of the world of the future."

Mickiewicz was a bohemian, more forthright and intimately observing than the spiritual Mazzini. To Fuller, he suggested, and apparently without any wishes of his own, that the first step in her deliverance "is to know whether you are permitted to remain a virgin."

When Mickiewicz came to Rome to recruit among the Poles living in exile, he stayed in her lodgings, and when she was suffering from illness brought on by her pregnancy, he was the first to be told

*Harry Rudman, *Italian Nationalism and English Letters*, p. 167.

the secret. "You are frightened at a very natural, very common ailment, and you exaggerate it in an extravagant manner," he told her. Mickiewicz was to be the child's godfather, but he was not about when Ossoli, determined upon the baptism both for his Catholicism and to legitimate the child, proceeded with the certification.

Fuller and Ossoli met in Saint Peter's Church, after an Easter service. Somehow, Fuller became separated from her companions, and while wandering about the church was asked by a young Italian if he could be of help. They walked back across the Tiber to the Corso. So, Mickiewicz said when he was told, it was at last to be, *"un petit Italien, dans l'église."*

Ossoli was twenty-seven, ten years younger. His mother died when he was a boy, and he lived in the family palazzo with his older brothers and sisters and their ailing father, whom he was taking care of. Later, much about Ossoli was obscured or questioned, either by malice, the secrecy of his connection with Margaret Fuller, or by his reserve and scant English. What seems to be true is that he was from an old family long attached to the Papacy, not rich, and certainly conventional in thought. His father and one older brother were high papal functionaries; two other brothers were in the Pope's Guardia Nobile. It seems, although it is disputed, that he had Republican sympathies before meeting Margaret Fuller, rather than that she swayed him in that direction. In any case, he joined the Civil Guard, put himself in much danger, and with the fall of the Republic would have had to flee Rome in any case.

The marriage, or the "underplot," as Henry James called it: Soon after their first meeting he proposed marriage, not necessarily legal. Margaret Fuller drew back. "The connection seemed so every way unfit." Instead, she went off to Florence and Venice as planned, but after a few months she changed her mind and returned to Rome, with almost nothing to live on.

Were they ever actually married? There is confusion here and no sure date or place. The impediments to marriage were many, among them the difficulty of getting a dispensation to marry a

Protestant and the confusion of bureaucratic documentation in the city's chaos. Also, Ossoli did not wish to be disinherited of the little property that was to come to him on his father's death. (His unfriendly brothers, owing to his Republicanism, managed to disinherit him in any case.) Then there is the question of whether Margaret Fuller cared about marriage vows. William Henry Channing argued that marriage was against her principles. Emerson thought otherwise: "When it came to be a practical question to herself, she would feel that this was a tie that ought to have the solemnist sanction; that against the theorist was a vast public opinion, too vast to brave." Some evidence can be made to support an actual marriage between the two, but uncertainty remains.

During 1849, Margaret witnessed the flight of the Pope, the announcement of the Constituent Assembly, the declaration of the Republic, and Mazzini's triumphant entrance into Rome. The happiness did not last long; French troops intervened, and the slaughter of the siege of Rome set in. She herself nursed the wounded, along with one of Europe's most celebrated beauties, the romantic, radical Princess Belgioioso. Margaret Fuller's conquest of the "radical chic" figures in Italy—and even of her conservative friend, the important, rich Marchesa Arconati Visconti—seemed to have come about in a natural, unexceptional fashion. She was not seen to be too *exalté*, aggressive, and learned—after all, they knew their Tasso, Dante, and the divine Raphael also.

There had been a cooling off, a winding down, we imagine, achieved by the surrounding acceptance of herself, her learning, her rapturous zeal and gift for friendship. She was as she was, interesting, unique in many ways, and companionable. Only her writing still suffered from orphic diffusion, from a sentimental femininity of accent. "Hard was the heart, stony and seared the eye, that had no tear for that moment."

Her dispatches to the *Tribune*, covering all the great events, were written in the first person and were personal in every sense, filled with pleading, and descriptive passages a bit commonplace. There is also concern for the diplomatic and military tangle of alliances and events. Her Republican bias is candid, in a manner that would not be thought suitable today. Indeed, her reports of disillusionment with the waverings of Pope Pius IX outraged the Catholic diocese in New York. Complaints were made, but Greeley published the accounts uncensored.

Toward the end of her stay in Rome, her writing begins to show a greater control and becomes more graceful and useful, with fewer "effects" that stress her own emotions.

> I entered the French ground, all hollowed and mapped like a honeycomb. A pair of skeleton legs protruded from the bank of one barricade; lower, a dog had scratched away its light covering from the body of a man, and discovered it lying face upward all dressed; the dog stood gazing on it with an air of stupid amazement.

By the end of June, the Republic had fallen to the French troops, and the losers were fleeing. The Ossoli family left for Florence and the following summer embarked for America. The last years of Margaret Fuller's life had been horrible: poverty, overwork, illness; her son nearly starved to death in the town of Rieti where she had left him with a wet nurse in order to return to Rome to make her living.

All the while, she had been preserving documents, taking notes, in addition to her dispatches, for a work to be called "History of the Italian Revolution." The loss of the book has been lamented. She had made inquiries about the possibility of publication in England, which were refused. Part of her reason for returning to America was that she thought it would help in making the arrangements for publication.

She asked Emerson's advice, and the answer shows that he was well aware of her "situation" with a husband, perhaps, and a little boy, certainly. Her family and various others had been informed.

(Earlier, when she was awaiting the birth of the child, she received a letter from Emerson, in Paris at the time, quite sweetly urging her to come home with him, where he said he would find a pleasant little house for her.) But now the possibility of the return of the irregular family was not so agreeable to imagine. He advised that Italy was an important advantage to her work. "It is certainly an unexpected side for me to support—the advantage of your absenteeism."

However, return she did, even if in a spirit of gloom about her reception, her devastating poverty, Ossoli's poor prospects, her ill health and exhaustion. They could not afford a steamer and took a merchant boat, a voyage of over two months. She packed all her documents, her notes, and the letters between herself and Ossoli, as well as others. The manuscript for the book was stored in another box.

The journey was a disaster from the start. The captain took sick of smallpox and died; the child contracted the disease but lived. The ship went on, reaching New Jersey for a landing in New York the following day. Trunks were brought from the hold, the child dressed in his best, America to be faced. A fierce storm came up in the night and the ship began to go down off Fire Island. It started to sink near enough to the shore for some of the passengers to make land by the use of a plank; some drowned in a like attempt. A steward tried to take the child to shore but was swamped by a wave. Margaret Fuller was last seen in a white nightgown, holding the broken mast. The body of the child was recovered and claimed by the Fuller family. The box of letters and other personal documents survived, but the manuscript box was lost. The bodies of Margaret Fuller and Ossoli were not recovered. Bell Chevigny came upon a note in the Harvard Library that indicated that the bodies were indeed found, put in coffins, and shipped to Greeley, who refused to take any kind of action. The captain of the boat in this account worried about his jurisdiction in the matter and buried the bodies at night on Coney Island.

"I have lost in her my audience," Emerson said. Thoreau, not the dearest of her friends, paid her the finest tribune—a journey to Fire

Island to look for the remains. Margaret Fuller was forty years old when she died.

———

Epilogue: Perfidious Hawthorne. The background is rather sketchy, although Hawthorne's dislike is not surprising. An early entry in his journal: "I was invited to dine at Mr. Bancroft's yesterday with Miss Margaret Fuller; but Providence had given me some business to do, for which I was very grateful."

Two years later, a more pastoral entry:

> After leaving the book at Mr. Emerson's I returned through the woods, and, entering Sleepy Hollow, I perceived a lady reclining near the path which bends along its verge. It was Margaret herself. She had been there the whole afternoon, meditating or reading.... She said that nobody had broken her solitude, and was just giving utterance to the theory that no inhabitant of Concord ever visited Sleepy Hollow, when we saw a group of people entering its sacred precincts.

Perhaps a bit of irony in the final clause.

Sophia Peabody Hawthorne, the placid, settled wife of the disturbed, settled Hawthorne, on "The Great Lawsuit":

> What do you think of the speech Queen Margaret Fuller has made from the throne? It seems to me that if she were married truly, she would no longer be puzzled about the rights of women. This is the revelation of woman's true destiny and place, which can never be *imagined* by those who do not experience the relation.

No doubt Hawthorne would have expressed it differently, as men and women married to those not concerned with the refinements of writing have good reason to know.

Hawthorne's *The Blithedale Romance*, in which the principal character, Zenobia, is often identified with Margaret Fuller, appeared in 1852, two years after her death. The death was a profound shock to the New England countryside, with the grieving family and old friends caught up in the tragedy and faced with the sharp conundrum of the life. While Hawthorne was writing *The Blithedale Romance*, the *Memoirs of Margaret Fuller Ossoli*, with an account of the history of the family and personal essays by Emerson, James Freeman Clarke, and W. H. Channing, was being composed and arranged. Both books appeared in the same year.

The "striking" remarks by Emerson do not altogether reveal his own and the others' great swell of reverence for their departed friend. The memorial volume edited, omitted, and even destroyed with a free hand; it also wished to assure that the object of veneration was safely married at the time of the conception of the child. Later scholars have been quick to point out the moral scrubbing of documents and to see the volume as a reduction of the vitality of the subject. Still, *Memoirs*, containing many letters and reminiscences of encounters among the group, is extraordinarily interesting and moving; it is possible to view it as the true salvaging of Margaret Fuller's life and thought, which otherwise might have been greatly shadowed in American literary history.

The setting of *The Blithedale Romance* is, as Hawthorne said, "based on my experiences and observations at Brook Farm," the hopeful and not quite practical socialist community established in Roxbury, outside Boston. Hawthorne also insists that the characters are fictional. Nevertheless, Zenobia, "the high spirited Woman, bruising herself against the narrow limitations of her sex," was thought by contemporaries to be a reflection of Margaret Fuller.

There are elements that correspond, but Hawthorne knew as a novelist that he could not have as the central figure a heroine he saw as wholly unappetizing. Had he drawn Margaret Fuller as he saw her, the results are not pleasing to anticipate, but the novel would have been less foolish, as in many ways it is; it might have been a strange modern fiction.

Zenobia is a great and riveting beauty; she is rich, with a mysterious past. She is a performer and a sort of writer with a "magazine signature." She is a feminist who "scorns the petty restraints that take the life and color out of other women's conversations." Zenobia, pretentious, nevertheless has no real culture, "her mind is full of weeds," which Hawthorne may have believed about Margaret Fuller, even though her culture was greater than his and greater than he needed.

In the book, the narrator, close to Hawthorne himself, has a sudden intuition about Zenobia. He divines, by some special mannish knowledge: "Zenobia is a wife! Zenobia has lived and loved!" The revelations about Margaret Fuller were distressing not only to the morals but to the vanity of the Concord circle. She was an "adulteress" and, if married at all, the wife of a titled foreigner, all rather exotic and *superior. The Scarlet Letter* was begun the year of the death off Fire Island. No just connection can be made but in practical reality Margaret Fuller was the big A in the experience of the countryside. In *The Blithedale Romance,* it may be noted that Zenobia, in a gruesome description, drowns herself because of love for an unworthy man.

In 1858, Hawthorne made his own Italian journey, and one of the things he did was to run down, like a detective, the Margaret Fuller and Ossoli affair. Hawthorne left in his notebooks an account of a conversation with Joseph Mozier, an Ohio merchant who had gone to Florence to become a sculptor and who had known Fuller. These strange unearthings, violent and above all relishing in tone, are contradictory to the facts and to the moral and emotional remembrances of Margaret Fuller in Italy and at home.

Hawthorne is concerned to remove the title "Marchese" from Ossoli and, if he cannot quite do that, to reduce him to a boy picked up on the street, an idiot, and to see Margaret Fuller as a sort of desperate procuress. His recording of his conversations with Mozier reflects as much his own feeling as that of one who had known Margaret Fuller in Italy.

Mozier... then passed to Margaret Fuller, whom he knew well. His developments about poor Margaret were very curious. He says that Ossoli's family, though technically noble, is of no rank whatever; his elder brother, with the title of Marquis, being at the time a working bricklayer, and the sisters walking the streets without bonnets—that is, being in the station of peasant girls.... Ossoli, himself, to the best of his [Mozier's] belief, was Margaret's servant, or had something to do with the care of her apartments. He was the handsomest man Mozier ever saw, but entirely ignorant even of his own language, scarcely able to read at all, destitute of manners; in short, half an idiot, and without any pretensions to be a gentleman.... As for her towards him, I do not understand what feeling there could have been, except it was purely sexual; as for him towards her, there could hardly have been even this, for she had not the charm of womanhood.... She had a strong and coarse nature, too, which she had done her utmost to refine with infinite pains, but which of course could only be superficially changed.... Margaret has not left in the minds of those who knew her any deep witness to her integrity and purity. She was a great humbug; of course with much talent, and much moral reality, or else she could not have been such a great humbug.

She had no manuscript, Hawthorne insists; it did not exist. And he concludes:

Thus there appears to have been a total collapse in poor Margaret, morally and intellectually, and tragic as her catastrophe was, Providence was, after all, kind in putting her, and her clownish husband, and their child, on board that fated ship ... a strange, heavy, unpliable, and in many respects, defective and evil nature ... she proved herself a woman after all and fell like the lowest of her sisters.

(*1986*)

Gertrude Stein

In the midst of her unflagging cheerfulness and confidence, Gertrude Stein can be a pitiless companion. Insomniac rhythms and melodious drummings: She likes to tell you what you know and to tell it again and sometimes to let up for a bit only to tell you once more: "To know all the kinds of ways then to make men and women one must know all the ways some are like others of them, are different from others of them, so then there come to be kinds of them."

Her writing, T. S. Eliot once said, "has a kinship with the saxophone." That could be one of her own throwaways, but she would not have used a word like *saxophone*. The saxophone is an object with a history, and she didn't care much for nouns with such unique significance.

What can Eliot mean? The saxophone, invented in 1846 by Adolphe Sax, has little standing in the hereditary precincts of the classical orchestra. So it must be that Gertrude Stein is a barbaric and illicit intrusion. Preceding the curiosity of the saxophone, Eliot said about her work: "It is not improving, it is not amusing, it is not interesting, it is not good for one's mind." No doubt, Eliot wasn't aware of the improvisations of the great American masters of the saxophone.

In any case, Gertrude Stein was born in 1874, nearly thirty years after the birth of the saxophone. Her family and its situation must have been the womb of her outlandish confidence, confidence of a degree amazing. She was, after all, determined to be, even if *in absentia*, or because of that exile, our country's historian. There is nothing hothouse in this peculiar American princess. For one thing, she is as sturdy as a turnip—the last resort of the starving, and native to the Old World, as the dictionary has it. A tough root of some sort; and yet she is mesmerized and isolated, castlebound, too, under the enchantments of her own devising.

Confidence is highly regarded by both citizen and nation; it is altogether warm and loving. Without confidence, fidelity to death, as it were, the work Gertrude Stein actually produced cannot easily be imagined. Other writings, perhaps, since possibility was everywhere in her; but not what we have, not what she did. In her life, confidence and its not-too-gradual ascent into egotism combined with a certain laziness and insolence. It was her genius to make the two work together like a machine, a wondrous contraption, something futuristic and patented for her use.

She wrote her Cambridge lecture at the height of her fame, while waiting for her car to be fixed. She sat down on the fender of another car and, waiting around, wrote "Composition as Explanation." Several hours it took her: "Everything is the same except composition and as the composition is different and always going to be different everything is not the same." So it was. And: "Now if we write, we write; and these things we know flow down our arm and come out on the page." Yes. So she told Thornton Wilder.

Many wires and pieces of string went into the contraption, the tinkering, and the one result was that she wrote at great length and used a vocabulary very, very small. It was her original idea to make this vocabulary sufficient for immensities of conception, America, Americans, being perhaps her favorite challenge. When she is not tinkering, we can see her like a peasant assaulting the chicken for Sunday dinner. She would wring the neck of her words. And wring the neck of sentences, also.

Miss Stein lived until 1946, through two world wars and much else. Perhaps she never seemed young, and everyone would certainly have wished for her to live on and on, since there is a Methuselah prodigiousness about her. Everything we know about her life contributes to her being.

When was she not a prodigy—and even without exerting herself to represent the exceptional in action? She went to Harvard and studied with William James. Anecdotes appeared on her doorstep, anecdotes quite enduring. No, she didn't want to take an examination because the day was too fine. William James understood and gave her the highest mark in the course, if we can trust the *Autobiography of Alice B. Toklas,* which we can and cannot.

Premedical studies at John Hopkins; that is part of her aura. Perhaps she's a scientist, so look, when the pages confuse, for the rigors of the laboratory. She abandoned the medical studies, and we must say that, too, added something to the whole. The willful simplification she practiced can make her, to some, appear to be a philosopher in the most difficult mode of our own period.

It will be said William James taught her that everything must be considered, nothing rejected. Simple enough and not quite a discovery. What you can say is that while she was not learning, actively not learning, other young women were going to finishing schools, primping, dancing, and having babies, and she was becoming Gertrude Stein. Every refusal was *interesting,* a word she liked very much.

Both of her parents were German Jews. Whether she thought of herself as Jewish is hard to say. Perhaps she didn't, or not quite. She didn't like to be defined and that helped her to stay on in Occupied France. Her brother Leo thought of himself as Jewish, even at Harvard—or (why not?) certainly at Harvard.

Her parents were, in terms appropriate for American history, early settlers. That she knew and took in seriously. If, as one can read, the definition of Old New York, of New York aristocracy, is to have made your money before the Civil War, the Steins were aristocrats. The Stein brothers, one of whom was her father, arrived in 1841; her mother's family had settled in Baltimore previously.

A Stein Brothers clothing store was set up in Baltimore with success, but Gertrude's father and the brother moved on to Allegheny, Pennsylvania, where she was born. Then quite soon the characteristic behavior of the family began to assert itself. They showed a desire to take off, for Europe. They are inclined to be Americans abroad.

The family finances are not easy to make out, at the beginning or at the end. But even when the Allegheny store was not quite flourishing, Amelia Stein took herself and the children to Vienna. There they lived with governesses and tutors, the lessons and practices of the upper class. The Steins early on must have realized that one could be almost rich in Europe at that time without being rich enough at home. And they liked to buy things, to go shopping. The mother and children went to Paris to buy clothes and trinkets and to have a good time. In a later period, while Gertrude and Leo remained abroad, the older brother, Michael, and his wife, Sarah, came back to stun California with their collection of modern paintings.

From Pennsylvania, the family settled in Oakland, California, and the father, Daniel Stein, went into the streetcar business—a good career move, it would be called nowadays, even if Daniel was not quite the master of it. He died when Gertrude Stein was seventeen, and she wrote about his disappearance: "Then our life without a father began a very pleasant one." But more of that later, about the pleasantness of not having family members and the strain when you have them.

The older brother, Michael, took over the family business and made good investments for the fine purpose of not having to work. He was able to set Gertrude and Leo up abroad: a princely situation. Michael and his wife, Sarah, were connoisseurs of the new, not of the refectory table from an old monastery or the great decorated urns to put in the hall and fill with dead reeds. For a time, they lived just outside Paris in a house designed by Le Corbusier.

In this family, you are not concerned with provincials—never at any point in their history. Not one of them seemed afflicted with puritanical, thrifty scruples, with denial or failure of nerve. Works of art were, in the end, their most daring and prudent investment. The paintings and the great international celebrity of the creative one, Gertrude, and even the fading claims of Leo make of the Steins one of the truly glittering American families. They stand in history along with the Adams and James families—along with if not quite commensurate with. They were immensely important in the history of American taste, by way of their promotion of modern painting through their collections and in their influence on the many painters, writers, and intellectuals who came to the *salon* on the rue de Fleurus.

The Cone sisters of Baltimore, contemporaries of the Steins, were to merit a kind of immortality when they used their cotton-mill fortune to buy Manets, Renoirs, Cézannes, and Matisses for the later glory of the Baltimore Museum. Acquisition has need of special conviction and taste, but neither of the Cone women could claim for themselves an art to rank with that of Cézanne and Picasso—a claim that Gertrude Stein did not hesitate to make.

Picasso, bewildered by the Stein entourage, coming and going in Paris, said: "They are not women. They are not men. They are Americans."

The Stein family was to be The Making of Americans. "It has always seemed to me a rare privilege, this of being an American, a real American, one whose tradition it has taken scarcely sixty years to create." There is no doubt Gertrude knows how to look at it, this subject of being American—the sixty years names it just right. An amused chauvinism—that is her tone. And elsewhere she notes that America is the oldest country in the world because it's been in the twentieth century the longest, something like that.

Still, it must be said Gertrude Stein feels more sentiment for

America than she does for her fellow Steins, except as a subject. The mother, the Baltimore bride, faded into illness and at last died when Gertrude was fourteen: "We had already had the habit of doing without her." Simon, older (Gertrude was the youngest), ate a lot and was slow. Bertha, well, she never cared for Bertha: "It is natural not to care for a sister, certainly not when she is four years older and grinds her teeth at night."

The alliance between Gertrude and Leo ended in bitter contempt on both sides. It was said that Gertrude gave Picasso's portrait of Leo to Etta Cone in order to get it off the wall. When Gertrude died, she and Leo were so greatly estranged he knew of her death only by reading about it in the papers. His comment was: "I can't say it touched me. I had lost not only all regard, but all respect for her." They were an odd lot, except for Michael, but then, as she put it herself: "It takes time to make queer people, and to have others who can know it, time and a certainty of means."

Three Lives was finished in 1906, published in 1909—in every way a work of resonating originality, even if no aspect of its striking manner will persist in the eccentric shape of the works that follow. The stories are composed in the manner of a tale. The characters are sketched by a trait or two, and they pace through their lives, as the pattern has ordained; and then each one dies.

Sometimes there is an echo of realistic fiction, the setting of a scene, the filling in of detail, but we are given almost everything by assertion, and thus there is an archaic quality to the tone. But, of course, the tone is new, partly because of this archaic picturing. No other writer would have composed these moving portraits as Gertrude Stein composed them. One, "Melanctha," is of a higher order than the other two, "The Good Anna" and "The Gentle Lena."

Nothing is sentimental. We are not asked to experience more emotion than the scene can render; the stories do not manipulate in excess of their own terms. A distance is maintained, a distance—perhaps it is objectivity—that provides a fresh, bare surface for the sketching of the lives of the two German women of what used to be called "the serving class" and the extraordinary daring of the picture of Negro life and character as she has imagined it.

"Melanctha" is the most challenging as a composition, and the character is the most challenging because she has an interior life. The presentation is for the most part in dialogue of a radical brilliance that lies on the page with a calm defiance. It is as stunning today as when it was first written.

Whether this dialogue is the natural rhythm of Negro speech is not altogether the point. Such a rhythm if discovered for transcription cannot be copyrighted; no author can own it for a certain number of pages. On the other hand, it is clear that the language of "Melanctha" is some kind of speech rhythm not written down before, some catching of accent and flow the reader recognizes without being able to name. Of course, it is a literary language, constructed of repetition, repeated emphasis, all with great musicality. There is a stilted openness to it; that is, it is both declamatory, unnatural, and yet somehow lifelike. It is a courteous dialogue and not condescending because it does not proceed from models, from a spurious idea, from the shelf of a secondhand store.

Inauthenticity is so often remarked when authors need to find a speech for those not from their own class or experience. Stephen Crane's powerful but badly written *Maggie: A Girl of the Streets* is an example of prefab ethnic or class speech. "Hully gee!" said he, "does mugs can't phase me. Dey knows I kin wipe up d'street wid any tree of dem"—Hell's Kitchen.

Gertrude Stein's way in "Melanctha" is so simple and arresting that her ear, in an offhand passage, does have a ghostly attuning. Note the distribution of the *yous* in a plain bit of dialogue spoken by Melanctha's father: "Why don't you see to that girl better you, you're her mother." Pure ear, quite different from the formal cadences of Dr. Jeff Campbell, the mellifluous suitor with his high-pitched arias to the "wandering" Melanctha: "It certainly does sound a little like I don't know very well what I do mean, when you put it like that to me, Miss Melanctha, but that's just because you don't understand enough about what I meant, by what I was just saying to you."

Hemingway learned from Gertrude Stein how to become Ernest Hemingway. Perhaps one could say that. He decided most of all to strip down his sentences. (It is curious to learn condensation from Stein, who stripped, reduced, and simplified only to add up without mercy, making her prose an intimidating heap of bare bones, among other things.) One can see it in 1921—before they had met, but not before he would have read *Three Lives*. Perhaps he learned more from the *yous* than from the more insistent rhythms in "Melanctha."

From "Up in Michigan":

> Liz liked Jim very much. She liked it the way he walked over from the shop and often went to the kitchen door to watch for him to start down the road. She liked it about his mustache.... She liked it very much that he didn't look like a blacksmith. She liked it how much D. J. Smith and Mrs. Smith liked Jim. One day she found that she liked it the way the hair was black on his arms and how white they were above the tanned line when he washed up in the washbasin outside the house.

And then he ends the paragraph: "Liking that made her feel funny." Gertrude Stein would not have written the last line. It is too girlish for her, and is a repudiation of the tone and rhythm that goes before.

Soon after *Three Lives*, *The Making of Americans* was resumed, since it had been started earlier. It was taken up—if that is not a contradiction of what it is, a dive into the deep waters of the Stein Sea. Down into the Stein Sea she went between 1906 and 1908, and the book was not actually published until 1925, for reasons not a mystery. It is very long. It swims about and about and farther and farther out with the murmurous monotony of untroubled waters.

The enormous ambition of the book is shown in the roundness of the title. It may be a sort of chronicle, imaginative history, of the

Stein family, but that's the least of it. It is the making of Americans, just as she says. That is the intention.

In his introduction, Bernard Fay writes, not without leaning in the direction of her own style: "She likes too much the present; she is too fond of words; she has too strongly the love of life; she is too far from death, to be satisfied with anything but the whole of America."

Consider her idea of the bottom nature of human beings: "A man in his living has many things inside him, he has in him his way of beginning; this can come too from a mixture in him, from the bottom nature of him." So we live and so we die. "Any one has come to be a dead one. Any one has not come to be such a one to be a dead one. Many who were living have come to be a dead one." The cold, black suet-pudding of her style, said Wyndham Lewis.

The "continuous present" is another of her rhetorical discoveries, and it seems to be just a circling round and round, a not going back or forward. *Four in America:* It is not clear how much she knows about her four Americans, how much she wished to know about Ulysses Grant, Henry James, the Wright Brothers, and George Washington. Her meditations do not run to facts or dates, and her vanity would preclude a quotation or even an appropriation. Instead, she asks herself what the four would have done had they been other than what they were. Suppose Grant to be a saint, Henry James a general, the Wright Brothers painters, George Washington a novelist.

What is the difference between Shakespeare's plays and Shakespeare's sonnets? "Shakespeare's plays were written as they were written. Shakespeare's sonnets as they were going to be written." Sometimes an interesting bit comes upon one suddenly, like a handout on the street: "Henry James had no failure and no success." Everything is process. There is no need for revision since the work celebrates and represents process itself, like an endless stirring on the stove. One gift never boils away: She is a comedian.

Such was her gift, and she created a style to display the comedy by a deft repetition of word and phrase. To display the comedy of what? Of living, of thinking? The comedy of writing words down on the page, perhaps that most of all. She was not concerned with creating the structure of classical comedy, the examination of folly. What she understands is inadvertence and incongruity. Imperturbability is her mood, and in that she is herself a considerable comic actor, in the line of Buster Keaton.

Remarks are not literature, so she said. But the remark is her triumph. She lives by epigrams and bits of wit cut out of the stretches or repetition, as if by a knife, and mounted in our memory. Her rival in this mastery is Oscar Wilde, with whom she shared many modes of performance: the bold stare that faced down ridicule, a certain ostentation of type, the love of publicity and the iron to endure it.

I like a view but I like to sit with my back to it.

What is the point of being a little boy if you are going to grow up to be a man?

Before the flowers of friendship faded friendship faded.

I am I because my little dog knows me.

Ezra Pound is a village explainer, excellent if you were a village, but if not, not.

Oscar Wilde was an aesthete. Gertrude Stein thought up something more stylish and impressive. She came forth as an aesthetician: more severe and riddling, yet dandyish in her handsome wools and velvety in her sentences.

"Continuous present": Her most valuable continuous present or presence was the alliance with Alice B. Toklas. It appeared she could achieve herself, become Gertrude Stein, without Leo, and she found him expendable. He combined her vanity with a down-turning contentiousness and tedious pretension, all bereft of her revolutionary accent and brilliant dogmatism.

But still she ponders ones and twos and twos not being ones and then had the luck to turn a corner and find this small, neat person from California, one with the intelligence, competence, and devotion to complete the drama of the large, indolent, brooding, ambitious sibyl, herself.

They are a diptych: figures gazing straight ahead, with no hint of Cubist distortion. A museum aspect to their image—wooden, fixed, iconographic in the Byzantine style. They are serene and a bit sly in the direct gaze.

Everything works, above all the division of labor. Carl Van Vechten considered that Gertrude couldn't sew on a button, couldn't cook an egg or place a postage stamp of the correct denomination on an envelope. Alice's labors over the manuscripts, the copying and proofreading, with a numbing attention to the mysteries of the commas that are and the commas that are not, make of her a heroine of minute distinctions.

The *Autobiography of Alice B.* overwhelms by charm and the richness of the cast and the rosy dawn in Paris at the time. The tone and the wit of the composition stand in an almost perfect balance to the historical vividness of the moment. The book is valiant in self-promotion also, boldly forward in conceit, but that is what spurs the recollection. Otherwise it would not have been worth the effort, Gertrude Stein's effort.

She enjoyed the *Autobiography* a good deal more than some of the great personages on the scene. More than one felt himself or herself to be wrongly presented. Matisse was not amused; he charged she knew nothing about painting. Braque was dismayed by her account of the beginnings of Cubism. Tristan Tzara called her "a clinical case of megalomania."

"Testimony Against Gertrude Stein" appeared in *Transition*. Eugene Jolas, who edited the pamphlet, wrote: "There is a unanimity of opinion that she had no understanding of what really was happening about her, that the mutation of ideas beneath the surface of the more obvious contacts and clashes of personality during the period escaped her entirely."

No matter, she was now a bona-fide international celebrity and had an American public. Books, poems, lectures, plays appeared—and she appeared in person. She returned to America in 1934 for a lecture tour, and everyone knew she had said a rose is a rose is a rose. Newspapermen came to the ship, crowds were waiting at the dock. She and Alice were photogenic, and Gertrude was ready with a reply to every question. It is Oscar Wilde landing in America in the 1880s with nothing to declare but his genius.

She returned to Paris, and then there was World War II and the Occupation—tragic, complex events not suitable to her talent and disrupting to her comfort. Her removal from large events, the hypnotic immersion in the centrality of her own being, made it possible for this very noticeable couple to stay on in France, move here and there, get food, in a sense to brazen it out and be there when the Americans arrived. And wasn't she first and last an American, a true example of the invulnerability of the New World? To be imperturbable, root strong, can be a kind of personal V-day.

Wars I Have Seen, published in 1945, covers these ruminating years in the countryside. It reads like a diary, the recording of events of the day. Perhaps it was dictated to Alice in the evenings. The landscape of the Occupation provided splendid vignettes and an awesome and rich cud of complacency. She did not understand the war, and she did not like things to be troublesome, and so she is increasingly conservative. Both Pétain and Franco pleased her—comfort requires order, that she understood.

But, at last, she had to mull over the question of Jewishness:

The Jews have never been an economic power as anybody knows who knows and as everybody knows who knows. But the Europeans particularly the countries who like to delude their people do not want to know it, and the Jews do not want anybody to know it, although they know it perfectly well they must know it because it would make themselves to themselves feel less important and as they always as the chosen people have felt themselves to be important they do not want anybody to know it.

If it were not for the fact that the reader supplies his own vision of Gertrude and Alice hanging on with the fortitude of lambs hunting for the sheepfold, the whimsicality of *Wars* would offend. "Oh dear. It would all be so funny if it were not so terrifying and so sad."

She lived a long time with her wondrous contraption, the Model T of her style, and sometimes she could run on things with a turn of phrase, but sometimes not. So, she opines, "Soviet Russia will end in nothing so will the Roosevelt administration end in nothing because it is not stimulating it will end in nothing." From the sheepfold, she took up dangerous challenges and offered a work called "Reflections on the Atomic Bomb." She found that the bomb was not interesting.

Anyway, she, the first American, loved the GIs, and they loved her. But she didn't know anything about the young men, and *Brewsie and Willie* (1946) is the aesthetician's defeat. The dialogue is atrocious. She had forgotten that she must fabricate speech, not believe she has captured it at the train station. By now, she is speaking in her own voice, just like any other old person, and confident always, she addresses the nation: "Find out the reason why, look facts in the face, not just what they all say, the leaders, but every darn one of you so that a government by the people for the people shall not perish from the earth, it won't, somebody else will do it if we lie down on the job." And so on.

Finally she emerged as a strange figure, competitive and jealous and also unworldly in her self-isolation. She could not understand why *Ulysses*, radical and difficult—or so she had been told for perhaps she hadn't read it—should have been selling more than *The Making of Americans.* Joyce is difficult because he has more knowledge, more language, more rhythmical musicality than the reader can easily summon. With Gertrude Stein we are frequently urged to forgetfulness, to erasure of tonal memory, so that we may hear the hypnotic murmurings of what is a literature in basic English.

Gertrude Stein, all courage and will, is a soldier of minimalism. Her work, unlike the resonating silences in the art of Samuel Beckett, embodies in its loquacity and verbosity the curious paradox of the minimalist form. This art of the nuance in repetition and placement she shares with the orchestral compositions of Philip Glass.

(*1987*)

The Fate of the Gifted

~~~

Djuna Barnes died in 1982 at the age of ninety. For forty-one years, this avant-garde 1920s figure had been living in a small apartment in Greenwich Village, surviving on her meager royalties and a stipend from Peggy Guggenheim. This stipend itself was a sort of survival if one considers the embattled relationship she had with Miss Guggenheim and, almost unfailingly, with everyone else. The last years were proud and sad, frugal and lonely, and unproductive except for a verse play, *The Antiphon,* completed in 1954. I was present at the first reading of the play at Harvard in 1956, and the evening was dismaying. Djuna Barnes's long silence had ended in this play, which had about it all the anxious, self-destructive tones of an impossibility into which great effort and hope had been poured. T. S. Eliot, in support of his long friendship with her, was in the audience, and he was also perhaps recklessly present in *The Antiphon,* a vehement, overwrought *Family Reunion* of badly written, declamatory verse and intense, unanchored bitterness of feeling. That night, Djuna Barnes, a writer of wild and original gifts, reminded me in her person of one of those *mutilé de guerre* posters of the First World War. She was a wounded hostage of some kind and somehow abandoned, but just what the line of her fate had been was difficult to know.

To her name there is always to be attached the splendor of *Nightwood*, a lasting achievement of her great gifts and eccentricities— her passionate prose and, in this case, a genuineness of human passions. A love of literary pastiche and parody made her earlier works, *Ryder* and *Ladies Almanack,* an astonishment of wit, as well as a wearying fluency of capital letters, archaic turns of speech, mannerism, and general mischievousness and amused perversity.

A certain balkiness seems to have been part of her character, and her career showed little aptitude for the sturdy and inspired exploitation that turned the most improbable of her contemporaries, Gertrude Stein, into an institution. For Djuna Barnes, Joyce was the inspiration and grandeur of the period. In Paris, she formed a friendship with him which was strong enough for him to have given her the original manuscript, with his annotations, of *Ulysses.* With her usual rotten luck, she was forced to sell it before it commanded a price that might have saved her from the penury and dependence of so many years of her life.

Andrew Field's biography, *Djuna: The Formidable Miss Barnes,* is not a work of any special vivacity. It is under considerable strain in all its parts and can only chatter along desperately about one who was noted for her silences. The title is the first indication of a perplexity. *Formidable* and *Miss Barnes* cannot easily draw us into the riddle, and the primness of the words does not telegraph the creative and personal hardships of the life. He tells of only one meeting with her, in 1977, and from that we conclude that he did not succeed in getting much out of her. Field's book is best when it reads like notes for another book. The portrait of certain Greenwich Village characters such as Guido Bruno, apparently the model for Felix Volkbein in *Nightwood,* and a nuisance named Elsa Baroness von Freytag-Loringhoven are amusing period pieces from the old days. The American expatriates in Paris—Hemingway, Natalie Barney, and others—are sketched in once more from the well-known documentation. There is a struggle with the written work of Djuna Barnes, but Field finds it hard to stay the course for fifteen rounds, and so there is a good deal of sparring with the names of characters and the names in real life and the name of Jake Barnes in *The Sun Also Rises* and what, if anything, the correspondence might indicate.

Djuna Barnes was born in Cornwall-on-Hudson, New York, in 1892. Her father, whom she hated we are told and believe, was a pretentious ne'er-do-well bohemian with mistresses and not much else. Her mother was English, having been born in Rutland. The parents were divorced and the grandparents were divorced and there is a tangle of half brothers and sisters. Quite early, Djuna had to undertake the support of her mother and three brothers, and she did this with admirable energy and talent in the New York newspaper world. The newspaper style of the time was jazzy enough but rather primitive as a vehicle for her talents. Nevertheless, a recent selection from this work, *Smoke and Early Stories,* shows her early mastery of a Firbank-like dandyism and theatricality. From "Paprika Johnson":

> The boy from Stroud's was a tall blond wimpet who had put his hands into his mother's hair and shaken it free of gold; a lad who had painted his cheeks from the palette of the tenderloin, the pink that descends from one member of a family to the other, quicksilver running down life's pages.

In Greenwich Village, she knew Edmund Wilson, Edna Millay, and Eugene O'Neill. She wrote for *Smart Set, Vanity Fair,* and *The Little Review.* She went to Paris and knew all the interesting artists of the time. The wonderful photographs by Man Ray and Berenice Abbott show her to have been extraordinarily chic and good-looking.

During this time, she wrote *Ryder, Ladies Almanack,* and *Nightwood,* and by 1940 she was back in New York, where she lived for four more decades.

The life of this remarkable American woman seemed to follow step-by-step the journey of the gifted of her time. Her experiences had a typicality about them: high literary ambitions, a lot of drinking, little money, London, Paris, Berlin and desperate encounters along the way. She was a lesbian in her life and in her work, although there were affairs with men, an abortion fairly late on. "I'm not a lesbian. I just loved Thelma," she said in Field's account. This is a remark. Field thinks of her as "basically heterosexual," whatever that might mean. In fact, "basically" appears to lean the other way, and there is little evidence that she anguished over the fact of lesbianism, even though the terrible Thelma Wood was an anguish indeed. Thelma is the Robin Vote of *Nightwood,* just as Djuna Barnes herself is, in the way of the transformations of literature, the Nora Flood.

Thelma Wood was an American who made sculptures with large feet rather like her own. In spite of that, she was a dashing beauty with a bit of money at times. She drove a red Bugatti, cruised the lesbian bars, drank enormously, lied, teased, was unfaithful, and gave Miss Barnes the miserable fate of wandering the streets at night looking for her. In *Nightwood,* she has the nature of a destructive, forgetful beast. Janet Flanner called her "the bitch of all times." So this love affair was a draining, spirit-crushing disaster, and at last it was broken off. After that, Miss Barnes stayed with Peggy Guggenheim in England, knew the lovers and friends collected there, was stormily friendly with Antonia White and rather more peacefully with Charles Henri Ford. But somehow her friendships did not work out much better than her love affairs. A difficult and unhappy nature she seems to have been—prickly, proud, and sarcastic.

Ryder is a daunting work, published in 1928 when the author was thirty-six. The dreadful father, here called Wendell Ryder, and his three women—mother, wife and mistress—are the center of this tale, as perhaps it can be called. There is an abundance of incident, some of it corresponding to known autobiographical details. Still, there cannot have been an intention to create the feeling of a genuine family chronicle, since events and persons are by style put at a distance of several centuries. In a chapter called "Wendell Discusses Himself with His Mother," the dialogue runs:

> Sometimes I am a whore in ruffled petticoat, playing madly at a pack of ruffians and getting thrippence for my pains; a smartly boxed ear, or a bottom-tingling clap a-hind … and once I was a bird who flew down my own throat, twangling at the heart cord, to get the pitch of my own mate-call.

Even the essential facts of narrative information are rendered in a mannered tone that often has the cadence of translation: "At the end of three weeks, his shadow was exceeding lean. On the coming of Saturday he was sacked. (His companions in clerking saying that it was due to his delivery of prussic acid to a weaning lady in Chiswick, in place of bismuth.)"

The pastiche, parody, and flow are accomplished with outstanding virtuosity of language, witty juxtapositions and reversals, and a wonderful ending line for the book and for Wendell: "And whom should he disappoint?" *Ryder* is a curiosity, showing its period, the 1920s, only in a sophisticated and conscious malice and in the studied, learned manipulation of styles. The zest and the jest are embraced perhaps too lovingly. The manner itself is the intention, and the ear is bookish and rather overwhelming.

The "Englishness" of Djuna Barnes's work, after her early apprenticeship, is perhaps to be laid at the door of her rejected American father. There is scarcely an American rhythm or cadence in her work, and even the description of Nora's American background in *Nightwood* has the generalizing aspect of something worked up rather than known from birth—for example, the atmosphere of Nora's house: "The Drummer Boy, Fort Sumter, Lincoln, Booth, all somehow came to mind; Whigs and Tories were in the air."

The famous Dr. O'Connor of *Nightwood* makes his first appearance in *Ryder*. And he is there as he will be—a monologist. Dr. O'Connor, an American going about Paris, talked and talked, both in life and in novels by Americans other than Djuna Barnes. Andrew Field runs the doctor down and finds that his performances received a mixed reception, with some remembering him as fantastical and amusing and others, of course, bored out of their skulls in his presence. In any case, his real name was Dan Mahoney, and he was a very noticeable queen around the Paris bars. He blued his eyelids and coated his eyelashes and covered his heavy beard with face powder. He claimed to have served in the navy and to be a medical doctor, but he was the sort whose name does not appear in the records of institutions. Aside from his fabrications, he spoke of himself, truthfully, as "poor Minnie Mahoney, the girl whom God forgot." Fashionable lesbians liked him, and he was cozy company.

"A slight satiric wigging," Djuna Barnes called *Ladies Almanack,* and it is just that. Many of the lesbian women in Paris appeared in this amiable calendar, which "featured" Dame Evangeline Musset (Natalie Barney), Lady Buck-and-Balk and Tilly-Tweed-in-Blood (Lady Una Trowbridge and Radclyffe Hall). The book was privately printed in Paris in 1929 and "hawked along the Left Bank by bold young women." It is a teasing and bold production and very much *written,* not tossed off, and again in the mock English Lit manner.

> Now this be a Tale of as fine a Wench as ever wet Bed, she who was called Evangeline Musset and who was in her Heart one Grand Red Cross for the Pursuance, the Relief and the Distraction of such Girls as in their Hinder Parts, and their Fore Parts,

and in whatsoever Parts did suffer them most, lament Cruelly, be
it Itch of Palm, or Quarters most horribly burning.

It is possible to see in this book and in *Ryder* a crippling facility for
inspired verbal cartooning. After the freedom, the parodying dash
and dazzle with no necessity for the restraints of verisimilitude and
narrative coherence, the small production of this large talent is a
loss not altogether surprising.

Nightwood is a novel of intrepid originality. It appeared in 1936,
published in England by Faber at the strong urging of T. S. Eliot.
Eliot supplied an introduction, thereby giving his unique impri-
matur to assist a daunting work of the imagination. Even this most
important and promising lift to a career in literature was met with
down-dragging decisions, some aesthetic and some practical. Djuna
Barnes herself cut the manuscript to a third of its original length,
and Eliot supplied the title. The expectation of loss caused the firm
to publish without an advance and to claim 25 percent of the
American rights.

The reviews in England, especially those by Edwin Muir, Dylan
Thomas, and Graham Greene, were favorable. In America the reaction was largely negative, and the "Elizabethan tragedy" claims of
Eliot's introduction were considered high-flown and dropped from
the second American edition. Considerable impertinence attended
this most sober and ambitious achievement in the work of Djuna
Barnes.

Nightwood opens in the formal, instructing manner of a European
novel, perhaps a German one. The beginning pages are laden with
ancestral claims, old furniture detailed in wood and decoration,
portraits on the wall, the lady in "great puffed and pearled sleeves,"
a gentleman on a charger. "The blue of an Italian sky lay between
the saddle and the tightened rump of the rider." Thus the introduction of Felix Volkbein, a stiff-necked Jew, with the false title of
Baron, a haughty, romantic obsequiousness and elaborate imitative
leanings. "He kept a valet and a cook: the one because he looked

like Louis the Fourteenth and the other because she resembled Queen Victoria." Some have questioned the more or less lengthy, in terms of this short book, intrusion of Volkbein at the beginning of a work to which he is not central. But he is attentive to structure and quite soon meets the human core of the novel—Dr. Matthews O'Connor, Robin Vote, and Nora Flood. Indeed, he rushes in and marries Robin, whom we first observe in a deathbed scene: "On a bed, surrounded by a confusion of potted plants, exotic palms and cut flowers, faintly over-sung by the note of unseen birds." Robin is not dead, she is only dead drunk.

Volkbein's elaborate aspirations for ancestral validation in no way prepare us for his marriage to the wayward Robin. Still, perhaps it is useful for a plot in which a hieratical and abstract conception of character almost precludes the usual conventions of psychological patterning. The characters are the subjects of a ruminating intelligence, and almost anything might be said about them by the author. Here, we do not have an accumulation of biography; instead, character is seen as a timeless intimation of universal buried life. Robin Vote: "Such a woman is the infected carrier of the past; before her the structure of our head and jaws aches—we feel that we could eat her, she who is eaten death returning, for only then do we put our face close to the blood on the lips of our forefathers."

Nightwood is a love story. Were it not, the high-pitched brilliance of the writing would offend by its disjunction from feeling. The love of Nora Flood for Robin Vote is a sort of sacramental agony, and for this affliction the devices of style, the demonism of the heavy night airs, have a ghastly appropriateness. Nora and Robin are American women who meet at a circus, under the gaze of a lioness with "her furious great head with its yellow eyes afire." Nora is said to be a Westerner, but there is no dust of Omaha or Sacramento about her. Like enchanted creatures, they immediately begin to travel to Munich, Vienna, Budapest, and Paris. The misery begins as each night Robin stands by the door, saying, "Don't wait up for me." Since Robin is the object of obsession, another American woman becomes obsessed and takes her off.

The nighttime misery of a desperate love holds the novel together and allows even the uncertain significations of Dr. O'Connor's monologues. He is a dog of the night, going from bar to bar, saying as he leaves a chance acquaintance, "The lady will pay." In the most powerful scene in the book, Nora seeks him out at home, or in the pitiful room that passes for the home of this person alive only in the presence of others. She finds him on a dirty bed in a woman's flannel nightgown:

> The doctor's head, with its over-large black eyes, its full gunmetal cheeks and chin, was framed in the golden semi-circle of a wig with long pendent curls that touched his shoulders, and falling back against the pillow, turned up the shadowy interior of their cylinder.

Dr. O'Connor is asked to think about the night and about love. He is ready, fully prepared; he is precocious, ludicrous, pedantic, and a consolation. To Nora's "What am I to do?" he answers:

> Be as the Frenchman, who puts a *sou* in the poorbox at night that he may find a penny to spend in the morning—he can trace himself back to his sediment, vegetable and animal, and so find himself in the odour of wine in its two travels, in and out, packed down beneath an air that has not much changed its position during that strategy.

Or he answers something else, at length. Dr. O'Connor, as I read it, is to be taken seriously because he is seen as providing in all his appearances the consolations of language itself, of memory, of jumbled information, of metaphor. "Was it at night that Sodom became Gomorrah? It was at night, I swear!" On and on. He is a fruitful creation of loquacity just as the animalistic Robin is a devastation by silence. But Eliot was wise to see the mischief of this rhetorical Satan going to and fro. As we have the novel now, we could not usefully have more of Dr. O'Connor.

Eliot's introduction sees the powerfulness of Dr. O'Connor and that "such a character needs other real, if less conscious, people in order to realize his own reality." He wants to insist upon the naturalness of the work as fiction, to see it as having some of the practical experience of human existence: "Felix and his child are oppressively real." Some of this is the kindness of the wish to aid in the marketplace a seemingly unmarketable inspiration. He ends: "What I would leave the reader prepared to find is the great achievement of the style, the beauty of the phrasing, the brilliance of wit and characterization, and a quality of horror and doom very nearly related to that of Elizabethan tragedy."

There is the Black Mass ending of *Nightwood* in which Robin in front of a "contrived altar, before a Madonna," and with two burning candles, turns into a dog to fight with a true dog nearby, both biting and barking until they give up, "lying out, her hands beside her, her face turned and weeping; and the dog too gave up then, and lay down, his eyes bloodshot, his head flat along his knees." This is revenge indeed, and a minor Elizabethan bloody finale it is.

As a work of its own period, *Nightwood* is not minor, though it is decadent. The literature of decadence with its ornamental style, artificiality, its relishing horrific incident, is common today in America with Norman Mailer and others, and so perhaps the charge is not impugning. Now, *Nightwood* appears more acceptable to the sensibilities than it might have in 1936, during the reign of documentary portrayal of what the actual was thought to be. It is a work of the imagination, a recognizable and frightening love story, accomplished with a high, cool, and loyal belief in the possibilities of words in place and out of place, vocabulary stretched and strained, incident and arrangement without practical preparation—all, in this case, instruments of revelation.

Andrew Field has learned what he could about Djuna Barnes, and it is not to his discredit that there isn't much to tell. There is a sadness in the life. She seemed to fall aside after she had done her best work. Her nature is not easy to take hold of. There was little luck, and to that she added a bit of obstructive paranoia. Thus, she suffered.

(*1983*)

Fictions
of America

～

Cheever;
or, The Ambiguities

~ ~ ~

In his last years, John Cheever, a man more disorderly than his proud art and his courteous, somewhat remote, manners revealed, tried to set his house in order. After a heart attack nearly fatal, he gave up a fervent addiction to alcohol, quit smoking—and all the while was preparing to die of cancer.

Cheever's was a lyrical talent quite mysterious in its movements. It was always plain that the writer was a New Englander. His stories of New York City and the surrounding prosperous suburbs are filled with men and women who seem, like himself, cast up on the shores of Manhattan's East Side and his suburban Shady Hill and Bullet Park as exiles from values less fretful and uncertain than they now know. Their expectations from life are high and yet reasonable, or so it seems to them. The poisoned dwellings they make for themselves take them by surprise.

The shadowy and troubled undergrowth of Cheever's stories brings to mind something of the temper of Melville and Hawthorne—and Cheever himself is a sort of *Pierre*, a study in ambiguity. His special tone is nostalgic, tender about memories of natural illuminations, the fine day, a sunset, the wind on the sea, and the first years of married love. The nostalgia is curiously, and with great originality, combined with a contemporary and rootless compulsion to destroy, even to crash by repetition, the essence of nostalgia, as when the remembered victories of the college track star become a drunken, fatal vaulting over the sofas in the living room ("O Youth and Beauty!").

In the beautiful early story, "Goodbye, My Brother," there is a characteristic balance or imbalance between the most destructive of family hatreds and the final melodies of celebration:

> The sea that morning was iridescent and dark. My wife and my sister were swimming—Diana and Helen—and I saw their uncovered heads, black and gold in the dark water. I saw them come out and I saw that they were naked, unshy, beautiful, and full of grace, and I watched the naked women walk out of the sea.

Beautiful, full of grace, black and gold in the water. The rapturous cadence seems to come from a vision of hope uncorrupted by the traumas this imagination so swiftly and deftly uncovers beneath the glistening of good taste, privilege, and hereditary goodwill.

"The Housebreaker of Shady Hill," about a man stealing from the houses of his neighbors, has the sweat of financial need and moral collapse lying on the pages. The atmosphere is overcast, clammy with the literal bankruptcy and the criminal solution of Johnny Hake, "conceived in the Hotel St. Regis, born in Presbyterian Hospital, raised on Sutton Place." The execution of the dark thefts is more brilliantly accomplished than Hake's atonement and return to the light world "become so sweet." Violence is to be contained by the memory of "summer nights, loving the children, and looking down the front of Christina's dress." The sentiments, the sacraments, secular and otherwise, are called upon again and again as a protection against self-destruction. It is by language, precise, original in its shaping, almost effortlessly evocative, that Cheever rescues the sentiments from sentimentality, from a mere consoling assertion.

In "The Swimmer," the suburban pools of house after house, backyard after backyard, are imagined to be a continuous river, a "quasi-subterranean stream that curved across the country." A disintegrating man passes through one after another, some surrounded by people eating peanuts and drinking cocktails, and some deserted. He is making his way home to what turns out to be an empty house, the gutters loose, the handles on the garage door rusty, the family gone, the swimming-pool river merely a deranged dream of reconciliation. This modern story is as resonant as an ancient tale. The suburban pools are elevated to a symbolical challenge like that faced by the wanderers in old forests.

Another homely object, "The Enormous Radio," is lifted beyond the anonymity of mere usefulness. On the radio, the nice wife, hoping for proper music, begins to hear the quarrels and distasteful dispositions of her apartment-house neighbors coming through the speaker. The radio gradually becomes a monstrous instrument of exposure, and there is something of the inscrutability of "The Turn of the Screw" about the story. Is it themselves the young couple is listening to?

Just who is the man, John Cheever, the Episcopalian anarch? Susan Cheever, his daughter, has written a memoir, *Home Before Dark,* about the writer as a son, a brother, and a father. She has chosen a tone of elegiac candor. The commemorative aspect is suitable to the 1982 death of this extraordinary man and to the pain of family grief. The candor is suitable perhaps to where the culture is now in matters of lapidary inscription. Candor has come to be the sum of the duties attending the documentation of lives by biography or by the reflection of autobiography. Weakness, temptation, indiscretion, infirmity—it must be said these are interesting. Revelations give "life" to the dead authors known previously to most only through their works and the shape of the head on book jackets. "O quiet form upon the dust, I cannot look and yet I must."

Susan Cheever has written novels, but none is as confidently composed as *Home Before Dark*. Here, she has had the assistance of the thirty volumes of the journals kept by her father. These are not mere jottings. Each excerpt she has called upon, and it is to be hoped the culling does not undermine the publication of this valuable testimony, shines with a limpid fluency and eloquence. The journals are passionately confessional, somehow a defiance of the other side of the coin, the appropriate John Cheever. Confession is the last resort, or even the first, of the captive, and what we learn in this memoir is that Cheever existed lifelong in captivities imposed by the complications of his nature, his masks, his loyalties, and the protection of his talent.

He had an unsettling sense of a lost or ambiguous heritage. New England, and especially the villages and towns around Boston, likes to greet each new dawn with the word "old": old families, old names, old money. This, by entail, becomes the right schools and occupations, "antique" woods in the parlors, Canton china, and so on. Genealogical support for the blue eye, fair face, and Anglo-Saxon name; affirming portraiture is a sort of kitchen scholarship.

Thus, Cheever liked to say that his family came to the new world by way of the passage of Ezekiel Cheever on the *Arbella* in 1630; "The roughnecks had come on the *Mayflower*." Susan Cheever puts the esteemed Ezekiel on the *Hector* in 1637. But no matter, the Cheevers were by the nineteenth century an "established Brahmin family," most of them engaged in seafaring. The ambiguous circumstances came in the branch; that is, the name endured among prosperous, greatly respected parts of the family, one of whom Susan Cheever rather apologetically calls upon, but status did not endure for all of the Cheevers, not quite.

As so often happens to a sensitive, insecure descendant, the real trouble, the downward slide, happened right at home. Cheever's father sold his interests in a shoe factory that bore his name, invested in stocks, and went broke: ruin at home. His mother set herself up in the genteel but socially déclassé gift-shop business, a move very galling to the men of the family. The father began to drink, and the parents separated amid the usual unrestrained household warfare. In the journals, some four decades later, we have Cheever's memories—written under the transformation of style, that proper affront to the crassness of reality. "An afternoon when he returned home from school and found the furnace dead, some unwashed dishes on the table in the dining room and at the center of the table a pot of tulips that the cold had killed and blackened."

There was trouble at Thayer Academy, and Cheever left school in his junior year. Just what brought about the expulsion is not quite clear: smoking, bad grades, fractious behavior—the accounts given by the delinquent student varied. An older brother, Fred, was a consolation and support, he being, or seeming in youth to be, a plausible and successful New England product. "His love for his older brother, who nurtured and supported him—and whom he was later called on to nurture and support—became the most complicated attachment in his life," Susan Cheever writes. Cheever himself remarked, "When it became apparent that it was an ungainly closeness, I packed my bag and shook his hand and left." Later, he told his daughter that he had wanted to murder his brother and at the same time to live with him after the family collapsed. "Much of the conflict in my father's heart, and many of the themes in his work, grew out of his love for Fred."

The brother's success did not last; indeed, his losses were great—job, money, marriage, and the decline, due in some degree to drink, into an embarrassing, empty heartiness. Thus, the common tendency of families to mistake who will make it to the finish line. The central role of the brother does not truly take shape in the memoir, and one has to accept it, unfleshed by dramatic characterization, as the repeated assertion of Cheever himself. Of the brothers in the fiction, one, Moses Wapshot, is a romantic projection of fulfilled hopes, quite unbelievable; two, the sullen, complaining intruder in "Goodbye, My Brother" and the murdered sibling in *Falconer*, are outstandingly vicious.

Cheever did not live with his brother. Instead, he came to New York. It was 1930, and he was eighteen, and that same year he published his first story, in *The New Republic*. In a few years, 1935, he had his first story in *The New Yorker*. The foundations of this precocity are not examined in the memoir, and we do not know what was read, studied, or the level of aspiration. That his literary hopes were not commonplace we can judge by the act of the submission to *The New Republic* and early publication in *Hound and Horn*, *Story* magazine, and others, and his fling with lowercase letters in the manner of Cummings. The reader we hear about is the reading of a father to his family, not the solitary reading of the writer. Throughout the daughter's memoir, Cheever's life as a writer is seen by the listing of publication of books, some successful, some less so, by his struggles with the opaque paternalism of *The New Yorker*, by the years of poverty and the years of spending, by late honors and prizes. Certain correspondences between the "candor" of the daughter's memoir, striking revelations, quite detailed, of pitiful bouts of drunkenness and homosexual inclination and flight from marriage, loyalty to marriage, and the use in fiction of these "themes" are offered in a perfunctory way. That certain masks might be required for the act of writing are overwhelmed by the masks of a social being, that is, the son and the father.

Cheever met his wife in 1938 when he was twenty-six years old, and they married three years later. That it was a profound attachment for forty years and that the knowledge of a strained and, inevitably, tormented union influenced his life greatly can be seen in his best stories about the married people they hoped to be or feared to be. Somewhat curtly, the daughter sums it up. "This pattern—my father as the alternately pursuing and rebuffed, resentful male, and my mother as the passive, coerced, resentful female—was held to as long as they were together." There were children, moves from here to there around Manhattan and the suburbs, and the final settling into the house in Ossining and the dogs, the neighbors, the garden.

In many ways my father's life can be divided into two distinct parts. The first forty-five years or so were devoted to a struggle for stability: the establishment of a professional reputation, the creation of a family, earning enough money to survive, and most of all the search for some kind of home—some place of his own that might confirm his credentials as a gentleman and soothe his insecurities.

And his last twenty years a struggle to escape the trap and "most of all to escape the pressure to continually surpass himself as a writer." But this cannot be true. Writing is not "the establishment of a professional reputation" as if one were a doctor or lawyer; it is not properly in the sentence with creation of a family and the purchase of a home.

Cheever came to New York in the 1930s, the Depression years. He was scarcely more than a boy, and his making his way as a writer of stories is quite astonishing. It was altogether saving that he came to New York. The North Shore or the South Shore around Boston would not have served. His own pretensions are to the point here. "His aristocratic New England background was partly sham, and his patrician airs were mostly his own invention." Displacement is at the center of his view, and, indeed, he was displaced, first from New England and then again in the literary landscape of his time. As a writer, he lived in a scene dominated at first by southerners and later by the arrival of brilliant Jewish fiction writers, neither congenial to his creative sources. He did not have at hand the small-town and rural grotesques of the southern sort, nor were his style and preoccupation similar to the intellectual aspirations and skepticism of the Jewish immigrant experience as seen by Saul Bellow, for instance.

He was poor in New York and, of course, given his own attraction to the pits and to risk, he was liberal in spirit. But he was not radical, not stung by the bees (or wasps) of the political battles of the period, although he knows the country and the minds in it. By the direction of the sentences, the ease of the meters in prose, by names, by floating images attached to stuffs and dishes and furniture, we are aware of a self-education as frenzied as that of any scarecrow in the public library.

The American bourgeois world and its pains are his quarry. Summers on the islands in Massachusetts, skiing weekends, going with your child to catch the private-school bus and meeting a mother and having an affair, spending too much in the memory of what one was supposed to have to spend. His was an Anglican New York and its suburbs a hungover Barchester. But because it was New York, it had the rocking unsteadiness of a metropolis quite different from the Edinburgh staunchness of Boston. The husbands had to catch the 8:10 into Manhattan and come home on the five o'clock quite uneasy, not knowing what they were bringing with them and not knowing either what they would find when they arrived.

The landscape of Cheever's fictions in the 1930s and 1940s did not pause at driveways where the dogs with names like Jupiter were family members. His branch of the family might have fallen back, but the mask of a well-bred patrician remained; he looked like one and spoke like one. Where no one knows your parents and your grandparents, inner being and surface at last unite against the provincial domination by fact. "There seemed to be money everywhere, and the Whittemores, who slept in their worn overcoats in the winter to keep themselves warm, seemed separated from their enjoyment of this prosperity by only a little patience, resourcefulness, and luck" ("The Pot of Gold"). This was the reality that produced the stories, and there was a certain price to be paid since the artfully out-of-place man was also dislocated for a time in the prevailing hierarchy of literature.

The New Yorker printed his stories, and this was fortunate, no doubt. At the same time, he was undervalued, not neglected but also not elevated by the attention of the best critics of the day such as Edmund Wilson and Alfred Kazin. It was felt that he was a minor John O'Hara, a talent much coarser than Cheever's.

The Way Some People Live (1942) and *The Enormous Radio* (1953), collections of brilliant short stories, appeared without causing a racket. We are not told how Cheever felt in these matters, but a dispiriting tension would be fitting to the bland reception to one's best work. It was not until his first novel, *The Wapshot Chronicle* (1957), that the general public and the prize committees took notice. This circumstance brings to mind the dismal delay in Faulkner's stock until after *Intruder in the Dust,* a near parody of his previous work.

There is something parodic in *The Wapshot Chronicle,* although not of the previous work but of the writer, the seafaring Yankee. Writing the novel, or trying to write a novel, took more than twenty years. The first pages are heavy with ancestral adornments, with the treacherous attractions of New England pedantry. The portrait of a not-long-dead founder of the Wapshot (Cheever?) family:

> He appeared in a yellow velvet cap, trimmed with fur, and a loose green velvet gown or bathrobe as if he, bred on that shinbone coast and weaned on beans and codfish, had translated himself into some mandarin or hawk-nosed Renaissance prince, tossing bones to the mastiffs, jewels to the whores, and swilling wine out of golden goblets with his codpiece busting its velvet bows.

Eccentric, rich aunts; eccentric, lovable father, Leander, who keeps a very mannered journal; the rather glamorized journey through occupations and love of the sons, Moses and Coverly.

Cheever is a disappointing novelist. The mellifluous style is always at hand, the courtesy and wistfulness of his way with dramatic encounters remain; and yet the novels fly apart, shred and shed as if some wind of inattention had overtaken them. High-flown backgrounds appear for characters who had otherwise seemed quite recognizable. Like the ancestor, they wear fur and velvet.

Bullet Park (1969) was a commercial failure, despite the success of *The Wapshot Chronicle.* In between, he did the stories in *The House-*

breaker of Shady Hill (1959), and these, like the earlier collections, are what he could so wisely compose in the pure and confident manner of his genius for the short form. *Bullet Park* is not quite serious, that is the trouble. Hammer and Nailles are the names of the two families; such is the beginning folly. Hammer, a suburbanite but actually the bastard son of outlandish, bejeweled parents, tries to immolate Tony, the beloved son of Nailles, in the chancel of Christ's Church and would have done so without the intervention of a kindly guru from the Temple of Light. A certain aspect of Halloween on the streets of Bullet Park.

The Wapshot Chronicle has a biographical interest. Here is the first of Cheever's confessions to homosexual inclinations and the first of what might be called his "gentrification" of the homosexual pass and of the homosexual affair in the later novels. Homosexuality and alcoholism return the thoughts to Susan Cheever's memoir, *Home Before Dark*. These two afflictions or profound wishes shoot out of the memoir with a marked propulsive force.

"It became clearer and clearer that my father was the worst kind of alcoholic. He seemed intent on destroying himself. I suppose he had always been an alcoholic." An invitation to teach at Boston University was accepted, with devastating results. "He narrowly missed being hit by a car as he crossed Commonwealth Avenue in a haze. The police threatened to pick him up for public intoxication—he had lain down on the grass in the Public Garden to share a bottle of hooch in a paper bag with a bum." At last, broken in health, he was sent to an alcohol-rehabilitation center in New York and on from there to AA and abstinence, no doubt painful. In the stories and novels, there is an unusual amount of drinking. Some of it is more or less unconscious stage business such as, "she said, fixing herself another drink"—that sort of line again and again. (A like stage business can be found in the fiction of many alcoholic writers.) But in the stories, drunkenness was often central to the action—cocktail parties, dinners with their insults, shameful outbursts, tears in the bedroom. In the period and the setting there was a naturalness to being drunk, and the plots it occasioned flowed into remorse and ruin and aroused, tenderhearted, forgiving emotions: "Oh, those suburban Sunday nights, those Sunday-night blues! Those departing weekend guests, those stale cocktails, those half-dead flowers, those trips to Harmon to catch the Century, those post-mortems and pickup suppers!" ("O Youth and Beauty!").

That was one thing, drinking. "My father's sexual appetites were one of his major preoccupations, and his lust for men was as distressing to him as desire for women was self-affirming and ecstatic." In the course of writing the memoir, Susan Cheever was telephoned by a young man who had "letters" and perhaps wanted to sell them; she interviewed another who had an unhappy story to tell. On one of his visits to a university, Cheever met Rip, "who would be his close friend, lover, confidant for the rest of his life." The writer's journals of 1978 tell it all:

> Absolute candor does not suit me, but I will come as close as possible to describing the chain of events. Lonely and with my loneliness exacerbated by travel, motel rooms, bad food, public readings and the superficiality of standing in reception lines I fell in love with Rip in a motel room of unusual squalor. His air of seriousness and responsibility, the bridged glasses he wore for his nearsightedness and his composed manner all excited my deepest love.

In his last years, John Cheever was much honored. His complete stories were collected, and the reception and sales were at last an acknowledgment of their fineness. He also wrote two novels, very curious both of them, and one of them, the bizarre *Falconer,* the best of his work in the long form.

Oh What a Paradise It Seems (1982) is the last of his novels. The confessional mode here is most charmingly engaged, and the torments of conscience and doubt poor Coverly Wapshot endured over a discreet homosexual pass have been swept away with a sunny air of innocence quite perverse. This short book is rich with the love of nature and memories of skating on ponds now being used as dump sites—and rich with embarrassments.

Lemuel Sears, "an old man but not yet infirm," stands next to a handsome young woman in the line at a bank. He is captivated and soon, after dinners and careful attentions on his part, it is a rainy night, people jogging on the street, and the girl, Renée, invites him to dine in her apartment. She meets him at the door wearing a wrapper, and as for him he is out of his clothes in a minute. "You were hardpacked," she says. A phrase from the army? It does some-how express the rather chirpy dash and potency of this distin-guished personage with two wives in the grave. The affair goes on for some weeks, and he arrives at the apartment one night to find her dressed, ready to go out. He nevertheless "unbuckled his trousers and let them fall to his knees." Her answer is, "I'm sorry, but I cannot help you." Thinking flowers might be "a seductive force," Sears goes out to buy them and comes back to find her gone.

> The elevator door opened. It was not she. It was the elevator op-erator. He was wearing street clothes and a hat. He went directly to where Sears stood and embraced him.... The stranger, whose name he hadn't learned, took him downstairs to a small room off the lobby, where he undressed Sears and undressed himself.

O, wishes and fantasies. The little idyll proceeds in a stately way. "We've got to find something else we can do together," Sears says, and so they go on a fishing trip. They sleep together quite peace-fully and Eduardo, his name, tells about his wife and sons and says that he will spend the rest of his vacation with his wife in Key West, a union package tour. Sears's last line when they part back in the city is, "Get a great tan."

Cheever is the straightest of homosexual lovers, and thus his last novels are not exactly a contribution to gay lit. The pastoral and nostalgic mood does not desert him, even at the cost of common experience. One might notice the absence of class tension or perhaps imagine that it exists in the passivity of Sears and also of *Falconer*'s Farragut, who are so sweetly taken, so accommodated without making a signal. Even the girl Renée appears in her wrapper to begin the seduction. In this winsome dream of Lemuel Sears's—too many autumn leaves.

Falconer is a perturbation. The Cheever artifice, the fall to the dust, and a precipitous act it is, rash and brilliant in the fall. Of course, there is a well-educated gentleman with one of those signifying, protective names, this one Farragut. (Falconer is the name of an old, brutal prison, based on Sing Sing in Ossining, where Cheever went to teach the inmates.) Farragut has been brought to "this old iron place on a late summer's day." Before we know his crime, we see him busy in his cell writing to "his wife, his lawyer, his governor and his bishop." *His bishop,* yes, writing to his bishop while longing for his methadone, since Farragut (his family came to America in 1672 on the *Nanuet*) is a heroin addict, but a fine fellow for all that. He has killed his gross, self-satisfied brother with a poker when the brother screamed that his father didn't want Farragut. "He had an abortionist come to the house. Your own father wanted you killed."

So Farragut is in prison for life. It is all to be inside, and Cheever has, without any previous indication of such powers, created a large cast from the underside of society, created guards and routines, obscene dialogues and mumbled, self-serving prison monologues, all with great imaginative force. There is a "radiant and aching" love affair with Jody. Jody is an ignorant, cunning, petty hustler in jail, or so he says, for burglary, pistol-whipping, and kidnapping of a candy-store operator in order to steal some parimutuel tickets. Their meeting, as we would expect, comes through Jody's initiative. He wants Farragut because "you ain't homosexual." No cash, no reward? "From what Farragut had read he had expected this to happen, but what he had not expected was that this grotesque bonding of their relationship would provoke in him so profound a love."

Jody escapes, dressed in drag as an acolyte of the cardinal who has made a ceremonial visit to the prison. Back in town, out of the vestments, the cardinal recognizes Jody for what he is, an escaped convict. And then a Theater of the Ridiculous scene follows. The cardinal and Jody prance about Madison Avenue, and all the while TV actresses and assorted others kneel to kiss the ring and be blown the sign of the cross. He takes Jody to a private room at a tailor's and orders him a suit of clothes for his new life. A miracle.

In Cheever's fiction there are, now and then, moments close to profanation of his insistent churchiness, just as he is compelled to deviation from his insistent passion for women. In prison, having left Jody's private brothel, Farragut writes "Oh, my darling" letters to a mistress, just as Lemuel Sears passes back and forth without mishap from his ecstasy with the girl, Renée, to the love of the elevator man, Eduardo. Whether this is naïveté, a startling unworldliness, willed illusion, or unguarded egotism is hard to say.

Cheever covers his tracks, but the writing dares his own horrors. And he will not give up the pastoral accent. Farragut, a heroin addict and a murderer, escapes prison by posing as a dead body on its way to the morgue. "He held his head high, his back straight, and walked along nicely. Rejoice, he thought, rejoice." And there you have it.

(*1984*)

Citizen Updike

~~ ~~ ~~

John Updike, the dazzling author, appeared, and still appears, to be one of Augustine's "fair and fit"—and never more so than when viewed among his male literary colleagues who often tend to show the lump and bump of gene, bad habits, the spread and paste of a lifetime spent taking one's own dictation. For this tall, one wants to say still young, man, despite certain dwindling days, September-song modulations in the composition of his memoir, *Self-Consciousness*, everything seemed to fall into place. An only child, treasured by nice intelligent parents who, if not particularly well-to-do, were prosperous in respect and plausibility; born in a pleasant Pennsylvania village, Shillington, with its "idle alleys and darkened four-square houses," its high school, movie house, stores, avenues, and streets whose names will have on his pages the curved beauty of Havana and Caracas, even if they are Pennwyn and Lynoak.

Updike went on to Harvard and, as a young writer, came under the benevolent paternalism of *The New Yorker*, married early, had children, moved to Massachusetts, and with an uncommon creative energy wrote stories, novels, poems, essays, and still writes on and on with great success about suburban landscapes or small-town ones efflorescent in observed detail, prodigal in image, and brashly knowing and accomplished in the rhythms of current dialogue and steaming with the orifices and bodily fluids of many fluent copulations.

And then, with an admirable and defiant gallantry, he designed in *The Coup* his African country, Kush, whose

> peanut oil travels westward the same distance as eastward our ancestors plodded, their neck-shackles chafing down to the jugular, in the care of Arab traders, to find in the flesh-markets of Zanzibar eventual lodgings in the harems and palace guards of Persia and Chinese Turkestan.

And then again, he, as productive of print as a Victorian, transmogrifies himself into a sluggish, anxious Jewish novelist, *Bech,* mooning on Riverside Drive with an exact ironical accent before taking off for a government-sponsored tour of the Soviet Union and various satellite capitals in Eastern Europe where he treads the ancient, war-worn stones and confers with the resident writers, one of whom says he plans to "defect as soon as he gets his laundry back."

A promiscuous, astonishing span, a labyrinthine talent through which the author makes a smooth, experienced, dashing, even dandyish passage. A bit of a parson, too, something icy inside the melting flesh of concupiscence.

Updike's memoirs bear the title *Self-Consciousness,* to indicate the natural authorial awareness and, more unexpected, to reveal a distress arising from the envelope of the self, the flesh and bones and organs that have been the source of pain and of the "self-consciousness" of hidden damage. He has lived with torments devastating, if not life-threatening, and it is a hard heart that could turn from these ills with a shrug. The greatest suffering has been a long battle with a virulent psoriasis. His account of the scabs, blisters, eruptions, and treatments is of such fullness and wounded feeling one would not want, in description, to substitute a version other than his own. The disease was not only hurtful and exhausting but also humiliating, as when he was required to learn to swim at Harvard. On a somewhat descending scale, he has endured bouts of stuttering, asthma, tooth and gum problems. So there it is, a host of imperfections and acute discomforts, woes rendered with an eloquent and almost sunny confidence.

My sufferings are purely physical, the aged, dying Santayana is supposed to have said in order to fend off the redemptive efforts of nuns and priests who might wish, at the end, to seduce him from the teasing ambiguity of "There is no God and Mary is His mother." Updike, far from the end and friendly to redemption, if it should come, has a way of translating the threat of moral ravage into symptoms. "I tried to break out of my marriage, on behalf of another, and failed, and began to have trouble breathing." Succeeding in the breakup, as determined people will, he writes: "My face broke out, my shoulders and neck became so encrusted I couldn't turn my head without pain."

He will go further, twirling, you might say, on a steel toe like a skater in the crisp New England air: "So wrapped in my skin, so watchful of its day-to-day permutations, I have little concern to spare for the homeless, the disenfranchised, the unfortunate who figure so largely in the inner passion of smooth-pelted liberals like my first wife." "A man's foes will be those in his own household," the Redeemer Himself opined. "Smooth-pelted liberal," sardonic locution, is attached to the sufferer's first wife, mother of four Updikes, daughter of a Unitarian clergyman. No doubt Updike regrets the homeless and the unfortunate as much as another. His distance here is atmospheric, a distaste for the fair, blue-eyed Unitarians in Cambridge, Massachusetts, the attachment to "causes" shown by the rosy-cheeked, trust-fund descendants of the balmy vapors coming from Concord and thereabouts. For Updike, the Over-soul Unitarians, brushing away the Trinity like dust in a dark corner, will not do, although he had a try with the placid church before settling down more or less as a Congregationalist and their "sweet bare rites descended from the Puritans."

Congregationalists are a mild enough church of choice for the census taker, not exacting or likely to be interfering or reforming in matters of conduct. It would not have been fitting to take a leap into the Roman Catholic Church where confession and forgiveness are followed by the intention to go and sin no more, a source of plot dilemma for Graham Greene and for the almost-forgotten Christian novelist François Mauriac. (Sartre: "God is not a novelist and neither is M. Mauriac.") The awesome basilicas, rituals, and elaboration of Christian duties in the Roman Church, appealing to the faith hunger of many converts, would be too richly aesthetic for Updike, too denying of Middle America, the other creed embraced in these confessions.

So it was the Congregational Church and its pleasant meetings— or was it? Updike was born a Lutheran, and there lives in him still a degree of the social conservatism of the great reformer who opposed the Peasants' War of the sixteenth century because it destabilized the state and the power of the Protestant nobles. So Updike shifts in the manner of the creative, leaves the Church and the site of his youth for self-definition and also, as his memoirs seem to say, to discover and to reclaim for his contribution to literature the meaning of who he was and where he was placed in the American scene.

Settling for the beauties of Massachusetts was not only a flight from Shillington but also from New York. Updike was happy, he tells us, in Ipswich, an old village on the North Shore of Boston with a number of quite dominating old families, a place notable for the charms of wooden saltbox houses, the wide shores and cold water of Crane's Beach, and, a formidable barrier to assimilation, the Myopia Hunt Club. And perhaps Ipswich is now notable for its transformation into Tarbox, the name of the town in Updike's novel *Couples.* Tar, an odorous viscous liquid, and box—well, guess. Of course, *Couples* is a work of fiction, and Tarbox need only be a convenient address of some status, the sort of town young-professional couples with children might feel a certain pride in attaching themselves to. In any case, Tarbox acts in a peculiar manner upon the pulsing libidos gathered there as if for some pagan festival of nymphs and satyrs and maenads or, perhaps, closer to the bone, a remembrance of Merry Mount, carnal and gun traffic with the Indians, frontier revels around the maypole before the English Puritans shipped Mr. Morton back to where he came from. Anyway, Updike was happy in the actual Ipswich—happy except for the period, the middle 1960s, coming like some loud neighbor's quarrel over the fence.

"On Not Being a Dove," the most striking section of the memoirs, is a sort of regimental assault, bayonets preceding, on the peace movement occasioned by America's fierce assault on Vietnam. It is meant to roil and rile the deracinated louts at their homefront barricades, the treasonable clerks in the literary establishment, the fashionable metropolis and its feathered dissent, the barefoot, braless flag-burners, the pious army deserters fleeing the hallowed shores for Sweden and Canada. Certainly, the inanities of the expressive side of the peace movement, the flower children, make love not war, the pouring of blood on this and that—on these antics anyone free from permanent brain shock might look back in embarrassment.

> The protest movement, which had begun in the solemn Fiftyish pronouncements of the Port Huron Statement and the orderly civil-rights strategies, by the time of the '67 Washington march and the '68 convention of mischievous voodoo and street theatre and, finally, a nightmare of anarchy, of window-smashing and cop-bopping and drug-tripping and shouting down.

That's one thing and not the whole of the peace movement, as the Dance of the Seven Veils is not the whole of the *Herodiade*. Updike's positions are not merely a shudder for the misdemeanors of broken windows and the heretical processions of candlelight blowing in the wind; he proposes a tangled support for the actual war in Vietnam, an implied, or rather insisted upon, duty that once in combat there is something cheap and hollow about agitating against the elected government, taking upon oneself matters of state that because of the horrible circumstances of war require patriotism, standing together, a national, if troubled, acquiescence. That's the way he sees it, altogether too much carrying on by the motley and mottled mob and worse by the scriveners, their wrists swollen from signing a thousand petitions. What do *they* know, who are they, poets and screen stars, to demand out-of-Vietnam or, for that matter, to change the scene to earlier foreign manifestations that toppled and diverted governments, to demand out-of-Suez, out-of-Algeria?

There are a number of points in his indictment, some about the nature of citizenship and others concerning the particularities of the Vietnam War.

One source of my sense of grievance against the peace movement when it came was that I hadn't voted for any of its figures— not for Abbie Hoffman or Father Daniel Berrigan or Reverend William Sloane Coffin or Jonathan Schell or Lillian Hellman or Joan Baez or Jane Fonda or Eugene McCarthy. I had voted for Lyndon Johnson, and thus had earned my American right not to make a political decision for another four years.

A peculiar idea of the franchise, considering the porousness of the mandate on this and that, the frenzied concentration in Washington at the end of the day on how "it played" on the evening news and in the polls, representing after all the raw opinion of the unqualified, on what came to the telephone operators computing the yeses and nos, what arrived in the legislative mail bag then, as always, casting a shadow over the morning D.C. sunlight.

Updike believes that Johnson was repudiated because he was not chic, altogether too down-home and as unmanicured as a coyote. "Cambridge professors and Manhattan lawyers and their guitar-strumming children thought they could run the country and the world better than this lugubrious bohunk from Texas." Henceforth, California began to run the country. And, true, not one of the successors could bring a tear to the eye like the memory of the un-buckled Johnson paddling nude in the White House pool or con-ferring on the toilet.

The war—Updike seems to come to rest on the dubious doctrine of "credibility," meaning the credibility of American power to sus-tain noncommunist allies wherever and whenever they were at-tacked. "Credibility must be maintained; power is a dirty business, but whoever said it wasn't?" Whether it was *prudent,* given the loss of lives, the waste and vast expense, still to be paid for, to send airplane after airplane each day with bombs, napalm, Agent Orange, soldiers, condoms, whiskey, cornflakes, and chewing gum—that's something else, the basis for dissent even among some skeptical, cautious men around Washington, along with the perception that the war was "unwinnable." And for the conscientious patriot Updike, should this war be morally allowable, considering the gross inequity of de-structive means between ourselves and the enemy?

Such, such were the days, and a little power struggle took place at *The New Yorker,* a filtering down or pushing up of conflict on West Forty-third Street, and Updike, an occasional political commenta-tor, was made to give way in "Notes and Comments" to Jonathan Schell and "more leftish hands."

"The world is fallen, and in a fallen world animals, men, and na-tions make space for themselves through a willingness to fight. Christ beat up the money-changers in the temple, and came not to bring peace, He distinctly said, but a sword." When Christ, who fa-mously blessed the peacemaker, spoke of not peace but a sword, He had no thought of wars between nations but induced instead the household declarations of war that would supply the troops for his crusade. (Matthew 10:34–35: "Think not that I am come to send peace on earth: I come not to send peace, but a sword. For I come to set a man at variance against his father, and the daughter against her mother, and the daughter in law against her mother in law.") Certainly, most of us would join the army rather than embrace the poverty and repudiation of family and earthly concerns these troublesome early Christians were to accept as their lot.

Neither Jahweh nor Christ can be, after the biblical period, slipped into war alliances even if it is natural, in the midst of wholesale death, that the suffering should seek divine sanction for their cause. Bavarian Christian leaders in the last war seemed to have no trouble piling up sanctions with or without the aid of divinity. Updike goes far afield to find advice, even from the Bhagavad-Gita: "Therefore you must fight.... Freedom from activity is never attained by abstaining from action." And in another obscure reference, obscure in intention at least, he thinks of men at war and of our national honor and writes: "In Sunday School, I had been much impressed by the passage where Peter denies Christ three times before the cock crows." The disciple Peter, with his noticeable Galilean accent, divesting himself of the beleaguered Christ, saying "I know not the man" thrice—this betrayal by propinquity or rhetorical extension seems to be attached to the milling throngs of the peace movement denying Johnson and Kissinger and Nixon. Perhaps the hippies should, like Judas in some accounts, hang themselves, as in an awful pop sense many of them did.... A slippery journey all this was. In a brilliant recent book about, among other matters, God and national policy in Victorian England up to the First World War, a young man recruited in 1914 is quoted as saying, "I've been a Christian all my life, but this war is a bit too serious."*

Updike's moral complexion is revealed with passion in his memoir and with a high degree of almost lapidary affection for the values of his youth, the war stamps and nickels in the church col-

---

*Derek Jarrett, *The Sleep of Reason: Fantasy and Reality from the Victorian Age to the First World War* (New York: Harper and Row, 1989).

lection plate, the mainstream in its decency, allegiance, and sacrifice. Along the way, he scolds the "anti-establishment militants" gathered for a summer on Martha's Vineyard, scolds Mailer and Philip Roth and even the long dead holdouts, New England with its "haughty disavowal of the Mexican-American War"—that skirmish, or those skirmishes, in which Mexico ceded two-fifths of its territory, which, being long accustomed to Texas and California, we were pleased to have.

Updike votes for the Democrats and is one of those Americans who retain from their parents a memory of the Depression and of the inspiration of Franklin Roosevelt. The upper-middle classes, he observed, voted Democratic out of "humanitarian largesse," because they saw it as the party of the left-out and needy. For himself, "I was simply poor and voted Democratic out of crude self-interest." He notes that his childhood contained the bicycles and so on beyond necessity and "when, many years later, I was recalling some of these happy circumstances in the company of my father, he interrupted me with an exclamation almost anguished, 'Oh, no, Johnny—we were *poor!*' "

The young man from Shillington is interesting indeed, and his autobiographical composition, the work of a master writer, is a document of some uniqueness in our contemporary literature, something like a desk full of stunningly local photographs preserved by accident; or it would be so if photographs had opinions. And yet, there is something droll about the picture of himself as déclassé while he wandered about Harvard, carrying with him his "humble beginnings" and his relative deprivation. With his Christianity and out-of-line distrust of the antiwar movement, he places himself as an object of aesthetic distaste like Johnson in politics, and in religion a lonely swimmer "sworn to seek / If any golden harbour be for me / In seas of death and sunless gulf of Doubt." Of course, he is the true and sweetly acceptable celebrity of art, that world of the self-made where attitude and pose have a license as plain as that of a mosquito.

A sort of citizen self-consciousness seems to accompany him as he goes into the Sunday-morning church service, there perhaps to sing the popular hymn, pleasantly negotiable for tenor and soprano, "Once to every man and nation comes the moment to decide," words actually taken from a Civil War poem by J. R. Lowell. Or to return home to the town meeting, home from the cynical caverns of New York.

> I walked with my suitcase, on a winter night, up to the high school, where the town meeting was in progress. I gave my name, was checked off and admitted, and stood there in the gymnasium-auditorium in my city suit, looking into the brightly illuminated faces of my fellow citizens.

"Among the repulsions of atheism for me has been its drastic uninterestingness as an intellectual position." Dear spotted atheism, the homely, wrinkled queen of heaven for the Big Bang, mother of the depressing claims of the prehistoric upright ape and the joke of the Piltdown Man—uninteresting? For this multiplex American talent, so various, as studious as a monk and as sly as a defense attorney with certain flashing difficulties in his case, here is the equation: "Down-dirty sex and the bloody mess of war and the strenuous act of faith all belonged to a dark necessary underside of reality that I felt should not be merely ignored, or risen above, or disdained."

"Down-dirty sex"—here the novelist can be seen to slip out the door of the prayer meeting and the vote on the zoning law, saying as he leaves to attend to business, "In Adam's fall, we sinned all." Updike began with *The Poorhouse Fair,* a charming fable about some old men in a country home. "It'll make a f.ing black mark in Connor's book," the dialogue goes, chaste typography of the year 1959, before the libertinism of the detestable sixties brought in the new-fangledness of typewriter fucking. Updike embraced the wide exemptions with a curious fervor, and his genius began to show a concubine's patience in the diversification of descriptions of the sexual act, not to mention the largest circus of performers. "Whoso list to hunt I know where is an hind."

To risk the opprobium of being against sex and candor in fiction, of withholding appreciation for the wearisome struggle with adjective, verb, and noun, the difficult rhythms of the alexandrines of copulation, brings on as much social uneasiness as not being a dove. Perhaps *Couples* and the cocky antics of *The Witches of Eastwick* are best thought of as Restoration comedies, fantasies of cuckolds, loose-girdled ladies, toffs, lecherous squires, theatrics free at last from the Roundheads. But then the triad: down-dirty sex, God, and country?

Updike himself worries the scab of the union of these three, one original with him perhaps. God knows all, and so cannot be shocked, he says. No, God is not easily shocked, but He is not one to forgo wrath about the evil and adulterous generations—a problem, yes, of Updike's own making, there's that to be said for it. We note in the crowd of characters those most sympathetically imagined, Piet Hanema in *Couples,* and Rabbit Angstrom in the trilogy devoted to him, are given a sort of club handshake: They go to church.

Roger's Version, a later novel, is prodigiously learned in theology ancient and modern, in physics, computers, whatever is necessary. There are four main characters: Roger Lambert, a professor of theology, rather cynical, tweedy, as he goes about giving lectures on Tertullian in a place like the divinity school at Harvard; his second wife, Esther, mother of their one child; Dale, a student, nerdish master of the computer who wishes to use its arcane possibilities to prove the existence of God; and Verna, Roger's niece, a foulmouthed flower child, with a child of her own, half black, whom she bangs about and injures sufficiently to be rightly accused of child abuse at the hospital.

In the novel, Dale, with his waxy pallor and acne, will have an affair with the professor's wife, Esther; the professor will sleep with his dreadful niece, Verna. Some justification, religious, is needed for this willful "cage of unclean beasts," as the Puritans were thought of in Holland. Remember, the text Updike quotes tells us, that Tertullian allowed: "There's nothing to blush for in nature. Nature should be revered."

Nature—Esther with Dale:

> He is coming. She stares at the little dark eye, the *meatus uranarius,* and with a stern helpfulness gives a downward tug at his engorged phallus ... and when the first gob comes, as if in slow motion on a pornographic film, she has to have it herself ... all that startling pure whiteness, ravenously nimble ... and holding him firm with that hand at his kicking root, centers her cunt above his prick quickly and impales herself.

And, etc.

Roger meanwhile at his desk, weary of translating Tertullian's difficult Latin, nods off to imagine, in quite pretty Kodachrome, his wife and Dale together:

> I pictured a white shaft: tense, pure, with dim blue broad veins and darker thinner ones and a pink-mauve head like the head of a mushroom set by the Creator upon a swollen stem nearly as thick as itself, just the merest little lip or rounded eaves ... overhanging the bluish stretched semi-epiderm where pagan foreskin once was, and a drop of transparent nectar in the little wide-awake slit of an eye at its velvety suffused tip.

Verna, in confrontation, with Uncle Roger: "Because you want to fuck me. You want to lick my cunt." At every point in this curious, yellow novel there are asides to make way for religious imagery and longer disquisitions about the Fall and meaning of flesh, all bringing to mind those philosophical longueurs in the Marquis de Sade that interrupt the tableaux and stagy criminality. Of course, Sade despises God, and Updike's is a domestic, harmless imagination.

What seems to make a remote connection between the two is the felt need for justification. When Verna and Roger are in conversation at the kitchen table and Roger instructs her in the Christian belief that "even little babies are bad," he elaborates from the unlikely pulpit: "Augustine did. Calvin did. All the best Christian thinkers did. You have to [believe in the badness of babies], otherwise the world isn't truly fallen, and there's no need for Redemption, there's no Christian story." (Pelagius thought Adam's sin was his alone and we must commit our own sins. But no matter.) There is much that is dismaying and unpleasant and tiresomely perfunctory in this violent congress between the pornographic impulse and Christian doctrine (e.g., the plastic cross that Dale, the callow Spinoza at his computer, wears and to which Esther, the divinity wife, gives whatever attention she has to spare).

If the novels, the hotter ones, need a vindication the need is not theological but aesthetic, a matter of fiction, and also a grounding in social credibility, the treadmill of fictional truth. The actors in the drama will be a biochemist, a Radcliffe graduate, a Congregationalist minister, an amateur violinist, all turned into colliding bodies, objects, to whom inhibition, anxiety, debts, the eye of the neighbors, the practical world, the overhanging aura of the divinity school, time itself, the bother, the bother, the boredom ("Fulfillment's desolate attic"—Philip Larkin) are completely absent. The matings of these married, switching couples do not take place in some 1920s demimonde or in Haight-Ashbury but are consummated in a wondrously laid-out realistic world, heightened by Updike's intense visual imagination. *Witches:*

> The night was moonless. The crickets stridulated their everlasting monotonous meaningful note. Car headlights swept by on Cocumscussoc Way, and the bushes by the church door, nearly stripped of leaves, sprang up sharp in the illumination like complicated mandibles and jointed feelers and legs of insects magnified. The air smelt faintly of apples making cider by themselves.

And *Couples:* "The blue fire, layer on layer, of swallowed starlight, was halved by a dissolving jet tail."

In the early pages of *The Great Gatsby*, the lower-class mistress makes a telephone call to the Buchanan estate at the dinner hour. This small event foretells the *tristesse* of the entire novel, sets the compositional tone for the eye and the special sensibility of the narrator. "Among the broken fragments of the last five minutes at table I remember the candles being lit again, pointlessly, and I was conscious of wanting to look squarely at every one, and yet to avoid all eyes." Saddest of all is the distant picture of the mistress at the telephone, she who literally doesn't know where she is with Tom Buchanan and his golden Daisy, she who can have no idea.

Updike's shimmering knowledge of the way things look, how they deface or illuminate the towns, the roads; his almost effortless command of the tradesman's shops, the houses, cars, sports, and the speech of America, his dialogue's wit, swiftness, and deftness in placement—in all this he is unsurpassed. But the greatly pleasurable gifts hang like white, puffy clouds around the humbly repetitive pandemonium of the relentless f.ings that do not advance the plot. On and on they go, fore and aft, signifying description itself, interspersed with the voyeur's homely and infidel conversation. "Neff allowed to Alexandra that Greta [his wife] was ardent but strenuous, very slow to come but determined to do so." In *Witches*, one of the women has a leaking pipe in the kitchen; the plumber is called ... and so on. At a point in their lovemaking, she suggests an unappetizing way of getting off, and the man of the people, the licensed journeyman with perhaps another leak on the intercom, says, "How about I give you a rain check on that?"

In the beauty of the lillies, Christ was born across the sea—this odd and uplifting line from many of the odd lines in "The Battle Hymn of the Republic" seemed to me, as I set out, to summarize what I had to say about America, to offer itself as the title of a continental *magnum opus* of which all my books, no matter how many, would be mere installments, mere starts at singing of this great roughly rectangular country severed from Christ by the breadth of the sea.

An extraordinary statement, beautiful in the quotation and in the lilt of the flow of aspiration. If Updike has done as he wished, he has done so in the Rabbit trilogy—*Rabbit Run, Rabbit Redux,* and *Rabbit Is Rich:* "I, who seemed to be full of things to say, who had all of Shillington to say, Shillington and Pennsylvania and the whole immense mass of middling, hidden, troubled America to say." True—the novelist's glory here is *saturation,* the jungle density of memory, experience, and imagination. The volumes span twenty years or so and they take place in a thick vegetation, crabgrass, and rotten dandelions pushing up over the lost basketball tournaments, the car lots, the aging elders, the songs and creaking beds, bad jobs, the growing and failing business of the lower-class and petit-bourgeois landscape. In these novels, it is the lived years of Harry—Rabbit as he is called—Angstrom and Janice, née Springer, that grow and grow with their mess, their cars, their flights, their domestic vagrancy, their inchoate sense of things, the spendthrift poverty and the TV dinners and hot dogs scrounged up on an evening.

Rabbit Angstrom is created out of recalcitrant materials, the high-school basketball court and finally the Toyota distributorship in Brewer—the facts, you remember, much like those of the truck-stop minimalism in favor just now. But in Updike there are no staccato notations; it unwinds and unwinds, scene after scene, a long flow of attention and feeling. It is difficult to describe just who this young man from Brewer might be because of the subtlety of his claim on our sympathy, the peculiarities of his unease, his "running," this is, running away in the first volume.

In earlier American fiction, the custom was to give a character like Rabbit, Middle Western, feeling cramped in spirit, to give him a touch of the poet, some little closet of Jude-like hesitant bookishness. But Rabbit is not leaving town, nor would he wish to exactly. He runs to get away, runs by car, and sometimes walks out of his too-early marriage to Janice because, well, as he puts it, "she's such a mutt." He has an inchoate sense of things "invisible" and goes to church where "the pressed suits of portly men give substance and respectability to his furtive sense of the invisible." He feels the need to ask forgiveness for his days at the used-car lot. "You see these clunkers come in with 80,000 miles on them and the pistons so loose the oil just pours through and they get a washing and the speedometer turned back and you hear yourself saying this represents a real bargain."

Rabbit is not a rebel against small-town hypocrisy and narrowness, the so-familiar plight. He's got a flag decal on his car, and he's a patriot in the barroom: "Poor old LBJ, Jesus, with tears in his eyes on television, you must have heard him, he just about offered to make North Vietnam the fifty-first fucking state of the Goddam Union if they'd just stop throwing bombs." If he has a spiritual quest it is to his old coach, Tothero, where he takes up with Ruth, a tired and realistic woman, available but not exactly a whore, just hanging on. He flees while Janice is back home experiencing their second child, and he leaves Ruth to return, leaving her pregnant after convincing her not to use the "flying saucer."

The years of Janice and Rabbit go on and lots of coitus, sometimes amid the residue of too much Gallo and too many bologna sandwiches for him and for her and, of course, with others. The Springers, the cabin in the Poconos, a couple-swapping trip to the Caribbean, very heavy, Rabbit's days as chief sales representative of the Toyota franchise in Brewer. "This is a Corolla.... This particular car has four-speed synchromesh transmission, fully transistorized ignition system, power-assisted front disc brakes, vinyl reclining bucket seats, a locking gas cap." *Saturation,* its reward. At the end, Rabbit is a grandfather. "Through all this she has pushed to be here, in his lap, his hands, a real presence, hardly weighing anything but alive. Fortune's hostage, heart's desire, a granddaughter. His. Another nail in his coffin. His."

These wonderful novels are acts of conservation, a gathering of plant specimens north of the Delaware River, a rare and lasting collection of the fertilities of Updike's genius. Along the way, his diversions, vacations perhaps, have been a sort of brilliant excess, as if thrown away; but the novels *Bech* and *Bech Is Back* are magical travel books, the best since Evelyn Waugh. His literary criticism, *Hugging the Shore* and pieces following, does not hug the shore but instead sails out in an open boat where his curiosity and great intelligence seem to sail on and on, wherever.

(*1989*)

Paradise Lost:
Philip Roth

~ ~ ~

Amerrican Pastoral is Philip Roth's twentieth work of fiction—an accretion of creative energy, a yearly, or almost, place at the starting line of a marathon. But his is a one-man sprint with the signatures, the gestures, the deep breathing, and the repetitiveness, sometimes, of an obsessive talent. Roth has his themes, spurs to his virtuoso variations and star turns in triple time. His themes are Jews in the world, especially in Israel, Jews in the family, Jews in Newark, New Jersey; fame, vivid enough to occasion impostors (*Operation Shylock*); literature, since his narrators or performers are writers, actually one writer, Philip Roth. And sex, anywhere in every manner, a penitential workout on the page with no thought of backaches, chafings, or phallic fatigue. Indeed the novels are prickled like a sea urchin with the spines and fuzz of many indecencies.

In *American Pastoral*, we are, on the first page, once more in Newark; and on page sixteen we are told "I'm Zuckerman the author." Nathan Zuckerman is the author of *Carnovsky* (*Zuckerman Unbound*), an alternative title like those sometimes used in foreign translations. In English, the novel is, of course, *Portnoy's Complaint*, which provoked among many other responses an eruption of scandal. The author of the book that brought about a fame and a "recognition factor" equal to that of Mick Jagger is Philip Roth. Or so it is in *Zuckerman Unbound,* where even a young funeral director, attending the remains of a Prince Seratelli, pauses to ask for the author's autograph—all part of this wild, very engaging minstrel show in which the writing of a book, not just *any* book, may serve as the lively plot for a subsequent book. Of course, we cannot attach Zuckerman or David Kepesh or Peter Tarnopol or Alexander Portnoy to Philip Roth like a fingernail. Not always.

However, if he follows Zuckerman to *The Anatomy Lesson,* the reader will gain or lose a shiver of interest if he knows that the late critic Irving Howe published in *Commentary* some forthright reservations about Roth's work and that Howe is the "source" of the character Milton Appel. Howe had written—among other thoughts, some favorable—that "what seems really to be bothering Portnoy is a wish to sever his sexuality from his moral sensibilities, to cut it away from his self as a historical creature. It's as if he really supposed the super-ego, or *post coitum triste,* were a Jewish invention."

Zuckerman or Roth cries out some years later in *The Anatomy Lesson:* "Milton Appel had unleashed an attack upon Zuckerman's career that made Macduff's assault on Macbeth look almost lackadaisical. Zuckerman should have been so lucky as to come away with decapitation. A head wasn't enough for Appel; he tore you limb from limb." If he is indeed torn limb from limb, this ferocious paraplegic author pursues Appel/Howe in a motorized wheelchair for almost forty pages.

The structure of Roth's fiction is based often upon identifying tirades rather than actions and counteractions, tirades of perfervid brilliance, and this is what he can do standing on his head or hanging out the window if need be. The tirades are not to be thought of as mere angry outbursts in the kitchen after a beer or two, although they are usually angry enough since most of the characters are soreheads of outstanding volubility. The monologues are a presentation of self, often as if on the stage of some grungy Comédie Française, if such an illicit stretch may be allowed. Here is Monkey, the trailer-park Phèdre of *Portnoy's Complaint,* in a cameo appearance:

> Picking on me all the time—in just he way you *look* at me you pick on me, Alex! I open the door at night, I'm so *dying* to see you, thinking all day long about nothing but you, and there are those fucking orbs already picking out every single thing that's *wrong* with me! As if I'm not insecure enough, as if insecurity isn't my whole hang-up, you get that expression all over your face the minute I open my mouth ... oh, shit, here comes another dumb and stupid remark out of that brainless twat ... Well, I'm not brainless, and I'm not a twat either, just because I didn't go to fucking Harvard! And don't give me any more of your shit about behaving in front of *The Lindsays.* Just who the fuck are *The Lindsays?* A God damn mayor, and his wife! A fucking *mayor!* In case you forget, I was married to one of the richest men in France *when I was still eighteen years old*—I was a guest at Aly Khan's for dinner, when you were still back in Newark, New Jersey, finger-fucking your little Jewish girl friends!

There you have Monkey and her expressive grievance.

For tirades and diatribes of a more demanding content, nothing Roth has written equals the bizarre explosions of *Operation Shylock,* a rich, original work composed with an unforgiving complexity if one is trying to unravel the design. It is about the double, the impersonator, the true self, one's own estimation, and the false self known to the public, the latter brilliantly examined in an account of the trial in Jerusalem of Ivan the Terrible, the allegedly murderous Ukrainian at Treblinka, who is also John Demjanjuk, "good old Johnny, the gardener from Cleveland, Ohio." And standing at not too great a distance from the actual ground of the novel we are reminded of the bad Philip Roth, creator for laughs of American Jewish life in its underwear; and, on the other hand, Philip Roth, artist, observer, inspired comedian, "the litanist of the fleas, the knave, the thane, the ribboned stick, the bellowing breeches"—comedian of the folkloric Portnoys and others of their kind.

In *Operation Shylock,* Philip Roth is in New York, recovering from depression and suicidal impulses brought on by the drug Halcion. (The doubling mystery of pharmaceutical messages—may cause insomnia or drowsiness. Remember President George Bush, reportedly on Halcion, ever windblown and smiling as he relentlessly raced up and down in his "cigarette" boat on the waters outside the summer White House in Kennebunkport, Maine.) Roth, from Halcion, down as a bottom-dwelling flatfish, is planning to go to Israel to interview the novelist Aharon Appelfeld. He learns, as if he had already departed and landed, that someone is giving interviews and lectures under his name, speaking on the radio and announcing an appearance in the King David Hotel on the subject of "Diasporism: The Only Solution to the Jewish Problem. A lecture by Philip Roth." The double, the imposter, given the fairy-tale name of Pipik, is one of the disputatious inhabitants of the mind of the actual Roth, who creates at interesting length the faux, but not altogether faux, debate on the present position of Israel in the world.

Diasporism: "The time has come to return to the Europe that was for centuries, and remains to this day, the most authentic Jewish homeland there has ever been, the birthplace of rabbinic Judaism, Hasidic Judaism, Jewish secularism, socialism—on and on. The time has come to renew in the European Diaspora our preeminent spiritual and cultural role." In questions and counterarguments between the true and false Philip Roth, the horror of the Holocaust is remembered but is now claimed to be a "bulwark against European anti-Semitism." The mad Pipik is arguing in effect: Europe's had that, it's over. "No such bulwark exists in Islam. Exterminating a Jewish nation would cause Islam to lose not a single night's sleep, except for the great night of celebration. I think you would agree that a Jew is safer today walking aimlessly around Berlin than going unarmed into the streets of Ramallah."

Pipik has in the name of Roth not only proposed his program of

diasporism, he has also organized A.S.A., Anti-Semites Anony-
mous, which leads to the appearance in the plot of a nurse who is
valiantly and with commendable self-discipline in "recovery," *she*
having taken the twelve steps. In this Israel, "the pasturalization of
the ghetto," prophets and pundits roam the streets, all the while
giving off the noise and fumes of opinion. Here, Philip Roth encounters an acquaintance from the past, a Harvard-educated Egyptian enrolled at Roth's time as a graduate student at the University
of Chicago and now a famous professor. His name is George Ziad
(*sic*). Zee, as he is called, is also a diasporist but for his own reason.
His program is to get the Jews out of Israel and thereby return the
land to his ancestors, the Palestinians.

Believing that the old Philip Roth of his acquaintance has been
transmogrified into the passionate diasporist of Pipik's caper, Zee
holds forth with feeling about the sufferings of the Palestinians
and the inferiority and provincialism of Israeli culture by comparison with that of the Jews in their true homeland, Manhattan.
"There is more Jewish spirit and Jewish laughter and Jewish intelligence on the Upper West Side of Manhattan than in this entire
country.... There's more Jewish heart at the knish counter at Za-
bar's than in the whole of the Knesset!"

Then the true Philip Roth, taking on the garments of the imposter Pipik, performs in his fluent rhythms about the greatest
diasporist of all, Irving Berlin.

The radio was playing "Easter Parade" and I thought, But this is
Jewish genius on a par with the Ten Commandments. God gave
Moses the Ten Commandments and then He gave to Irving
Berlin "Easter Parade" and "White Christmas."...Easter he turns
into a fashion show and Christmas into a holiday about snow.
Gone is the gore and the murder of Christ—down with the cru-
cifix and up with the bonnet!... If supplanting Jesus Christ with
snow can enable my people to cozy up to Christmas, then let it
snow, let it snow, let it snow!

So goes this curious, hilarious work of a profligate imagination unbound.

Along the way, it dashes into subplots of many befuddlements and allocations of adventures offered with the pedantic assurance of a mock court indictment. It is suggested, or more or less sworn to, that Philip Roth, the living author, acted as an agent for the Mossad, the CIA of Israel, by spying upon "Jewish anti-Zionist elements threatening the security of Israel." Serving counterintelligence by impersonating the impersonator? The novel is subtitled: *A Confession.* The preface claims that "the book is as accurate an account as I am able to give of actual occurrences that I lived through during my middle fifties and that culminated, early in 1988, in my agreeing to undertake an intelligence-gathering operation for Israel's foreign intelligence service, the Mossad." A solemn affidavit? Not quite. A note to the reader at the end of the book reads, "This confession is false." An operatic divertissement? Aida, the Ethiopian princess stealing war plans from her Egyptian lover for the benefit of her country. Or the false Dimitri and at last old Boris Godunov, Philip Roth, saving the state from the diasporists and in a cloud of redemption expiring.

The talent of Philip Roth floats freely in this rampaging novel with a plot thick as starlings winging to a tree and then flying off again. It is meant perhaps as a sort of restitution offered in payment of the claim that if the author has not betrayed the Jews, he has too often found them to be whacking clowns or whacking-off clowns. He bleeds like the old progenitor he has named in the title. Since he is, as a contemporary writer, always quick to insert the latest item of the news into his running comments, perhaps we can imagine him today as poor Richard Jewell, falsely accused in the 1996 Olympic bombing in Atlanta because, in police language, he fit the profile but was at last found to be just himself: a nice fellow good to his mother.

And yet, the impostor, the devil's advocate for the diaspora, has, with dazzling invention, composed not an ode for the hardy settlers of Israel but an ode to the Wandering Jew as a beggar and prince in Western culture, speaking and writing in all its languages.

After fame and mischief on the streets of Jerusalem, Roth in a sort of recidivism returns to the passions of his youth with a "hero," Mickey Sabbath, certainly not in his first youth, but shall we say, still trying. *Sabbath's Theater,* a much admired book, is seriously filthy. *Portnoy's Complaint,* by comparison and to put the best face on it, is lads and lassies a-Maying. *Sabbath's Theater* is mud, a slough of obscenity with some lustrous pearls of antic writing embedded in it. The first line: "Either forswear fucking others or the affair is over." That is Drenka, a fifty-two-year-old Croatian voluptuary with ovarian cancer of which she dies, but not before thirteen years of insatiable carnality with Sabbath and more years than that with others.

Sabbath, now sixty-four, refuses to forswear, saying it would be repugnant to him to break the "sacrament of infidelity." And that is, perhaps, why he is given the name Sabbath, the day of worship, to suggest a sort of Black Mass of fucking. The world is out to crucify the master puppeteer of his Indecent Theater, but the aging, arthritic, disheveled puppeteer is irresistible to all except his wife Roseanna, who spends her days in an alcoholic stupor and when at last belligerently sober, by way of AA, takes off with a lesbian and often turns her thoughts to the penis clipper, the well-named Lorena Bobbitt.

Among the breathlessly accommodating are a Barnard girl; Christa, a runaway German au pair; and Rosa, a Spanish-speaking maid, "four childs," another in her belly; and a student at a liberal-arts college from which Sabbath is fired as an adjunct professor of puppet theater, owing to the discovery of a taped telephone conversation of outstanding lasciviousness, published in full at the bottom of the pages, a priapic academic footnote. This leads to an apologia, attributed to Sabbath, which can be attributed to the author, Philip Roth.

Not even Sabbath understood how he could lose his job at a liberal arts college for teaching a twenty-year-old to talk dirty twenty-five years after Pauline Réage, fifty-five years after Henry Miller, sixty years after D. H. Lawrence, eighty years after James Joyce, two hundred years after John Cleland, three hundred years after John Wilmot, a second earl of Rochester—not to mention four hundred after Rabelais, two thousand after Ovid, and twenty-two hundred after Aristophanes.

To the challenge of white satin, spring flower epithalamia, the "realist" offers the rude, raging insistence of Nature. In Roth's novels, the erotic pushes and thrusts where it will, even in imagination to the iconic Anne Frank and Franz Kafka. In *The Ghost Writer,* a young female student, a refugee from Europe at the time of the Holocaust, turns up as an assistant to the esteemed writer Lonoff, living in Massachusetts, the snowscape Yankeeland. Zuckerman, young and only on the first arc of the happy curve of his talent, enters the shrine of literature as a guest in Lonoff's house. He soon imagines the attractive assistant to be a living Anne Frank, rescued from death only to be sent in the still of the night to the bed of Lonoff, or he to her bed.

In *The Professor of Desire,* David Kepesh this time, rather than Nathan Zuckerman, goes on a journey to Prague, the holy city of the painfully reserved, tubercular genius, Franz Kafka. In a dream, a jeu d'esprit, Kepesh is taken to see "Kafka's whore," a hideous old fraudulent tourist attraction, and a foul scene follows.

Sabbath's journey into the underworld is sex and death, the classical Manichaean union. He is haunted by his mother, who was haunted by the death of his brother, Morty, shot down in the Philippines during World War II. Sabbath, at the end of his tether, or so you might put it, masturbates and pisses on the grave of the exuberant Drenka of the "uberous breasts." He is found there by her son, a cop, whose outrage is so great he will not arrest or shoot him to death, as Sabbath wishes. Let him lie in the muck. "You desecrate my mother's grave. You desecrate the American flag. You desecrate your own people. With your stupid fucking prick out, wearing the skullcap of your own religion!" So Sabbath is doomed to life. "He could not fucking die. How could he leave? How could he go? Everything he hated was here." Here is Drenka's cemetery, in America, in the spurious romanticism of lovemaking, marriage, fidelity? Sabbath and his theater of indecent puppets like Drenka, Christa, and so on are not a happy band of buskers. There is illness, prostate affliction, ovarian cancer, madness, drunkenness, the scars of his brother's death and his mother's annihilating grief. Perhaps he is saying he cannot bring himself to suicide because of the life-giving force of hatred—an idea indeed. But it is not always useful to seek abstractions in fiction. When you turn to the last pages of *Sabbath's Theater* not much is clear beyond the anarchic brilliance of the swarm of characters, the rush of language, the willful chaos of the inspiration.

American Pastoral: Paradise remembered: The Fall; Paradise Lost in New Jersey, Philip Roth's singular turf, Newark "before the negroes," its raucous, fetid airs memorialized by his art as if they were the zephyrs in a sportsman's sketches. Zuckerman is called to tell the story of the fate of Seymour Levov, a supreme high-school athlete, called "the Swede." His is a life that began in gladness and came to an end in a conflagration of appalling desolation. The Levov family, the marriages, the children, the business, the houses are the landscape of toil and success, an ever-upward curve horribly deflected by the America of the 1960s. The elder Levov has through his unceasing labor and shrewdness, his toughness, built a business in the manufacture of ladies' gloves, the firm going by the name of Newark Maid Leatherwear.

Newark Maid at the time of the novel's action has moved to Puerto Rico, but the roots of the family go back to the old Levov grandfather, who arrived in America in the 1890s and "found work fleshing sheepskins fresh from the lime vat." The slow, punishing development of Newark Maid by Lou Levov, the father of Swede and his brother Jerry, is the ancestral cord of blood and sweat that will be broken in subtle ways by the agreeable Swede and in violent ways by the bomb-throwing murders committed by Swede's daughter, Merry, a child of the 1960s.

The elder Levov was "one of those slum-reared Jewish fathers whose roughhewn, undereducated perspective goaded a whole generation of striving, college-educated Jewish sons." Lou Levov went to work at the tannery at fourteen: "the tannery that stank of both the slaughterhouse and the chemical plant from the soaking of flesh and the cooking of flesh and the dehairing and pickling and degreasing of hides." At the workhouse, "the temperature [rises] to a hundred and twenty degrees ... with hunks of skin all over the floor, everywhere pits of grease, hills of salt, barrels of solvent— this was Lou Levov's high school and college." The labor, powerfully imagined and researched here, brings to mind the Lower East Side tenements and the brutal hours at the sewing machines that led in time to the garment district on Seventh Avenue.

On the domestic scene, the increasing prosperity of Newark Maid gloves sends the Levov family from the streets of the lower- and middle-class Jews to "Keer Avenue ... where the rich Jews lived." They become Keer Avenue Jews, "with their finished basements, their screened-in porches, their flagstone front steps,... laying claim like audacious pioneers to the normalizing American amenities." Swede, the athletic, tall, blond Levov, "as close to a goy as we were going to get," survives the Marine Corps, plays baseball at Upsala College in East Orange, New Jersey, turns down a club contract offer, and joins his father's business. And in a sort of sleep-walking way, out of natural inclination, he crossed a line—or what would seem to be a line to the old inbred Levovs: he married Miss New Jersey. "Before competing at Atlantic City for the 1949 Miss America title, she had been Miss Union County, and before that Spring Queen at Upsala.... A shiksa. Dawn Dwyer. He'd done it."

As the novel opens, the Swede is almost seventy, and he has sent a letter to the author, Zuckerman, asking for a dinner meeting. The old Levov had died at age ninety-six, and the son is struggling to write a memoir about him to be distributed to family and friends. He wants to discuss his father with Zuckerman, who is a friend from high-school days. In the note, he says about his father that he suffered "because of the shocks that befell his loved ones." Indeed, the shock that caused the old man to keel over dead was the discovery that Seymour's daughter, Merry, had, after a somewhat fortuitous connection with young radicals in New York City, fallen under the spell of violent resistance to society, the Vietnam War, rejection of family, the whole package. One early morning, she planted a bomb at the post office of her town and blew up the popular town doctor who was picking up his mail. She went into hiding at the home of her speech therapist, for little Merry suffered from a stutter; in time, she "connected" again and after robbery and rape and gross ill treatment took part in an "action" that killed three people in Oregon.

This is the fall, paradise lost, the dramatic center of the novel. Yes, it could have happened; young men and women better educated than Merry Levov blew up a house in Greenwich Village, killing some of their own, went underground, and later some of them, low on funds, held up a Brinks money truck, killed the black driver, and subsequently went off to jail. There are other bombings and deaths listed in the book. So poor Seymour, the Swede, still well meaning and now a suburbanite, must wake up one morning like the Mayor of Casterbridge and say: I am to suffer, I perceive.

The bomb-throwing plot is not altogether convincing on this particular stage. Merry must make a passage from her Audrey Hepburn scrapbook days to a loquacious, sneering radical life that has to be accepted as given. The most provocative shift in the portrait of Merry as a death-dealing 1960s revolutionary is that she later passes from radicalism to the old Indian religion of Jain, which sought to release the spirit from the bonds of the flesh. Merry adds her own self-destructive interpretations of Jain, with its passivity and pacifism. She eats almost nothing out of regard for the integrity of animals and also that of plants. When found by her father, she is shrunken, living in filth, wandering alone in dangerous spots of Newark with the serenity of the abandonment of selfhood. This reminds us of the cultist aspect of the American revolutionaries of the sixties, sometimes a small band bound together by their rants, paranoia, and above all the exaggeration of their power and the foolish underestimation of the power of society. Even the militia groups of the nineties with their guns and explosives are swollen with a cultish sense of empowerment, a poisonous edema of stockpiling, camaraderie on the rifle range—until the transition of indictment for murder turns them into whimpering, plea-bargaining, helpless victims of consequence. Little Merry Levov takes instead the spiritual life in a drastic extension, but Roth, if he must have her as a bomber, has shown imagination about the loss of revolutionary enthusiasm when the aftermath must be faced alone.

That the Levov family is to suffer, by way of Merry, a catastrophe remote in a statistical sense, undermines the interesting close calls on the road of the Swede's American journey. The Swede has made a right turn into the highway of assimilation and this, it appears, is the true direction of the novel's intellectual and fictional energy. First, the Swede has married the beauty queen, Dawn Dwyer, a Roman Catholic. Even though Dawn surreptitiously had Merry baptized in the faith, they are, in the words of Seymour's brother Jerry, a bullying, big-time coronary surgeon in Florida, a "knockout couple. The two of them all smiles in their outward trip into the USA. She's post-Catholic, he's post-Jewish, together they're going to go out there to Old Rimrock to raise little post-toasties."

Old Rimrock is a posh bit of the New Jersey countryside to which Seymour takes himself and Dawn in a sort of paroxysm of enthusiasm for open fields and great old trees. Old Rimrock in WASP, Republican Morris County. His father had wanted him to settle in a modern house in the "rock-ribbed, Democrat" Newstead Development, where he could live with his family among young Jewish couples. No, for the Swede it is to be a hundred acres of land, "a barn, a millpond, a millstream, the foundation remains of a gristmill that had supplied grain for Washington's troops." And an old stone house and a fireplace "large enough for roasting an ox, fitted out with an oven door and a crane to swing an iron kettle around over the fire." Why shouldn't it be his? Why shouldn't he own it? "Out in Old Rimrock, all of America lay at their door. That was an idea he loved. Jewish resentment, Irish resentment—the hell with it." Dawn is somewhat concerned with Protestant ill feeling about Catholics, but for the Swede, "the Protestants are just another denomination. Maybe they were rare where she grew up— they were rare where he grew up too—but they happen not to be rare in America. Let's face it, they *are* America."

In the 1940s, Jews might have felt some anxiety about their reception in a rich enclave of old-family inhabitants viewing them with condescension if not rudeness. Such would not be true today, when a Jewish media billionaire would, if such an opportunity arose in a period of regal retrenchment, be urged to buy an ancient bit of land in the woods of Windsor, where he could, on an occasional weekend, tramp about over the bones of Queen Victoria. In Old Rimrock, the Levovs make the acquaintance of an architect, Bill Orcutt, from a Morris County family that has filled the local cemetery with worthies for two hundred years.

The Swede, by the time he meets Zuckerman in a New York restaurant, has been divorced from Dawn and has a new wife and children; and Dawn, brought near to suicide by the cruel biography of her daughter, has returned to life with a Swiss face-lift and, in a thunderous rush of plot, made an alliance with the tombstone genealogist, Orcutt. It didn't work out, as the saying goes, the idyll of the young couple. Jerry, the angry sawbones brother, turns Merry in to the FBI, and along the way, driven by his fraternal jealousy of his paragon brother, denounces the life Swede and Dawn shaped for Merry. "Out there with Miss America, dumbing down and dulling out. Out there playing at being Wasps, a little Mick girl from the Elizabeth docks and a Jewboy from Weequahic High. The cows. Cow Society. Colonial old America. And you thought all that façade was going to come without a cost. Genteel and innocent. *But that costs, too, Seymour.* I would have thrown a bomb. I would become a Jain and live in Newark. That Wasp bullshit!" But Seymour in his love and grief for his daughter knows better. "It is chaos. It is chaos from start to finish." America gone berserk.

Among the ruins of time is the city of Newark, where Roth reared the author, Zuckerman, with his elegiac memories of interiors, "the microscopic surface of things close at hand ... the minutest gradations of social position conveyed by linoleum and oilcloth, by yahrzeit candles and cooking smells, by Ronson table lighters and venetian blinds." And outside, autumn afternoons on the football field; down the main drag to movies on a Saturday afternoon; record shops offering Glenn Miller; and at the high-school reunion, damaged faces that still carry the trace of teenage beauty.

When the Swede and Zuckerman meet so many years later, Newark has been the scene of devastating riots in 1967. It is now the "car theft capital of the world"; shops are boarded up; houses, once the shrines of relentless homemakers, are now smashed and splintered orphans; gunshots split the air, causing no more wonder than the screech of big trucks backing into parking spaces: Newark, long ago the little Jewish Eden of Roth's youth.

American Pastoral is a sort of Dreiserian chronicle of the Levov family. Their painfully built fortune, even without the disgrace, might have declined owing to obsolescence. Maids have not for some decades been in need of the finely stitched, soft leather gloves

In the Wasteland:
Joan Didion

~ ~ ~

Joan Didion's novels are a carefully designed frieze of the fracture and splinter in her characters' comprehension of the world. To design a structure for the fadings and erasures of experience is an aesthetic challenge she tries to meet in a striking manner: the placement of sentences on the page, abrupt closures rather like hanging up the phone without notice, and an ear for the rhythms and tags of current speech that is altogether remarkable. Perhaps it is prudent that the central characters, women, are not seeking clarity since the world described herein, the America of the last thirty years or so, is blurred by a creeping inexactitude about many things, among them bureaucratic and official language, the jargon of the press, the incoherence of politics, the disastrous surprises in the mother-father-child tableau.

The method of narration, always conscious and sometimes discussed in an aside, will express a peculiar restlessness and unease in order to accommodate the extreme fluidity of the fictional landscape. You read that something did or did not happen; something was or was not thought; this indicates the ambiguity of the flow, but there is also in "did or did not" the author's strong sense of willful obfuscation, a purposeful blackout of what was promised or not promised—a blackout in the interest of personal comfort and also in the interest of greed, deals, political disguises of intention.

Joan Didion's novels are not consoling, nor are they notably attuned to the reader's expectations, even though they are fast paced, witty, inventive, and interesting in plot. Still, they twist and turn, shift focus and point of view, deviations that are perhaps the price or the reward that comes from an obsessive attraction to the disjunctive and paradoxical in American national policy and to the somnolent, careless decisions made in private life.

> I have the dream, recurrent, in which my entire field of vision fills with rainbow, in which I open a door onto a growth of tropical green (I believe this to be a banana grove, the big glossy fronds heavy with rain, but since no bananas are seen on the palms symbolists may relax) and watch the spectrum separate into pure color. Consider any of these things long enough and you will see that they tend to deny the relevance not only of personality but of narrative, which makes them less than ideal images with which to begin a novel, but we go with what we have.
>
> Cards on the table. (*Democracy*)

This writer is the poet, if you like, of the airplane and the airport. Offhand journeys to Malaysia or to troubled spots in Central America are undertaken as if one were boarding the New York–Washington shuttle. For the busy men, we learn somewhere in the pages that any flight under eight hours is called a "hop." So, we head out for the blue yonder by air as earlier novelists wrote of signing up for a term on ship. "Sailors are the only class of men who now-a-days see anything like stirring adventures; and many things which to the fire-side people appear strange and romantic, to them seem as common-place as a jacket out at elbows" (Melville, preface to *Typee*). Flying round the world every day is for her characters just a "jacket out at elbows." Nothing unusual. Trying to keep pace with an ethereal mobility now become as mundane as a dog trot is a mark of this writer's original sensibility: "She had been going from one airport to another for some months; one could see it, looking at the visas on her passport.... People who go to the airport first invent some business to conduct there.... Then they convince themselves that the airport is cooler than the hotel, or has superior chicken salad" (*A Book of Common Prayer,* 1977).

And from her most recent novel: *The Last Thing He Wanted.*

> I see her standing in the wet grass off the runway, her arms bare, her sunglasses pushed up into her loose hair, her black silk shift wrinkled from the flight, and wonder what made her think a black silk shift bought off a sale rack at Bergdorf Goodman during the New York primary was the appropriate thing to wear on an unscheduled flight at one-thirty in the morning out of Fort Lauderdale–Hollywood International Airport, destination San Jose, Costa Rica but not quite.

Her first novel, *Run River,* appeared in 1963. It is rich in talent and also rich in the virtues of traditional fiction: families, generations, births and deaths, changes of fortune, betrayals. Set in the Sacramento Valley between 1938 and 1959, it begins with a gunshot: "Lily heard the shot at seventeen minutes to one." ("Seventeen minutes to one" brings to mind the surgical precision of the information that will be offered in the later fiction.) The intervening pages and chapters explain what went before the opening shot. In the final pages of the last chapter, we read, "She sat on the needlepoint chair until she heard it, the second shot." The first shot was the husband killing the wife's lover, and the second shot was the husband killing himself. Some families in *Run River* are descendants of the pioneers who made the trip of hardship and promise across the Great Plains. There are hardship passages in the subsequent fictions, although not in a covered wagon but in an airplane carrying your uncertain identity in a six-hundred-dollar handbag.

Her nerves are bad tonight in the wasteland of Haight-Ashbury; she has migraines, generalized and particular afflictions that bring on tears in "elevators and in taxis and in Chinese laundries." Joan Didion's revelation of incapacity, doubt, irresolution, and inattention is brought into question by the extraordinary energy and perseverance found in *Slouching Towards Bethlehem, The White Album,* and the later collection, *After Henry.* If she has "nerves," she also has "nerve" in the sense of boldness and fortitude. She will do the lowest work of a reporter; make the call, try again when the promised callback is not forthcoming. She scouts the neighborhood, finds the houses, and once inside notes the condition of the sink, the baby lying on a pallet and sucking its thumb, and the five-year-old on acid—"High Kindergarten." She spends time with Otto and Deadeye, among other stoned hippies; visits that need the self-denial of a Sister of Charity, although what she brings is a presence, free of strategies of redemption.

At three-thirty that afternoon Max, Tom and Sharon placed tabs under their tongue and sat down together in the living room to wait for the flash. Barbara stayed in the bedroom, smoking hash. During the next four hours a window banged once in Barbara's room.... A curtain billowed in the afternoon wind. Except for the sitar music on the stereo there was no other sound or movement until seven-thirty, when Max said, "Wow!" (*Slouching Towards Bethlehem*)

Moving down the coast from the numb deprivation of Haight-Ashbury to the alert consumerism of Ronald and Nancy Reagan in the governor's mansion in Sacramento and then in the White House, Didion finds them apart from the usual politicians who cherish, or so pretend, their early beginnings in Hyde Park, Kansas, or Plains, Georgia. The Reagans' habits, or perhaps their modes of operation, do not spring from marks left by their placement on the national map. The Reagans come from the welfare state of Dreamland; their roots are Hollywood.

> This expectation on the part of the Reagans that other people would take care of their needs struck many people, right away, as remarkable and was usually characterized as a habit of the rich…. The Reagans were not rich; they and this expectation were the product of studio Hollywood, a system in which performers performed, and in return were cared for…. She [Nancy Reagan] was surprised to learn ("Nobody had told us") that she and her husband were expected to pay for their own food, dry cleaning, and toothpaste while in the White House. She seemed never to understand why it was imprudent of her to have accepted clothes from their makers when so many of them had encouraged her to do so…. The clothes were, as Mrs. Reagan seemed to construe it, "wardrobe"—a production expense, like the housing and catering and first-class travel and the furniture and paintings and cars that get taken home after the set is struck—and should rightly have gone to the studio budget. (*After Henry*)

Play It as It Lays (1970) is the first of the digressive, elusive novels, typical in style and organization of the challenging signature of a Joan Didion work. Shadowy motivation, disruptive or absent context in a paragraph or pages here and there are not properly to be read as indecision or compositional falterings. They display instead a sort of muscular assurance and confidence, or so one is led to believe in the face of a dominant, idiosyncratic style that if nothing else scorns the vexation of indolent or even sophisticated readers who prefer matters and manners otherwise expressed. But, as she says, we go with what we have. The author is in control of the invention, and if the machine is a little like an electric automobile or one running on pressed grapes instead of gasoline in a field of Chevrolets, the autonomy—it does run—puts the critic in an uneasy situation.

The opening sentence of *Play It as It Lays* is: "What makes Iago evil? Some people ask. I never ask."

"I never ask" is a useful introduction to Maria Wyeth: the sound of the extreme negativism, withdrawal, depression, or terminal disgust of this still young woman, a marginal figure in the movie business, brought up in Silver Wells, Nevada, by her drifting parents, divorced, finally in the book from her husband, a director. One might, however, question that the unanswerable evil of Iago would be on her mind, an evil that led even the great Coleridge to fall back upon "motiveless malignity." But who's to say she has not at a bar heard a discussion of the ecstatic treachery of Iago that makes its tragic progress to the suffering and death of Desdemona and Othello? It's just that the inclination to pedantry in instances of piddling, measly inconsequence are sometimes the only protection one has against the witchery of this uncompromising imagination, the settings so various and the sometimes sleepwalking players who blindly walk through windows and fall into traps of great consequence such as the Vietnam War or the world of the Contras.

The women in the novels suffer losses, serious blows from fate that enshroud them like the black dress European peasant women wear lifelong for bereavement; but they are not wearing a black dress except for stylish definition, like the black dress of Anna Karenina in her first appearance at the ball. Maria Wyeth in *Play It as It Lays* has a damaged daughter off somewhere in a hospital; she loves the girl obsessively, but there is no reciprocation from the screaming, indifferent child. Maria has had a cruel abortion. At the end of the book, a lover or sometime lover dies in her bed from an overdose of Valium, saying "because we've been out there where nothing is."

In *A Book of Common Prayer*, the daughter of Charlotte Douglas has disappeared and is wanted by the police for a political bombing. In *Democracy* (1984), Inez Victor's daughter is a heroin addict and Inez's father, in an onset of lunacy, has killed her sister and another person. Inez has also had cancer. In *The Last Thing He Wanted*, Elena

McMahon has lost her mother and in walking out on her rich husband has lost the affection of her daughter. The interior in which the women live is a sort of cocoon of melancholy, but their restlessness is modern and cannot be expressed like that of a country wife sighing at the moonlight as it hits the silence on the front porch. Maria Wyeth sleeps by her pool when she is not driving the L.A. freeways all night, stopping only for a Coke at a filling station. But she is driving a Corvette. The women have credit cards, bank drafts, an Hermès handbag, or a large emerald ring. In the heart of darkness, men fall in love with them, bereft and downhearted as they are. The sheen of glamour is useful to give entrance to the melancholy adulteries and to the plot of costly wild travels and also, in some cases, to politics that come out of the Oval Office or some room in the White House basement and turn up on the runway in Saigon or Costa Rica.

A Book of Common Prayer is a daring title, a risk, even, some would name a presumption. Perhaps the title is meant to bring to mind: "Have mercy on us in the hour of our death ... *Prega per noi.*" Charlotte Douglas is wandering the earth by air, aimlessly hoping to run into her daughter, Marin, "who at eighteen had been observed with her four best friends detonating a crude pipe bomb in the lobby of the Transamerica Building at 6:30 am, highjacking a P.S.A.L. 1011 at the San Francisco Airport and landing in Wendover, Utah, where they burned it in time for the story to interrupt the network news and disappeared." Charlotte Douglas goes to a miserable, corrupt little place called Boca Grande, an ungoverned and ungovernable country near Caracas. Her plane took her there with the blinkered idea that her daughter must be somewhere—and why not Boca Grande? Charlotte is killed by some machine-gun-toting activist in the almost weekly coups and countercoups. And meanwhile, Marin, the Berkeley Tupamaro, is actually in Buffalo. *A Book of Common Prayer* is an odd and most unusual study of secular violence and, in the case of the wandering mother, a sort of heathen inanition. Unable to think on the appalling plight of her daughter, Charlotte fills her mind with memories of her happy at the Tivoli Gardens in Copenhagen, devouring coconut ice under "the thousand trunks of Great Banyan at the Calcutta Botanical Garden."

Democracy: Washington, Honolulu, Hong Kong, Kuala Lumpur, Saigon, and Jakarta appear along the road in this novel of outlandish ambition, justified and honored by the scope, the subtlety, the agenda, as they call it. The time is 1975, the aftermath of Vietnam still in the air, and we go back to the way of setting the scene, a sort of computer lyricism:

> I would skim the stories on policy and fix instead on details: the cost of a visa to leave Cambodia in the weeks before Phnom Penh closed was five hundred dollars American. The colors of the landing lights for the helicopters on the roof of the American embassy in Saigon were red, white, and blue. The code names for the American evacuations of Cambodia and Vietnam respectively were EAGLE PULL and FREQUENT WIND. The amount of cash burned in the courtyard of the DAO in Saigon before the last helicopter left was three-and-a-half million dollars American and eighty-five million piastres. The code name for this operation was MONEY BURN. The number of Vietnamese soldiers who managed to get aboard the last American 727 to leave Da Nang was three hundred and thirty. The number of Vietnamese soldiers to drop from the wheel wells of the 727 was one. The 727 was operated by World Airways. The name of the pilot was Ken Healy.

One of the leading characters in the novel, Jack Lovett, is in love with Inez Victor, who is married to Harry Victor, a member of the United States Senate and a onetime candidate for president, easy to believe since it is the dream of everyone who has ever had a term in the state legislature of whatever state. Lovett is perhaps CIA but not a villain, instead a realist who can say, "A Laotian village indicated on one map and omitted on another suggested not a reconnaissance oversight but a population annihilated. Asia was ten thousand tanks here, three hundred Phantoms there. The heart of Africa was an enrichment facility." In these novels, you do not just take an airplane from Florida to Costa Rica, you board a Lockheed L-100; and in another aside, if such it is, you learn how to lay down the AM-2 aluminum matting for a runway and whether "an eight-thousand foot runway requires sixty thousand square yards of operational apron or only forty thousand."

This author is a martyr of facticity, and indeed such has its place in the fearless architecture of her fictions. You have a dogged concreteness of detail in an often capricious mode of presentation. The detail works upon the mind of the reader, gives an assurance, or at least a feeling, that somewhere, somehow all of this is true, fictional truth, or possibility. It could have happened, and Inez Victor did in fact go off to Kuala Lumpur to work in the refugee camps. And that is where we leave her after her love for Jack Lovett and after her escape from a somnambulistic time as a politician's wife who must say over and over, "Marvelous to be here," and be "smiling at a lunch counter in Manchester, New Hampshire, her fork poised over a plate of scrambled eggs and toast." That is, you may accept or allow for the aesthetically doubtful because of the interesting force of the factual in which it is dressed.

In any case, every page of the books is hers in its peculiarities and particulars: All is handmade, or should we say, hand cut, as by the knife of a lathe. Some unfriendly reviewers, knowing Didion has written screenplays, will call the frame or action cinematic. But the fictions, as she has composed them, are the opposite of the communal cathedrals, or little brown churches in the vale, built by so many willing slaves in Hollywood. The first cry of exasperation from the producers, script doctors, watchful money crunchers with memories of hits and flops would be, What's going on here? What's it about?

If you can believe that Robert "Bud" McFarlane, Reagan's national-security adviser, could fly off to Iran, carrying with him a cake and a Bible in order to make a deal for the shipment of arms to the Contras, you can believe the less bizarre happenings in *The Last Thing He Wanted*. In this novel, Joan Didion has placed a woman, Elena McMahon, on a plane filled with illegal arms bound for Costa Rica, or the off-the-map border installations set up by the Americans, the Freedom Fighters. At the end of the flight, she is to collect the million dollars owed her dying father, a man who does "deals." Collect the money and fly back, or so she has been led to imagine. In the usual percussive Didion dialogue, Elena says, "Actually I'm going right back.... I left my car at the airport." The pilot says, "Long time parking I hope." She doesn't return and at the end of an elaborate plot is assassinated by "the man on the bluff with the pony tail"—the same sinister man who had met her at the landing strip in Costa Rica.

And there is Treat Morrison, the romantic lead you might say, who first sees Elena McMahon in the coffee shop of the Intercontinental Hotel, where she was "eating, very slowly and methodically, first a bite of one then a bite of the other, a chocolate parfait and bacon." The odd menu is mentioned several times but does not give up its meaning beyond the fact that the parfait and bacon had bothered him, Treat Morrison. Morrison is an "ambassador at large" for the Department of State, a troubleshooter, a fixer. Like Jack Lovett in *Democracy*, this is another love-at-first-sight matter, and, odd as it might be, not necessarily as hard to imagine as some of the more portentous occasions. The attractions are ballads: I saw her standing there and my heart stood still—something like that. Treat Morrison and Jack Lovett are attractive men of the world, at work, as the collision of romance leads them to the forlorn, needy women standing there, waiting.

In *The Last Thing He Wanted*, Joan Didion appears on the page directing, filling in, being, often, a friend from the past or a journalist on the case. "For the record this is me talking. You know me, or think you do." Here she is a moralist, a student of the Contra hearings. "There are documents, more than you might think. Depositions, testimony, cable traffic, some of it not yet declassified, but much in the public record." Of course, Elena McMahon is a fiction, but we are to remember the actual people "all swimming together in the glare off the C-123 that fell from the sky into Nicaragua." Among those caught in the glare was "the blond, the shredder, the one who transposed the numbers of the account at the Credit Suisse (the account at the Credit Suisse into which the Sultan of Brunei was to transfer the ten million dollars, in case you have forgotten the minor plays)."

The Last Thing He Wanted is a creation of high seriousness, a thriller composed with all the resources of a unique gift for imaginative literature, American literature. There remains in Didion's far-flung landscapes a mind still rooted in the American West from which she comes. When in *Slouching Towards Bethlehem* she visits the venerable piles in Newport, Rhode Island, she remembers the men who built the railroad, dug the Comstock Lode for gold and silver in Virginia City, Nevada, and made a fortune in copper.

> More than anyone else in the society, these men had apparently dreamed the dream and made it work. And what they did then was to build a place which … led step by step to unhappiness, to restrictiveness, to entrapment in the mechanics of living. In that way the lesson of Bellevue Avenue is more seriously radical than the idea of Brook Farm.… Who could think that the building of a railroad could guarantee salvation, when there on the lawns of the men who built the railroad nothing is left but the shadow of the migrainous women, and the pony carts waiting for the long-dead children?

She is saying that Bellevue Avenue in Newport is not what the West was won for.

(1997)

Reckless People:
Richard Ford

~ ~ ~

From the stories in Richard Ford's collection *Rock Springs* (1987): "This was not going to be a good day in Bobby's life, that was clear, because he was headed to jail. He had written several bad checks, and before he could be sentenced for that he had robbed a convenience store with a pistol—completely gone off his mind." Bobby's ex-wife is giving him his last breakfast, and the man she is now living with is telling the story, with some disgruntlement ("Sweethearts").

In the title story, the narrator, Earl, with his daughter, Cheryl, her dog, Little Duke, and Earl's girlfriend, Edna, are driving through Wyoming in a stolen car.

I'd gotten us a good car, a cranberry Mercedes I'd stolen out of an opthalmologist's lot in Whitefish, Montana. I stole it because I thought it would be comfortable over a long haul, because I thought it got good mileage, which it didn't, and because I'd never had a good car in my life.

The car develops trouble in the oil line, and they have to abandon it in the woods. Somehow, the little group gets to a Ramada Inn, and after a bit of food and lovemaking Edna accepts Earl's offer of a bus ticket and takes off.

There he is, Earl, with Cheryl, the dog, and no car. They might as well be a stone urn of wilting geraniums outside the inn. In the dark of night in the parking lot: "I walked over to a car, a Pontiac with Ohio tags, one of the ones with bundles and suitcases strapped to the top and a lot more in the trunk, by the way it was riding." Standing beside the car, Earl's inner soliloquy runs:

> What would you think a man was doing if you saw him in the middle of the night looking in the windows of cars in the parking lot of the Ramada Inn? Would you think he was trying to get his head cleared? Would you think he was trying to get ready for a day when trouble would come down on him? Would you think his girlfriend was leaving him? Would you think he had a daughter? Would you think he was anybody like you?

Another story, "Optimists," begins: "All of this I am about to tell you happened when I was only fifteen years old, in 1959, the year my parents were divorced, the year when my father killed a man and went to prison for it, the year I left home and school, told a lie about my age to fool the Army, and then did not come back." The father was working in the railroad yards when a hobo tried to jump off a train and was cut into three pieces. The father comes home ashen and trembling from the horrible accident he has seen. At home some recent acquaintances of his wife are playing cards. The visitor, more or less a stranger to the father, turns out to work for the Red Cross. He interrupts with a pedantic interrogation about tourniquets, resuscitation, all the while insisting that technically, as it were, the hobo didn't have to die had the father acted properly.

In a rage of grief and at the presumption of the lecture, the father hits the man, who is killed by the blow. The father goes to prison, comes out in a state of deterioration, begins drinking and brawling, and disappears off somewhere. The years pass, and one day the son sees his mother with a strange man shopping for groceries at a mall. The son and mother talk briefly, but with a good deal of inchoate affection. And that is more or less it. "And she bent down and kissed my cheek through the open window and touched my face with both her hands, held me for a moment that seemed like a long time before she turned away, finally, and left me there alone."

The smooth and confident use of the first-person narration in these brilliant stories is especially remarkable when they are told by petty thieves, the stranded and delinquent. Here the "I" is not remembering or recasting but living in the pure present, in the misbegotten events of the day. The focus is of such directness, the glare of reality so bright, that the shadow of the manipulating author does not fall inadvertently on the deputed "I"—who is in no way a creature of literary sensibility. The tone and the rhythm of the composition, the feat of being inside the minds or the heads as they make their deplorable decisions infuse the pages with a kind of tolerance for false hope and felony and rotten luck.

The Montana landscape in *Rock Springs* is empty and beautiful and lonely. The men do whatever kind of work turns up and are always being laid off. There is nothing but hunting and fishing, sex, and drinking and fighting. Wives go off to Seattle or Spokane, just for a change. Young girls and not-so-young men turn up in the taverns and get into a lot of trouble for themselves and others. So your wife has taken off with a groom from the dog track, and a couple of huge, rough women turn up at your door with a deer gruesomely slain lying in their pickup; and you will be glad for their knock, for the company, which will be a mistake. Recklessness is the mode of life, but what the stories seem to be saying is that people are not always as bad as what they do, something like that. No judgment is solicited, and yet the desperation and folly arouse pity, the pity that everywhere sends girlfriends, mothers and children, grandparents and old pals trundling out to the prisons for visiting hours.

In the novel *Wildlife* (1990), a son is the observer of the sudden defections and panics of his parents. "In the fall of 1960, when I was sixteen and my father was for a time not working, my mother met a man named Warren Miller and fell in love with him." The tactful, muted eloquence of the tone is a sort of balance for the unstable inner and natural landscape. It is Great Falls, Montana, and the forest fires of summer are still smoking and glowing in the autumn sky. The parents have lived and been to college in Washington State and have come to Montana from Idaho, thinking money could be made from the oil boom. But prosperity does not extend itself to them, and so the father works at the air base two days a week and otherwise as a golf pro at the local country club. He is rudely laid off at the club because of a false accusation. In Ford's fiction, the West, with its fabled openness under the big sky and all that, is a place of emotional collapse from forced or glumly accepted idleness, an invitation to dangerous brooding over the whiskey bottle. After such an acute brooding and character upheaval the father somehow gets a chance to save his soul, or self-image, by being allowed to take a place with the knowledgeable firefighters in the forest, although he had no experience beyond the flaming egos on the golf course.

The mother is alone for three days. She and the son visit the voracious Warren Miller, a man with a limp and soon to die of a "lengthy illness," a man with lots of money, grain elevators, and other assets, and a wife who has gone off somewhere—a man with a house. In the house, the mother and son spend the night after the older folks have been drinking and dancing. The unresisting mother is seduced on the spot, decides to leave her husband and set herself up in a rented flat, there to accommodate what she foolishly believes will be a better life with Warren Miller. Shifts in direction, improvisations, sleepwalking into calamitous consequence seem to be in the fiction part of the effect the Western states have upon the mind. The characters are still pulling the wagon across the frontier, looking for a place to settle.

The father comes down from the burning hills to meet his domestic surprise. In a fury ignited by betrayal and alcohol, he picks up a can of gasoline at a local pump and, thinking his wife is inside, sets fire to Miller's house; the fire is not serious and no charges are filed. Indeed, Miller fled the scene with another woman in tow, not the wife. After some years of wandering, the mother returns to Great Falls, and the son reflects that something has died between them but something remained. "We survived it." A benign accent in the style of narration covers *Wildlife* in a forgiving mist. The quiet pacing through the threat of the landscape and the predatory challenge of experience is a compromise, the rain falling on the blackened trees.

Before he went West, so to speak, in his stories and in *Wildlife*, Richard Ford had published three books of fiction: *A Piece of My Heart* (1976), *The Ultimate Good Luck* (1981), and *The Sportswriter* (1986). *A Piece of My Heart* is an elaborate, stylistically ambitious, and complex novel, somewhat in the Southern Gothic vein. The setting is Mississippi, and there are two old people in their decayed mansion, the man a relentlessly loquacious, cursing, shrewd old fellow. The estate is connected by boat to an island where people from town pay to hunt duck and for the turkey shoot in season. Two young men, each of whom has an alternating section of the book, come to the spread. One is a Columbia graduate student enrolled in the University of Chicago Law School; he's in a slump, and his girlfriend thinks that, since he is a native Mississippian, he might pull himself together by a spell at the estate owned by a relation of hers. This character, perhaps an echo of Faulkner's Quentin Compson, is not entirely successful, owing to the mingled yarn in the knit of his rather far-flung situation.

The other young man, named Robard, could be a character in one of the stories in *Rock Springs*. His fate is powerfully and alarmingly conceived in the intense thicket of the action. Robard wakes up in the dark of early morning, looks at his wife peacefully sleeping, and, although he has gentle feelings for her, takes off without leaving a word. His journey, his hardscrabble trek to the swamp of sex, has come about from a curious, oblique feeling of obligation to experience. Some years before, Robard had picked up a young woman on the road when her car broke down. They ended up in a motor court for a raw, lascivious night or two, and for Robard that was the end of it, but not for her, Beuna by name. Beuna is a seriously dreadful encounter, a sex fiend, a sort of barnyard creature of befoulment.

Time has passed, and Beuna is married to W.W., a broken-down bush-league ballplayer and deputy sheriff. Beuna does not find much satisfaction in W.W., and since she knows where Robard lives, she begins to send messages to him and to make disturbing phone calls, delivered with a panting absolute demand for a reunion. Robard finally takes off to meet her. His emotions are murky and guarded, and he means to return. Beuna's insistence over the weeks and months gives Robard the sense that something has entered his life he can't altogether deny. He is broke, and to complete his destiny he takes a job at the estate, acting as a guard on the island to keep poachers away.

His true "business," as he calls it, is to go into town in the evening to find Beuna. They meet and bed down in a scabby rent-a-cabin place, where she says the proprietor wouldn't care if you took a "goddamn sheep in here." For the tryst, Beuna has brought a plastic bag of excrement. There is a merciful blackout of the subsequent congress, but at last it is the cue for Robard to climb out of the pit of eros, find his truck, and get back to the island. W.W. is nosing after him in his Plymouth, shotgun at the ready. Almost free of the pursuing furies, Robard meets his death, his release, when he is thought to be a poacher and shot by a boy who is taking his place as guard on the island.

The backcountry landscape, the waters of the river at night, the woods, the sullen towns are rendered with a tireless fluency. As a principal in a sordid tangle of compulsion, Robard, nevertheless, is conceived in tragic terms and is the most touching of Richard

Ford's doom-stricken young men, rushing to certain destruction, to Beuna, who, by the unfortunate meeting on the road, has become "a piece of my heart."

Ford's second novel, *The Ultimate Good Luck,* is another trip altogether, this time to Mexico, around Oaxaca. It is a steamy ride through the south-of-the-border labyrinth, with characters who are defined by situation, plot, intrigue, and dénouement. They have a certain brittleness as they act out their roles; and there is a cinema-noir aspect to the landscape of drug smuggling, prisons, bribery, disappearances, threats of murder, and actual murder. Quinn, a Vietnam vet, and his mistress or whatever, Rae, are engaged in an effort to get Rae's brother, Sonny, out of the hell of a Mexican prison. Sonny has been picked up for drug smuggling, and his escape or release is to be accomplished by bribery, mysterious connections, and enigmatic maneuvers under the direction of a shadowy lawyer named Bernhardt, who, along the way, is murdered for his efforts in the matter or perhaps for some other malfeasance.

The language of the novel is rich; there is, or so it seems, a haunting absorption of the countryside, the bars, the alleys, the prison, the midnight world. No one is sympathetic; there's not much to be said for Quinn, and Rae, embarked on her act of charitable rescue, is stoned most of the time. Sonny is not an object of moral concern since he is stupid, greedy, and a natural loser. *The Ultimate Good Luck* has a curious sheen of high glamour as a genuinely imaginative example of a genre, if that is the proper word for this visit to the underworld.

The Sportswriter followed the first two novels and preceded the Western stories and *Wildlife*. Frank Bascombe is a sportswriter, living by choice in Haddam, New Jersey, a pleasant suburban town of moderate physical and social dimensions, suitable to Bascombe's moderate expectations from life. He has published a book of stories that did moderately well, started and abandoned a novel, and is moderately content to be something of an oddity in the arts, where an early kiss from the Muse is likely to leave a lifelong discoloration on the cheek. He is not a failed writer but one who fails to write another fiction or poem. What is to prevent your writing, dear? the forlorn wife in George Gissing's *New Grub Street* asks of her miserable husband trapped in the period of the three-decker novel. Bascombe's answer would have been a cheerful I prefer not to.

But even Bascombe's cheerfulness is moderated by the dark wings of melancholy after the death of his son Ralph and the divorce from his wife, here called X. The most remarkable aspect of this engaging character is his remove from paranoia, the national and literary mode of the time. Bascombe is offered a job on a well-known sports magazine, published in New York, to which he chooses to commute. Needless to say, he does not take sports or sportswriting with undue seriousness.

> I make my other calls snappy—one is to an athlete shoe designer in Denver for a "Sports Chek" round-up box I'm pulling together on foot injuries…. Another call is to a Carmelite nun in Fayetteville, West Virginia, who is trying to run in the Boston Marathon. Once a polio victim, she is facing an uphill credentials fight in her quest to compete, and I'm glad to put a plug in for her in our "Achievers" column.

The scene shifts, as it often does in this work crowded with incidents and people met along the way, this time to a trip to Detroit to interview Herb Wallagher, an ex-lineman who lost his legs in a ski-boat accident and is now in a wheelchair. The interview is not profitable, even though the sportswriter tries to rouse Herb about the game of football: "But I'd still think it had some lessons to teach to the people who played it. Perseverance. Team work. Comradeship. That kind of thing." To which, Herb replies: "Forget all that crap, Frank."

The trip to Detroit is made with Vicki, cute and with far greater common sense than Bascombe, she being a nurse. She talks about a "C-liver terminal, already way into uremia when he was admitted, which is not *that* bad cause it usually starts 'em dreamin about their pasts and off their current problem." Scenes and characters flow into this suburban novel on the wide stream of Bascombe's obstinate receptiveness. The Divorced Men's Club, which Bascombe attends, brings him into an encounter with poor Walter Luckett, whose wife has taken off to Bimini with a man named Eddie Pitcock. Walter has a secret he wants to share. After a few drinks with a Wall Street colleague, he finds himself going to bed with him in the fellow's New York apartment, not once but again and again. Walter is troubled and as naive as a country-boy sailor on his first shore leave in Naples. In what could be called a sentimental confusion, for that is his nature, he commits suicide one night.

One of the most brilliant scenes is Bascombe's Easter Sunday visit with Vicki's family. Her father, a turnpike toll-taker, has somehow gotten an old Chrysler into his small, wet basement and is restoring it fin by fin, with full attention to broken and rusted chrome. Her brother, Cade, a boat mechanic, is on the waiting list at the Police Academy. Cade has already "developed a flat-eyed officer's uninterest for the peculiarities of his fellow man." Lynette, the father's second wife, is working on the crisis line at the Catholic church. She has "transformed her dining room into a hot little jewel box, crystal-candle chandelier, best silver and linens laid" for "the pallid lamb congealed and hard as a wood chip and the ... peas and broccoli flower alongside it cold as Christmas." In the midst of all this, Bascombe's thought is: "What strange good luck to be reckoned among these people like a relative welcome from Peoria."

The Sportswriter is a sophisticated book that celebrates life as it comes and speaks in its voice, often with devastating humor. Easter Sunday: "the optimist's holiday, the holiday with the suburbs in mind." The sermon about the Resurrection: "Well now, let's us just hunker down to a *real* miracle, while we're putting two and two together.... Let's just let plasma physics and bubble chambers and quarks try to explain *this* one." The vitality of the novel lies in the freedom and expressiveness of this first-person excursion through

New Jersey, Detroit, the Berkshires, and the bearable shambles of Bascombe's life.

Independence Day, Richard Ford's most recent novel, returns to Frank Bascombe. *Rabbit Redux?*—not quite. Bascombe is an upscale ruminant, now in his forties, with opinions about everything, and Emerson's "Self-Reliance" in the glove compartment. There is no outstanding typicality in him; instead, he has the mysteriousness of the agreeable, nice person, harder to describe than the rake, the miser, or the snob. As a professional, or as a working man, his résumé is unsteady: short-story writer, sportswriter, and now a "realtor." The wobbly nature of Bascombe's status makes him a creditable collector; nothing need be rejected, not the trash of the road signs, clichés produced with a ring of discovery, the program on TV, the decor of the Sleepy Hollow Motel on Route 1, or the "fanlights, columned entries and Romany-fluting" of the houses on the better streets.

Selling real estate is a good way to get about town but a poor way to reach "closure." The business is a serial plot of indignities—tune in tomorrow. Joe and Phyllis Markham have decided to get out of their hand-built house in Vermont, "with cantilevered cathedral ceilings and a hand-laid hearth and chimney, using stones off the place," to try a suburban New Jersey lifestyle and better schools for their daughter. They "have looked at forty-five houses—dragging more and more grimly down from … Vermont." The fearsome negotiations, or lack of them, provide a miserably comic underpinning to Bascombe's days and nights.

The other block of the story is a hazardous trip, a Fourth of July journey with his son, Paul, to the Basketball Hall of Fame in Springfield, Massachusetts, and the Baseball Hall of Fame in Cooperstown, New York, where they stay in The Deerslayer Lodge. Paul is a thoroughly complicated and unpredictable young man of fifteen. He has stolen boxes of condoms, for which he had no use, from a pharmacy; he barks like a dog in memory of his dead dog and probably in memory of his dead brother, Ralph. Underneath his basket of misdemeanors and off-tone noises, he is a gentle teenager and will probably come to resemble his father's more acceptable waywardness. At the Baseball Hall of Fame, Paul seriously damages an eye in the batter's cage, a tourist attraction that allows one to seem to swat a ball like Babe Ruth. His mother, now remarried to a rich architect, comes up in a helicopter and takes him to New Haven for surgery.

There are many other diversions: Sally, Bascombe's girlfriend, the renters of a house he owns, old friends, or a new passerby. And as always with Richard Ford, the sense of place, towns, houses, highways is luminous in lavish, observed detail.

> I drive windingly out Montmorency Road into Haddam horse country—our little Lexington—where fences are long, white and orthogonal, pastures wide and sloping, and roads ... slip across shaded, rocky rills via wooden bridges and through the quaking aspens back to rich men's domiciles snugged deep in summer foliage.... And here, wedges of old-growth hardwoods still loom, trees that saw Revolutionary armies rumble past, heard the bugles, shouts and defiance cries of earlier Americans in their freedom swivet, and beneath which now tawny-haired heiresses in jodhpurs stroll to the paddock with a mind for a noon ride alone.

In passing, it might be remarked that Ford is the first, if memory serves, to give full recognition to the totemic power in American life of the telephone and the message service. At one point, he pauses at the Vince Lombardi Rest Area, across from Giants Stadium, to check his messages. There are ten of them, listed with content, among them obscenities from Joe Markham, client. Often, Bascombe will interrupt the plot to make a dreamy call to a former lover, who might not immediately place him or might be cooking dinner. In *The Sportswriter,* the call is to Selma, a friend from his spell as a teacher at Berkshire College. In *Independence Day,* he gets on the line to Cathy, a medical student he spent time with in France a few years back. He's hoping for "a few moments out of context, ad hominem, pro bono phone treatment." Ring, ring, ring, click, click, and the machine answers: "Hi. This is Cathy and Steve's answering mechanism. We're not home now. Really. I promise." In Frank Bascombe's world, a good deal of the information necessary to move forward is given over the phone.

(Recently, in the O. J. Simpson criminal trial, the prosecution, following week after wearying week, month after month building its beaver dam of circumstantial particulars, spent quite a lot of time with the record of Simpson's car phone around the time projected for the murders. The record keeper for the phone company dutifully went down the list, the purpose seeming to be that the number of busy signals and no answers might slip into the minds of the jurors as yet another twig in a rage that led to double homicide.)

Independence Day, if you're taking measurements like the nurse in a doctor's office, might be judged longer than it need be. But longer for whom? Every rumination, each flash of magical dialogue or unexpected mile on the road with a stop at the pay phone, is a wild surprise tossed off by Richard Ford's profligate imagination as if it were just a bit of cigarette ash. *The Sportswriter* and *Independence Day* are comedies—not farces, but realistic, good-natured adventures, sunny, yes, except when the rain it raineth every day. The new work, *Independence Day,* is the confirmation of a talent as strong and varied as American fiction has to offer.

(*1995*)

Biographies

Katherine Anne Porter

~ ~ ~

Katherine Anne Porter died at the age of ninety. She had one of those very long lives the sickly, with their bronchial troubles and early threats of tuberculosis, achieve as a surprise to us and perhaps to themselves. It was just two years ago, in September 1980, that she died and now we have a biography devoted to this long life.

Biographers, the quick in pursuit of the dead, research, organize, fill in, contradict, and make in this way a sort of completed picture puzzle with all the scramble turned into a blue eye and the parts of the right leg fitted together. They also make a consistent fiction, the fiction being the arrangement, artful or clumsy, of the documents. Biography casts a chill over the late years of some writers and, perhaps from their reading the lives of those they had known in the too solid flesh, has often provoked the insistent wish that no life be written. Among those who wished for no life after life were W. H. Auden, George Orwell and T. S. Eliot. The result has been two lives already of Auden and Orwell, and Eliot's life is in the making, waiting to be lived again by way of the flowing bloodstream of documentation.

Sometimes very fine writers and scholars undertake biographies, and their productions have at least some claim to equity between the subject and the person putting on the shoes. Others hope to establish credentials previously lacking by hard work on the abounding materials left by a creative life. In any case, a biography appears to be thought of as a good project, one that can at the very least be accomplished by industry. And if there is a lot of busywork in it— many visits to the libraries, a store of taped interviews, and, of course, the "evidence" of the writer's work itself (the last rather a difficulty since it is not precisely to be understood by research)— the book gets written, and the "life of " is, so to speak, born.

In her eighty-sixth year, Katherine Anne Porter appointed Joan Givner to undertake the re-creation of her many decades. The biographer might be thought to be in luck since Miss Porter advised her to "get at the truth," an always murky command when ordered on one's own behalf. The real luck about the truth turned out to be that the distinguished writer was unusually inclined to fabrication about her past. These fabrications, dashing often and scarcely news and only mildly discrediting, seem to be the driving engine behind Joan Givner's accumulation of the facts of life.

How certain human beings are able to create works of art is a mystery, and why they should wish to do so, at a great cost to themselves usually, is another mystery. Works are not created by one's life; every life is rich in *material*. By the nature of the enterprise, the contemporary biographer with his surf of Xerox papers is doing something smaller and yet strikingly more detailed than the great Victorian laborers in the form. Our power of documentation has a monstrous life of its own, a greater vivacity than any lived existence. It makes form out of particles and finds attitude in a remembered drunken remark as easily as in a long contemplation of experience—more easily in fact. It creates out of paper a heavy, obdurate permanency. Threats to its permanency will come only by way of other bits of paper, a footnote coup d'état. No matter— a territory once colonized in this way has had its indigenous landscape and culture put to the heel.

In Joan Givner's book, the root biographical facts have the effect of a crushing army. Everything is underfoot. Each character and each scene of Miss Porter's fiction is looked upon as a factuality honored by its provenance as autobiography. And separate fictions are mashed together as bits of the life recur or are suggested in different works. Miss Porter, in a manner impertinently thought of as dilatory, did not often translate experience in a sequential fashion. So she is writing "Hacienda" while she is "living" *The Leaning Tower.* She is boarding the ship of fools before the Mexican stories have been accomplished. It is something of a tangle to get this particular life and its laggard production into time slots, and the result is an incoherence in regard to the work. Information about when each story was actually completed, when published and where, is lost in the anecdote of days and nights. No doubt the information is somewhere among the pages, but it is a slogging task to dig it out.

The life—some scandal and a considerable amount of folly: Katherine Anne Porter was born in a log cabin in Texas and grew up in hardship without a really good education. She knew a genuine struggle to provide for herself and slowly to define herself. Gradually, along the way, after her stories became known, she slipped into being a Southern belle and into being to some extent a Southern writer after *Flowering Judas.* The role was there for the choosing since to be a belle and to be a Southern writer is a decision, not a fate. (Poe, for instance, was a Southerner but not a Southern writer.) Perhaps under the influence of the very talented Southern Agrarians—Allen Tate, Caroline Gordon, and others— she began to appropriate a rather frantic genealogy of Daniel Boone and certain Southern statesmen; in addition, she developed some soothing memories of plantation dining rooms, "several Negro servants, among them two aged former slaves," and so on. In this way, she filled in the gap between what she was and what she felt like.

She was handy, too, in disposing of the traces of her various mismatings, the first a marriage at sixteen. "I have no hidden husbands," she once said. "They just slipped my mind." She was beautiful, a spendthrift, an alert coquette, and, since she lived long, a good many of her lovers and three of her husbands were younger than she was. She lopped off a few years here and there. The book goes into a determined sorting out, and the husbands are lined up, the years restored.

Her serious work was slow in coming about because of a scratchy, hard life after she literally ran away from her first husband—just ran off, as they say. She tried acting, did very provincial newspaper work and finally got a job on the *Denver Post*. Everything was hard, poorly paid, hand-to-mouth. During this period, she seems quite Western or Middle Western, like someone in a Willa Cather story trying to find the way out. Her story "Maria Concepción" was published when she was thirty-four, and her first book, *Flowering Judas,* appeared when she was forty. Fortunately for her future work, she went to Mexico as a reporter; she was in and out of Greenwich Village, where she met writers and no doubt increased her sophistication about literature and the act of writing.

At this point, the shape of her life falls into a sort of twenties pattern. She went to France and to Germany with her third husband, Eugene Pressly—her second husband, a person named Ernest Stock, "deadly Ernest," as she called him, having been run away from while he was sleeping. In Mexico, she met the Russian film director Eisenstein; in Germany in 1932 she met Göring; in Paris, she met Hemingway. Eisenstein became Uspensky in *Hacienda,* the ship upon which she traveled from Mexico to Germany became the *Vera* in *Ship of Fools.* In Berlin, she stayed on alone, having encouraged Pressly to return to America for a holiday without her. She never liked the constant presence of her husbands or lovers and did not like, she soon found out, to be alone—a dilemma in one shape or another common to most of mankind. The pension where she stayed in Germany went, with little need for renovation, into *The Leaning Tower.*

Research finds that in Germany, Katherine Anne Porter did not always conduct herself with generosity or moral refinement. She had a young friend, Herb Klein, a newspaper reporter, who tells years later of her leaving a seamstress without paying for a dress she had ordered—leaving the dress, too—and in this way embarrassing Klein's mother, who had brought the two together. He also discredits her claim to have met Hitler and feels strongly that she did not move widely or knowledgeably about the Germany of the time. So, a little more unstitching of the embroidery here.

Also, and again many decades later, she made in an interview slanderous, nasty remarks about Sigrid Schultz, a reporter in Berlin in the thirties for the *Chicago Tribune*. All of this, no doubt rightly, brings on a fit of temper by the biographer, who finds that the German experience, as the chapter is called, "forms a dismal record of cheating, lying, slander and malice." She sees ruthlessness, alienation (?), and brutality at the "beginning of her fifth decade." Garrulousness and a certain untidiness in 1932 are excavated and rebuked in 1982, showing at least one of the dangers of living. The celebrated do not understand that they are chatting away in a bugged universe.

The few times in the biography that a particular work comes under Joan Givner's critical scrutiny—divorced for the moment from her main concern, which is the presumed umbilical attachment of life and fiction—the same inclination to outrage flares up. She finds Braggioni, the revolutionary in *Flowering Judas*, to be a "complete caricature." She adds that he "looms in the story like a grotesque Easter egg in shades of purple and yellow."

Katherine Anne Porter wrote:

> He bulges marvelously in his expensive garments. Over his lavender collar, crushed under a purple necktie, held by a diamond hoop; over his ammunition belt of tooled leather worked in silver, buckled crudely around his gasping middle; over the tops of glossy yellow shoes Braggioni swells with ominous ripeness.

So, the animadversion of the biographer is not quite to the descriptive point. And to be a revolutionary is in some sense to assume a pose. Costume, gesture, personal style, slogan, poster become personification of idea, especially in Latin America.

Perhaps in this remarkable early story, the pure, tasteful, puritan elegance of the American girl, Laura, is somewhat extended beyond credibility. Yet this girl, who has been born a Catholic and is now living among the Mexican revolutionaries, provides an outstanding instance of the magical detail that gives the stories their preeminence.

Laura sometimes slips into church, but no suitable emotions come to her. "It is no good and she ends by examining the altar with its tinsel flowers and ragged brocades, and feels tender about the battered doll-shape of some male saint whose white, lace-trimmed drawers hang limply around his ankles below the hieratic dignity of his velvet robe." It is not always clear that the biographer understands the elegance of the prose. Instead, she knows from her file cabinet that it was Mary Doherty, an interesting radical living in Mexico, who was probably the model for Laura.

On the subject of Adam, the young soldier in *Pale Horse, Pale Rider*, Mrs. Givner is also casually dismissive: "An insubstantial figure, completely lacking in vivid details and turns of phrase that usually animate the characters based on people whom Porter knew." "Completely" implies the self-evident in what is a sketchy opinion. The young soldier who is to die of influenza after looking after and being enchanted by the infected Miranda—who does not die but recovers—is necessary to the structure of the story. He serves it well by the charm of his dialogue; the irony of the romantic, accommodating American gives a tragic force to this thoughtful creation about a moment in history, the devastating influenza epidemic of 1918.

The influenza epidemic, Mexico in the days of the Revolution and after, the feeling of World War I, Berlin in the thirties, the Irish in America: The situations in Katherine Anne Porter's stories show the unexpected felicities of "homelessness." Afterward, she came to disown the log cabin that sent her out to the highway, and she fell back, still with her stylistic gracefulness, on nostalgia and memory, or the aura of it, of a more traditional kind.

In what are called the "Miranda" stories, Miranda seems to stand for the author's sensibility, if not for the actual author. These stories often combine scenes contemporary with Miranda's (Porter's) life mixed with family anecdotes about dead relations—the "old order." The old order is a cavalier landscape of powerful grandmothers; a former slave, Old Nannie; the scandalous, bewitching Aunt Amy; the little girls, Miranda and her sister; their attractive father who reads from Spenser, Shakespeare, and Dante and brightens their childhood with prints from Dürer and Holbein—all the pleasant baggage, supposedly, of the old Southern aristocracy. It does not seem to the point that this was not the author's life, that it is a burial of the detested log cabin in which she was born. The eye that looks across the track might be dangerous to Southern presumption, but what we have so often in the "old order" work is an eye that is too readily assimilating. Miranda's present is nearly always more vivid and original than her past. The present is harder, more shaded with sadness and uneasy defiance, and in the long run more genuinely dramatic. "Old Mortality" is elevated as a conception by the bitter alcoholic collapse of Uncle Gabriel, his decline into a brilliantly observed social seediness by way of his hysterical, misplaced hopes at the racetrack.

"Noon Wine" is a success indeed, a story of plot, a sort of realistic tale, tightly composed in the manner of *Ethan Frome*. In this story, felt to be odd because of the backwoods setting, there is no doubt that Porter knows where she is. She knows in transfiguring detail what a dairy farm is like. "The churn rumbling and swished like a belly of a trotting horse." And hens "dying of croup and wryneck and getting plagues of chicken lice; laying eggs all over God's creation so that half of them were spoiled before a man could find them, in spite of a rack of nests." If this knowledge came from the time she lived on a relative's farm outside Buda, Texas, and from certain characteristics in the dairy farmer, Mr. Thompson, that can be traced to her own father—"ambivalence" toward whom figures gravely in the biographer's grave quilt of patches—that is only the beginning. The story has its roots in pioneer and rural American fiction and even in Faulkner. The ancestry of literature is, of course, another story of kinfolk.

Katherine Anne Porter, from the first appearance of her stories, made her mark and impressed other writers by the way she wrote. It is not easy to define her purity of style. The writing is not plain, and yet it is not especially decorative either; instead, it is clear, fluent, almost untroubled. Everything necessary seems at hand: language and scenery, psychology and memory, and a bright aesthetic intelligence that shapes the whole. Sometimes she claimed to have written certain stories at one sitting, but it is known that many were started and abandoned, taken up again and made into something new. She was dilatory perhaps, but the completed work as we now have it does not reveal any deformation of character, and indeed is expansive enough in theme and achievement to satisfy the claims of her high reputation. She was very vain as a beauty and just as vain as a writer, and this latter vanity perhaps accounted for a good deal of the waiting and stalling, a stalling filled with romantic diversions.

Joan Givner, throughout, sees what are often creative problems as problems of life, usually linked to an unsteady childhood that weeps its lacks and resentments right up to the age of ninety. In the case of a complicated egoist like Katherine Anne Porter, the biographer is altogether too insistent upon the writer's "longing for love." A typical passage reads: "It should be remembered, however, that Porter's need for love was far beyond the ordinary, a desperate, compulsive need inspired by the nagging, ever present sense of her deficiencies." The biographer's rather smug provincialism distorts the worldly and amusing mishaps of a woman who was not made for marriage and thus married four times. It is agreeable to come upon the writer's sniffs in the midst of the biographer's rampaging "longings" and doubts of "self-worth." When she happened to remember the fiftieth anniversary of her first marriage, Miss Porter observed that the fiftieth was a lot more pleasant than the first.

Ship of Fools was a long novel and long in the making: from 1941 to 1961. The book made over a million dollars and, of course, for poor Miranda that made a difference. Its reception was very favorable at the beginning, but thereafter followed some fierce reservations. The setting of the book is 1931, a ship going from Vera Cruz to Bremen with a passenger list very long and outlandishly challenging. A fixed arena in which persons who would not ordinarily meet can be realistically gathered together would seem to be a gift of structure, in the manner of large hotels or prison camps or hospitals. But the gift of this natural and ordained diversity is claustrophobic, like a sea journey itself. Characters are given their traits, their tics of manner, their past histories. But then they are trapped in them in the dining room, on the deck, in the bar. Diversions of distress or comedy are offered with great skill, but the sea rolls on and the characters roll on, clutching their gestures.

The significant promise of the novel lies in the date and destination: It is 1931, and the boat is on the way to Germany, carrying with it Germans who must somehow prefigure what is to come by way of German arrogance and moral limitation, what is to come for the poorly conceived solitary Jew—an unattractive man who makes his living selling Christian religious objects—and what is to come for the German whose wife is Jewish but scarcely knows it, an assimilated person answering to the name of Mary. The historical promise is too pressing for the imagination in the novel. All is too static, and the implied parable is never quite achieved. There is something a little musty, like old yellowing notes. The flawless execution of the single scenes impresses, and yet the novel remains too snug and shipshape for the waters of history.

With the publication of *Ship of Fools,* Katherine Anne Porter was past seventy, but since she was to live twenty more years, there was time for a daunting accretion of foolishness. She can fight with faithful friends and relatives, she can spend, she can fall in love, she can drink too much, she can buy a large emerald ring, a "longing" from which she did not run away. She also has time for her increasing anti-Semitism: "Everybody except the Jews knows the Jews are not chosen but are a lot of noisy, arrogant, stupid, pretentious people and then what?" She pronounced on desegregation, leading her close friend Glenway Wescott to declare that "her poor brain is just simply one seething smoking mass of molten lava."

Biographies inevitably record the demeaning moments of malice and decline and have the effect of imprinting them upon the ninety years. In the biographies of today, all things are equal except that the ill winds tend in interest to be—well, more interesting.

Katherine Anne Porter did not have a happy life. She was better at sloughing off love than retaining it. She was often lonely in between her rushes to attachments. Her egotism was disabling. Throughout her life, the most useful condition for her work and for her sense of things came from the part of her that was an audacious, immensely gifted, independent Sister Carrie who knew about poverty and rooming houses and bad marriages and standing alone. The folly of the claim to represent somehow an aristocratic example of taste and moral excellence was not wisdom but just the downward path.

The ending of the biography, a flourish, is an unhappy image of the limitations of the method of composition. It reads: "At the very end she lay, like La Condesa on the *Vera*, drugged and demented, bereft of her home and jewels, but defiant until the last moment when on September 18, 1980, the little point of light flickered and failed." The truth is that Katherine Anne Porter was drugged and demented from strokes and the ghastly illnesses of extreme old age. It is not a useful summarizing sentiment to think of her as a fiction, just as it has not been altogether wise to think of her fiction as her life, or for that matter "the life of" as precisely her life.

(1982)

Wind from the Prairie

Roll along, Prairie Moon,
Roll along, while I croon.

Around World War I, writers from the American Middle Western states began to appear on the literary scene. In fiction, there were Theodore Dreiser, Sinclair Lewis, and Sherwood Anderson, and also the three known as the Prairie Poets, Carl Sandburg, Vachel Lindsay, and Edgar Lee Masters.

Looking into the new biography of Carl Sandburg, a work of exhaustive, definitive coziness in the current American mode of entranced biographical research, I was reminded of having some years ago taken from the library stacks a curiosity, a biography of Lindsay written by Edgar Lee Masters. If Carl Sandburg can be said to have managed shrewdly the transactions of his declamatory, bardic career as a national treasure, born in Illinois on a corn-husk mattress, the other two rose and fell disastrously and literally. Vachel Lindsay committed suicide, and Masters died in want, having been found broke and sick in the Chelsea Hotel in New York and rescued to die in a nursing home.

The two men, Lindsay and Masters, are not quite soul mates. Their union is geographical, a territorial, circumstantial linkage to a mythographic Middle West, the putative spiritual grasslands of the vast native country. Lindsay was a naive, manic evangelist, preaching the Gospel of Beauty, and carrying with him on his incredible cross-country hikes the Christian fundamentalism and Anti-Saloon teachings of his youth—along with, of course, the prairie, the conviction of being the voice of some real America, *in situ*, that must be honored, as if under threat of extinction by a flood. As a versifier he had no more caution than a hobo hitching a ride, but somehow his voice prevailed for a time, even with some of the respected critics of the day. He appeared and appeared, willing to recite at a high-school reunion as well as in London, where, according to a later biographer, Eleanor Ruggles, "he and his mother met Robert Bridges, venerable laureate and defender of the tongue [*sic*], and John Masefield, always Vachel's admirer, came in from Boars Hill to pay his respects." Feverish days, but, toward the end, in Washington, D.C., an audience of two hundred walked out, puzzling the performer and Edgar Lee Masters but attributed in the Ruggles biography to a microphone failure of which the poet was unaware.

Edgar Lee Masters, for a good part of his life a successful lawyer in Chicago, was a lot smarter than Vachel Lindsay and certainly more worldly—but then everyone was more worldly than Lindsay. Masters was in religion a freethinker, set against the "hypocrisy" of the preachers, even more exasperated by the temperance movement, and along the way set against puritanical sexual inhibitions. He was a handsome man who, step by hesitating step, nevertheless made a rashly uncomfortable marriage to a fundamentalist, teetotaler young woman. He had children, stayed on, was unfaithful (listing in his autobiography nearly as many female loves as Goethe), finally divorced, and remarried a young woman—indeed, thirty years younger than he. Lindsay was one of those too friendly boosters with their often strange imperviousness and faltering sense of the appropriate. Masters was splenetic, the cemetery headstone his natural memorial, cranky in opinion, and, although very productive and for a time immensely successful, there was in his life a feeling of being undervalued, and even of seeing the whole country in an enormous displacement from virtue, pioneer and otherwise.

Of Lindsay, Masters said he was "impelled to write something about the poet who was native to Illinois, as I am in reality, and who knew the same people and the same culture that I do, and who practiced the art of poetry, as I have, in the same part of America, and under the same social and political conditions." In the end, as he reaches Lindsay's declining audience and death, he begins to see the life as a social rather than a personal tragedy, to view the native "singer" as a victim of the East, the money-grubbing, alienated world that preferred the poems of Robert Frost and E. A. Robinson, poets Masters finds essentially "English" in tone and landscape rather than American.

There's more to it than that from this strange man about his stranger fellow bard:

> The motley stocks and alien breeds which have taken America cannot be American until there is an America to mold them into Americans.... Lindsay might sing himself hoarse of the old courthouse America, the old horse and buggy America, the America of the Santa Fé Trail, of Johnny Appleseed.... Did the East, did these alien stocks want to be American? This is what Lindsay was up against. In this connection mention must be made of the Jews who are enormously numerous, powerful and influential. Jews are not Americans in the sense that the Jews are English or French, according to habitat.

Ezra Pound described Vachel Lindsay as a "plain man in gum overshoes with a touching belief in W. J. Bryan." Yes, there was "Bryan, Bryan, Bryan, Bryan," the poem celebrating the Free Silver populist, fundamentalist, and prohibitionist in his losing campaign against McKinley. Almost three hundred lines in which Bryan is seen as "the prairie avenger ... smashing Plymouth Rock with his boulders from the West." His defeat was the "victory of Plymouth Rock and all those inbred landlord stocks" (perhaps it was) and also, in a wild extension, somehow the defeat of the "blue bells of the Rockies and the blue bonnets of old Texas."

Lindsay's life was one of intense, sentimental aggressiveness; and yet there is something unprotected about him. His unanchored enthusiasm has the dismaying aspect of being genuine and unforced, a sort of hysterical innocence, or so it seems. The cheerful, round-faced, fair-haired country boy was in fact town bred, born in Springfield, Illinois. Fate put his birthplace next to the house in which Lincoln had lived, and this—the nearness of the great, solemn son of the prairie, the hallowed walker of the streets of Springfield—had the effect of igniting the boy like a firecracker. Lincoln in Illinois had quite a contrary effect on Edgar Lee Masters, who wrote a long, scathing biography of the fallen president, composed with the racing eloquence of contempt for the man and for the "tyrannous plutocracy" that followed the Civil War.

Both Lindsay and Masters come from professional families. Masters's father was a self-made lawyer, a conscientious man of some influence in Illinois and given, at least in part, to liberal causes and worthy cases. The Lindsay family was an older combination of beliefs and habits. The father, as a young man in impecunious circumstances, worked his way through an Ohio medical school, set up practice in Illinois, and, after the death of his first wife, somehow saved enough for further study in Vienna. On the boat going to Europe, he met his future wife, a teacher of art and other subjects in Kentucky. Throughout their lives, with or without their children, the couple traveled quite a lot, going several times to Europe and even as far as Japan and China, but there were less cosmopolitan strains in the mother. She passed on to her son the ornamental, provincial "art-loving" claim of certain small-town American wives and also a good measure of the missionary qualities he displayed. Mrs. Lindsay was the organizer of church spectacles, liked to officiate in group meetings, attend conferences, and so on.

Her family was attached to the Campbellite Church, also known as the Christian Church. The church had been founded by Alexander Campbell and his son Thomas, originally Presbyterians and then, coming to believe in baptism by immersion, united with the Baptists, before finally breaking away—in one of those organizational disputes so peculiar to the Protestant denominations—to found their own Campbellite sect. From these roots, Vachel Lindsay got his fundamentalism and prohibitionism, the Gospel of Beauty, and a flair for expounding preacher-style. He was sent to the Art Institute of Chicago and later, in New York in 1905, studied with William Merritt Chase and Robert Henri but did not make notable progress as a painter or as a cartoonist.

All the time, Lindsay had been writing verses in his hymn-tune rhythms, reciting at the YMCA, and turning himself into a peddler. With his verses and drawings, the plain, open-faced, clean young man wandered the streets of New York, knocking on the doors of fish markets, Chinese laundries, and bakeries, stopping people to listen to his wares, canvassing, as it were, Hell's Kitchen. A curious, impervious nuisance, bringing to mind the intrepid appeals of the Jehovah's Witness bell ringers. And then he began his years of quite literally tramping across the country, pamphlets and verses for sale, doing missionary work for the Gospel of Beauty. He carried with him a character reference from the YMCA.

It was in California that Lindsay learned of the death of General William Booth, founder of the Salvation Army. And thus he came to write one of his first bizarre incantations, an unaccountable success for which the mind glancing back on our literary history is, well, dumbstruck.

GENERAL WILLIAM BOOTH

ENTERS INTO HEAVEN.

(To be sung to the tune of "The Blood of the Lamb"
with indicated instrument)

The works opens with bass-drum beats and:

> Booth led boldly with his big bass drum—
> (Are you washed in the blood of the Lamb?)
> The Saints smiled bravely and they said: "He's come."
> (Are you washed in the blood of the Lamb?)

The thing flows on apace and concludes:

> He saw King Jesus. They were face to face,
> And he knelt a-weeping in that holy place.
> Are you washed in the blood of the Lamb?

The submission appeared in an early issue of *Poetry* and Harriet Monroe in the annual prize giving of 1913 awarded it $100. A prize for $250 went to William Butler Yeats, the latter having been pushed for by Ezra Pound. Sometime later, when Yeats was in Chicago, Miss Monroe invited Lindsay to a dinner at which the various important writers on hand were invited. That evening Vachel Lindsay recited the whole of "The Congo" and was apparently "well-received" in spite of its being over two hundred fiercely resounding lines. This most extraordinary embarrassment in our cultural history achieved a personally orated dissemination scarcely to be credited. Anywhere and everywhere he went with it—the Chamber of Commerce, high schools, ladies' clubs, the Lincoln Day banquet in Springfield, the Players Club in New York, where Masters tells that its noise greatly irritated certain members.

"The Congo" is the supreme folly of Lindsay's foolhardy career.

There is a sad, no doubt unconscious, complacency in its concussive hilarity, the compositional shove coming from

an allusion in a sermon by my pastor, F. W. Burnham, to the heroic life and death of Ray Eldred. Eldred was a missionary of the Disciples of Christ who perished while swimming a treacherous branch of the Congo.

The work is subtitled "A Study of the Negro Race," and part one lies under the heading "Their Basic Savagery." The imagery, if such it can be called, is blackface American minstrel, except for a strophe about Leopold of Belgium in hell with his hands cut off.

With a "deep rolling bass," the prairie evangelist sets out on his crusade:

> Fat black bucks in a wine-barrel room,
> Barrel-house kings, with feet unstable ...
> Beat an empty barrel with the handle of a broom ...
> Boomlay, boomlay, boomlay, BOOM ...
>
> THEN I SAW THE CONGO, CREEPING THROUGH
> THE BLACK,
> CUTTING THROUGH THE FOREST WITH A
> GOLDEN TRACK....
>
> Tattooed cannibals danced in files;
> Then I heard the boom of the blood-lust song....
> Boom, kill the Arabs,
> Boom, kill the white men,
> Hoo,Hoo,Hoo....
> Mumbo-Jumbo will hoo-doo you.

The second section has the title "Their Irrepressible High Spirits." Here, on the Congo River, we run into a round of crap-shooting, whoops and yells, witch-men dressed to kill, "cake-walk princes" in tall silk hats, coal-black maidens with pearls in their hair, and more Boom, Boom, Boom. In the third section, "The Hope of Their Religion," the Apostles appear in coats of mail and, to the tune of "Hark, ten thousand harps and voices," ordain that "Mumbo-Jumbo will die in the jungle." The forests, the beasts, and the "savages" fade away, whispering, in a pianissimo, the dying strains of "Mumbo-Jumbo will hoo-doo you." The "bucks" are thus converted, all now down-home Campbellites.

What the far-flung audiences made of this infernal indiscretion is hard to imagine. There is always a market for "carrying on" in public, as we can confirm today. No doubt there was more condescension in the air than the reports would suggest. A performance organized in 1920 at Oxford University by Robert Graves can be read as an elaborate prank on the pretensions of the dons rather than as a tribute to the prairie poet—indeed, the sweating reiterations of the amateur elocutionist might recall Tom Thumb at Queen Victoria's court.

In any case, scholars can excavate in the old magazines many alarming commendations of this native genius, fresh voice, America's Homer, and so on. Harriet Monroe, a promoter of poetry and of the Middle West in tandem, wrote the introduction to the book publication of *The Congo and Other Poems*. The praise is short but unfortunately ranging in reference, like a kangaroo leaping over rich and spacious plains. Whistler and Whitman are called forth before a landing by Miss Monroe on the "old Greek precedent of the half-chanted lyric." The "Greek precedent" is one of those critical jokes like "the Jane Austen of the Upper West Side," but the claims of the Prairie Poets and subsequent idolators to the example of Whitman is an unending irritation.

"The Santa-Fé Trail" is another noisy work, the theme seeming to be that the sound of the automobile—Crack, Crack, Crack—is trying without success to overwhelm the song "sweet, sweet, sweet" of a local Southwest bird known as Rachel-Jane. Then there is a salute to the firemen, "Clang, Clang, Clang," and an evocation of Jesus in "I Heard Immanuel Singing."

> He was ruddy like a shepherd.
> His bold young face how fair.
> Apollo of the silver bow
> Had not such flowing hair.

Tramping and reciting, forever in manic locomotion with note-book in hand to scribble whatever came into his head, head to be laid down at night on a YMCA pillow, leaving little time for romantic life. Actually, Lindsay comes across as more than a little girl-shy in spite of crushes here and there, one falling on the poet Sara Teasdale. But she married a rich shoe manufacturer and for a time was set up grandly in New York, until she too was mowed down by the drastic scythe of taste and died divorced, no longer rich, reclusive, and em-bittered. At last, Lindsay married a young woman from Spokane, a high-school teacher of English and Latin. She was twenty-three, and he was forty-six. They had two daughters and were always in finan-cial distress, since his income came largely from recitations and a good portion went to agents and expenses. On the road, the listeners forever calling for "Congo" and "General Booth," Lindsay was to ex-perience the pathos of repetition: exhaustion and insolvency.

Along the way, uphill and downhill, Lindsay wrote a most inter-esting book, fortunately in prose: *The Art of the Moving Picture,* first issued in 1915, revised in 1922, and later reprinted with an excellent appreciation of its worth in an introduction by Stanley Kauffmann. After the rant and carelessness of the verses, Lindsay concentrated his mind on the movies. Here it is, he must have decided as he rested his vocal cords in the darkness of the old cinemas—American, popular, infinite in variety, flung out to the folk with a prodigality very similar to his own production methods. He tries to organize what the films can do, sort out the types, explain the power of di-rectors such as D. W. Griffith.

For instance, "The Action Picture":

> In the action picture there is no adequate means for the develop-
> ment of full-grown personal passion. The Action Pictures are
> falsely advertised as having heart-interest, or abounding in
> tragedy, but though the actors glower and wrestle and even if
> they are the most skillful lambasters in the profession, the audi-
> ence gossips, and chews gum.

There are the Intimate Photoplays, the Splendor Pictures, which
divide into Crowd Splendor, Patriotic Splendor, Religious Splendor, and so on. Concerning the intimate photoplay, he writes:

> Though the intimate and friendly photoplay may be carried out
> of doors to a row of loafers in front of the country store, or the
> gossiping streets of the village, it takes its origin and theory from
> the snugness of the interior. The restless reader replies that he
> has seen photoplays that showed ballrooms that were grandiose,
> not the least cozy. These are to be classed as out-of-door scenery
> so far as theory goes, and are discussed under the head of Splen-
> dor Pictures. The intimate Motion Picture ... is gossip *in extremis.*

The movies and their vagrant images for him, the lonely traveling
man, had the seductive power of the saloon for others of his kind. He
was seduced into a contemplation and wish for coherence absent from
his verse making. Thus, he finds "noble views of the sea," common
to early camera effects, allied to "the sea of humanity spectacles":

> the whirling of dancers in ballrooms, handkerchief-waving masses
> of people on balconies, the hat-waving political ratification meet-
> ings, ragged, glowering strikers, and gossiping, dickering people in
> the market-place. Only Griffith and his disciples can do these as
> well as almost any manager can reproduce the ocean. Yet the
> sea of humanity is dramatically blood-brother to the Pacific, the
> Atlantic, or Mediterranean.... So, in *The Birth of a Nation,* the Ku

Klux Klan dashes down the road as powerfully as Niagara pours over the cliff.

A film version of Ibsen's *Ghosts* came to town, and Lindsay reports that it was not Ibsen and should have been advertised under the title "The Iniquities of the Fathers. An American Drama of Eugenics, in a Palatial Setting." The style of these reflections, offhand and colloquial, is usefully attuned to the subject and to his casual but transfixed attentions. Returning from the showing of Larry Trimble's *The Battle Hymn of the Republic,* he recorded that the girl at the piano played "Under the Shade of the Apple Tree" throughout. Among the virtues of the films are their usefulness, nonalcoholic, to the working classes, who, in the heat of summer, "under the wind of an electric fan, can witness everything from a burial at Westminster to the birthday parade of the ruler of the land of Swat."

Los Angeles is the Boston, the Florence of this great flowering, and the stars are national monuments. He pens a tribute to Mary Pickford, "doll divine," which will proceed to rhyme with "valentine." And Blanche Sweet: "Stately are her wiles / filling oafs with wisdom, / Saving souls with smiles." *The Art of the Moving Picture* is the prairie singer's finest, most lasting tribute to the American West, to Hollywood.

He was fifty-two years old when he committed suicide. It is not easy to be certain what was going on in his mind, but there seem to have been frightening mood swings, ups and downs, suspicions followed by remorse, in every way a sad collapse. Doctors were called in, but before a decision could be made for treatment, Lindsay drank Lysol, saying, "I got them before they got me—they can just try to explain this if they can."

Edgar Lee Masters was asked by Lindsay's wife to write a biography and given access to the papers—a very large fund of jottings, since Lindsay showed a self-preoccupation quite precocious, if that is the way to look at his keeping a daily diary almost from the time he first learned to write. Masters's work is rich in thorny attitudes, and that gives it a certain cross-grained interest, especially when compared to the ruthless coverage of the pertinent and impertinent, the sense of being on a long trip with the subject in the family car, that defines the research of Lindsay's other biographer, Eleanor Ruggles, as it does so many other conventional and academic biographies.

Lindsay's limitations are, if not stressed, at least acknowledged when Masters writes:

> Lindsay dwelt forever in cuckoo cloudland.... He never grew up. The curled darling became a man of great emotional strength; but the memory of himself as the apple of his mother's eye, as the child wonder of grammar school.... a sort of Santa Claus grown up and made suitable for adult wonder and devotion.

On the other hand, we are asked to view the fantastical footnote, Lindsay, in conspiratorial terms:

> Not being Eastern American he made only a slight impact upon it; and after the first excitement about his poetry subsided he was treated with supercilious indifference, and the field he had broken and harrowed and sowed was taken and reaped by pro-English artists.... They preferred the Arthurian legends to Johnny Appleseed and Andrew Jackson.

The accent of grievance, neatly correspondent to Masters's cast of mind, is not to the point in the matter of Vachel Lindsay, and in any case the shape of an individual career is mixed with so many contingencies it cannot easily support a translation to the general. But all that is nothing beside the fact that if Lindsay had some sort of talents, they were not for poetry. He did not write poetry, he wrote jingles and hymns and scenarios for his public appearances. The true melancholy of the life lies in the broad encouragement of his naïveté, the span of his performances, which would inevitably weary. His books were published, he was "famous," and yet somehow he remained a door-to-door peddler.

Edgar Lee Masters was born in 1869, and his major work, *Spoon River Anthology,* did not appear until 1915, although a few of the portraits in it had been published earlier under a pseudonym. He entered his father's profession of law and practiced in Chicago for almost thirty years. He was unhappily married and wrote in his autobiography: "Somehow little by little I got the feeling that my wife in spite of her almost meek compliance was enervating me and cutting off my hair and putting out my eyes." A bitter divorce finally came about, and Masters moved to New York with a new young bride and settled into the Chelsea Hotel, his wife going back and forth to teach in Pennsylvania.

In many ways a companionable man, friend of Mencken, Dreiser, and others who liked their cigars and schnapps, member of the Players Club, somehow Masters seemed to drift into reclusion. We may notice that although he was in partnership for almost eight years with Clarence Darrow in Chicago, the well-known lawyer does not appear in Masters's autobiography. Masters's son, by the first wife, in a memoir attributes this gap to the scandal of the divorce and the appearance on the scene of her replacement, some thirty years younger. Perhaps, he suggests, Darrow took at best a neutral attitude, and the estrangement followed. Also the son tells of visiting his father at the Chelsea. Ellen Masters, now his stepmother, did not seem to be on hand. Present, however, was another young woman, Alice Davis, who lived in the hotel and helped with manuscripts and whatever else she helped with.

In 1944, *The New York Times* printed a story telling that Masters had been taken to Bellevue Hospital suffering from pneumonia and malnutrition. The Authors League and the American Academy came to his rescue, the wife packed him off to a Pennsylvania nursing home, near to where she was teaching, and there he died six years later at the age of eighty-one. Not a happy roundup, even if there is a hint of self-willed recoil and collapse when one remembers

the great industry Masters showed throughout his life in the production of works in many forms—verse, plays, novels, biography,
and autobiography.

Spoon River Anthology (1915)—a book could scarcely be more of a
success. Said to have sold more copies than any other previous
work of American poetry, it was translated into all the European
languages as well as into Arabic, Korean, and Chinese; it was also
transformed for the stage and used as the libretto for an opera, per-
formed at La Scala. The book is an "anthology" of the gravestones
around Spoon River, an area near to Lewistown, Illinois, where
Masters grew up. The dead come forth to speak the epitaphs of
their lives, each one a short free-verse recollection, a sort of *conte*,
very often remembering injuries or spoken with a surly ruefulness.
The unquiet graves, some 214 of them—"all, all, are sleeping on
the hill"—were thought to be somewhat cynical and degrading
to the quality of life lived in the Illinois villages of Masters's youth
and from which he drew his ruminating characters.

The first one is "Hod Putt," who died by hanging for a robbery in
his days of poverty after a life of toil. Seeing an opportunity for the
last word, he notes with satisfaction that he lies next to a crook
who prospered from clever uses of the possibilities of bankruptcy.
"Now we who took the bankrupt law in our respective ways, /
Sleep peacefully side by side." The verses today strike one not as
acerbic so much as generally soulful, "filled with longing" poems;
good, simple people seeking transcendence. "Of what use is it /
To rid one's self of the world, / When no soul may ever escape the
eternal destiny of life?"

The public appeal of the work must have been in the framing:
first, the lachrymal country churchyard with the darkening granite
of the tombstones lying in random placement as in village life;
then, the brief, anecdotal summations, many of them reading like
those civil-court cases that scrape the skins of the litigants into
eternity. To this must be added the candid moral framing of the
little stories, the accent on the scorned, the unlucky, the eccentric

from whom the smothering "hypocrisy" of the village would exact its punishments.

The "valiant" departed one, "Jefferson Howard," is "Foe of the church with its charnel darkness, / Friend of the human torch of the tavern" and hounded by the "dominating forces"—Republicans, Calvinists, merchants, bankers. In Spoon River, fate deals out repetitive cards, like the equalizing aspect of death itself. The aesthetic default of the work, pressing upon the mind as one name after another approaches its declaration, is that it could go on forever, the flat proseness of the language contributing, as the rocks in the sod are turned over again and again. There was indeed a second collection of Spoon River tales, a replication and consequent deflation of the original invention. (Another monologue-portrait was published during these years, "The Love Song of J. Alfred Prufrock.")

A biography, *Lincoln: The Man,* appeared in 1931. Hara-kiri, blood on the floor, Masters's as well as Lincoln's, an insult to the prairie, to Illinois, and perhaps to Carl Sandburg, or so Vachel Lindsay thought. The first part of Sandburg's Lincoln book, *The Prairie Years,* had been out for five years, and if its success embittered Masters, the emotion had its source in the picture of Lincoln rather than in the author's success in the market.

Masters's character is a puzzle, and it is hard to understand why this attractive and intelligent man, successful as a lawyer and a writer, should be such a sorehead. He is the village iconoclast, atheist, free lover, and more than a bit paranoid in the matter of local and national forces. He has *ideas* as some have freckles, and the book on Lincoln puts many of them on display with a good deal of eloquence, however alienating. The notion of the book is that the Civil War should not have been fought and that the aftermath— the domination of plutocrats, merchants, bankers, and the later imperial adventurism—was a disastrous drift. "Hebraic-Puritanism" is Masters's phrase for the moral insufficiency of the country. By this he does not appear to indicate anti-Semitism; instead, he felt a corrosive resentment of the Bible, Old Testament and New, and its power to shape the ethical climate of the nation. After the Civil War,

> as if in sublime malice, the choking weeds of Hebraic-Puritanism were sown; and thus the evils of empire and ancient privileges began to thrive, scarcely before the new wheat was started. Ages may be required for creative vision to stand externally in this field and its epos.

The overwhelming offense of the biographer was its picture of the character of Lincoln, who is seen as a creature of swamp-bred shrewdness, a sort of wary, calculating Snopes, retaining in the midst of certain superficial refinements the qualities of his father, Thomas Lincoln, who out of shiftlessness had sunk into the fetid habits of the "poor white" class. Masters stresses the fact that Nancy Hanks, Lincoln's mother, was illegitimate and in the enveloping mist of parental uncertainty had discovered or imagined her supposed father to be a well-bred Virginia planter. Lincoln claimed the presence of his more promising qualities to have come from the absent grandfather. "Lincoln was profoundly ashamed of the poverty of his youth, and of the sordid surroundings in which he grew up." Thus, his life was ruled by the determination to rise above his beginnings, "unlike the more honest Andrew Jackson and Walt Whitman."

The distinction and beauty of Lincoln's prose and of his platform style must be conceded—and also reduced. For Masters, this accomplishment and talent are suffused and diseased with the poison of the Bible: "Lincoln, whose only literacy was out of the Bible, and who developed an oratory from it, inspired by its artifice of emotional reiteration, and equipped with its sacred curses and its dreadful prophecies, its appeal to moralities where there was no thought, no real integrity." The Gettysburg Address is unfavorably compared to Pericles' funeral oration and subjected to a textual analysis on the matter of truth: "It was not true that our fathers in 1776 had brought forth a new nation; for in that year our fathers brought forth thirteen new nations, each of which was a sovereign state." Lincoln as a statesman and a thinker is accused of the "Hebraic-Puritan principle of assuming to act as one's brother's keeper, when the real motive was to become one's brother's jailer."

Out of indignation and obsession, Masters dug his own grave and sadly inscribed his own tombstone with the acid of the Spoon River meters. The resentment of the Civil War soldier, "Knowlt Hoheimer," killed in battle and lying up on the hill, might be his own epitaph:

> Rather a thousand times
> the county jail
> Than to lie under this marble
> figure with wings,
> And this granite pedestal
> Bearing the words, "Pro Patria."
> What do they mean, anyway?

Carl Sandburg lived to be eighty-nine years old, and he spent those years going here and yon, a hardy tumbleweed of a populist, blown by the wind across the plains. More than forty books to his credit and what for some would have been a burdensome accretion of honors, each one to be accepted and attended like the duties on the court calendar. Of course, he was sustained by the old pioneer energy, and as an early pop-art king his act—writing free-verse poems, collecting and performing *The American Songbag*—was inexhaustible. The six volumes on the life of Lincoln, "a folk biography" some critic was happy to describe it, spread over more than ten years, but of course he was on the hoof a good deal of that time.

These reflections come about from the strenuous busyness of Penelope Niven's new biography of Sandburg: over seven hundred pages, followed by another hundred of notes. This effort is a sort of rival to Sandburg's *Lincoln: Prairie Years, Chicago Years, National Hero Years*. Professor Niven says in her preface that her previous scholarship was of the sort to exclude the claims of this bygone figure, fallen from eminence, but "a decade after his death, I went to his Carolina mountain home," and then it appears that she fell into the corncrib, so to speak. That is, the vast Sandburg papers in libraries, in possession of the family, lying about in cartons. After this great haystack, the fodder of the book, was pulled apart, she began the Carl Sandburg Oral History Project of more than 150 interviews.

Having gone through the heap, settled into the poet and each member of the family, reliving their nights and days with an intrusive intimacy, the biographer wants to record each scrap. The index cards or data sheets come to have a claim of their own, and the affirmation, the yes, yes, of Sandburg's scurry through life is her own affirming journey. The book is tedious and sentimental and long, long, long. She likes participial descriptions such as "hearty and vigorous," or "erect and vigorous"—and who can doubt that's exactly what the wily old campaigner was, even though the biographer had never encountered him in life. The scholar of the papers, of *the life of,* knows, like some celestial Xerox machine, details that consciousness erases overnight.

One of the amusements of this biography is that it is a kind of informal history of the radio and television shows of the period, not unlike listening to the "golden oldies." Sandburg hit them all: the *George Jessel Show*, the *Milton Berle Show*, the *Dave Garroway Show*, the *Bell Telephone Hour*. Ed Murrow comes in more than once, and with Norman Corwin, the prince of radio Americana, Sandburg had a "fruitful" relationship. At the Philharmonic Auditorium in Los Angeles, he was introduced by Edgar Bergen (sold out, standing ovation); the publication of the *Second American Songbag* had an introduction by Bing Crosby. Penelope Niven again and again calls Sandburg the "eternal hobo," but as his fame grows he is usually on his way to the studio or the auditorium.

For a number of years, or for a good part of them, the prairie poet was in Hollywood under contract. Two producers from MGM sought his services for an "epic film about the USA," an undertaking not designed to be a mere motion picture but a "great, ringing message to the people." Sandburg was to write a novel, following in shape a scenario written by Sidney Franklin. The novel would be published, then made into a film. For this he was given $100,000, and the project was a "challenge Sandburg could not resist." The end of it all, after story conferences, residence in the film colony, after years and years, was that the novel appeared under the name of *Remembrance Rock,* 1,067 pages of the American Dream, never made into a film, a critical failure, but in no way a money loss for the author. The second Hollywood adventure was a year and a half of work with George Stevens on *The Greatest Story Ever Told.* "He was not only a pioneer, but an adventurer and an explorer, in his own words a Seeker," Sandburg's biographer writes, her words ever echoing those of her subject.

Sandburg made a bold identification between his own career and the history of the great country itself. Roosevelt wanted him to run for Congress, we are told. He collected Harvard and Yale honorary degrees, among many others, Pulitzer Prizes for history and poetry, invitations to address a session of Congress—a lot of this adulation arising from assuming the mantle of Lincoln as a friend of the Family of Man, and so on. He missed out on a few things such as the Nobel Prize and felt a certain annoyance when President Kennedy, whom he had supported, invited Robert Frost to read a poem at his inaugural rather then himself.

Oscar Wilde called the prairies "blotting paper," and if they are so looked at Carl Sandburg can be said to have sucked up all the nutrients in the soil. His beginning voice in *Chicago Poems* (1916), celebrating the "City of the Big Shoulders," and lamenting the lot of the dispossessed, sustained him, it seems, into the Depression period and the years of the New Deal. As a child of Swedish immigrants, Sandburg was part of the Social Democratic movement in the Middle Western states, and that marked the rhythm of his life:

the man, the striker, the dreamer, the immigrant toiler, friend of all mankind. His particular politics were New Deal and the Democratic Party. On and on he goes, each of his affirmations self-affirming.

The People, Yes is 179 pages long, with 107 sections—a statistical plenitude as typical of the Prairie Poets as of the wheat acreage of the region. In his notes, Sandburg writes of the work as coming out of "Piers Plowman, seven hundred years ago, a far better handbook and manual of democracy than either Dante or Donne"—a statement of such historical incongruity it raises questions of familiarity with the last two and maybe also the first of the antecedents named. No matter, the sprawl of the work is a "modern epic" and an "odyssey deep into the American Experience," in the reading by the biographer. In some ways, her spacious accommodations arouse sympathy since an attempt to analyze Sandburg's lines flowing down the pages would be profitless. His people, yes or no, are actually just indentured servants, and they did his work, sunup to sundown. The poet's acres and the house in the Carolinas are "open to the public as a National Park and National Historic Site." And that's it.

Spending time with the metered, or unmetered, minstrels of the Middle West is to invite a special melancholy, one not only aesthetic, although that defect predominates since they come into history as poets, not as preachers, philosophers, politicians, or entertainers. Birth or youth in Illinois marked them, a tattoo appropriate enough as experience, the turf of the imagination. Still, they were not ordinary citizens, state proud, but ones making a claim for what were, for the most part, hasty, repetitive, and formless verses, unlike, for instance, the inspirations of Hart Crane of Ohio.

Elitism, belief in the existence of exceptional talents, will here be scorned as a threat to the demotic voices of the prairie. Of course they, too, by publication, must make their entrance into the long tradition, an inescapable transition in the arts. As outlandishly successful as these poets were, the happy circumstance was, as usual, not sufficient, because of the wish for a higher validation that haunts the dreams of the popular.

All three had a proprietary feeling about the country, a longing to transform its restless genetic material into a *folk,* to fashion the inchoate strains into a hardy stock with the name "American" on it, like a packet of sunflower seeds. A futile parochialism for a nation that has ever been, to expropriate a phrase from Kafka, "a cage seeking a bird."

(*1991*)

Edmund Wilson

~ ~ ~

Edmund Wilson, one of our country's supreme men of letters, is sometimes remembered as being autocratic and intimidating. My own memory, not the most intimate, is of a cheerful, corpulent, chuckling gentleman, well-dressed in brown suits and double martinis. As a literary and cultural critic, Wilson produced many volumes on an astonishing range of subjects. And beyond that, every scrap of his diaries, his letters, and his autobiographical writings appear to have been collected and published. He liked to write about himself, his friends, his wives, his love affairs, his days and nights, sometimes formally composed in an essay, sometimes transformed, more or less, into fiction or preserved in his voluminous daily jottings. With the author having left so few gaps, it is not surprising that the present biography by Jeffrey Meyers can be said to be the first devoted to Wilson.

A "first" is something of a rarity for the very productive Meyers, who has practiced his craft in the prevailing scene of biography, in which the lives of writers and the remains of certain flamboyant artists and musicians are examined in one large volume after another. A new letter here or there, an untapped acquaintance, a passing stranger remembering a misdemeanor, might offer what is called in court "a window of opportunity." In any case, Jeffrey Meyers has produced biographies of Fitzgerald, Hemingway, Robert Lowell, Joseph Conrad, and others. In this field study, each new digger will need to explore the previously looted pharaonic tombs in search of an overlooked jewel in the stone eyes prepared for eternity.

If Jeffrey Meyers has broken the tape in the matter of Wilson's biography, he might not hold the title for long. The scholar Lewis Dabney has been "working on Wilson" for some years, and his labor is known as "authorized." What that distinction means is not always clear. Is it to be thought of as similar to the Queen of England's stamp on Pear's Soap? For a biographer, authorization seems to indicate the choice and support of family or heirs by providing access to papers, letters, drafts, mementos, photographs not available to all and sundry. In fact, almost everything or its equivalent—another photograph, for instance—is available to all and sundry, leaving the family members or others interested in restriction with not much beyond the power of refusing a personal interview.

Papers are sold, deposited, given as gifts or charitable deductions to libraries and other institutions suitable for preservation, cataloging, and reproduction, and they are for the most part open to academics and others with useful credentials. Collections are not meant usually as an honor to the collector but as a source of cultural history. If a biographer sets about his task, writes letters and receives replies about the subject, goes here and there for interviews, visits birth and burial sites perhaps, reads the work and the critical response to it, offers or stresses a few preferences, then with reasonable experience in doctoral programs or independent critical work, a biography can be produced. They are far from being, in most cases, a rich source of income; a lot of time is consumed, and if one is led to wonder just to whom the works are addressed, there is always one answer—the subsequent biographer.

Auden, George Orwell, and T. S. Eliot come to mind as distinguished writers who pleaded that there be no biography. They were like old wanderers on the road in Russian fiction, crying, "Have mercy on me, good folk!" The prayer seemed to have been heard as an impertinence and certainly an alert. Each got his biography and not one but several, the "interpretation" of Eliot's life flowing down to *Tom and Viv* on the stage. Scandal, or merely selfish and imprudent behavior, can be found in most lives as surely as the dates and ancestral records. It happened, didn't it? The unguarded moment or lifelong indiscretions, yes, or most likely, and so the biographer proceeds, as if under oath "to the best of my knowledge."

In the Victorian period, great figures often shared some of the majesty of the monarch, but even there the authorized memorialist could turn out to be somewhat less awed by the connection than the great one had imagined. Carlyle asked his friend and more or less disciple, the historian James A. Froude, to edit his memorial to Jane and to tell the tale, as it were. Froude wrote: "Carlyle never should have married." A curious emendation or explosion about the celebrated couple who lived together for forty years and famously reigned at 5 Cheyne Row. This assertion later led the unreliable Frank Harris to report that a doctor had examined Jane in her forties and found her to be "virgo intacta."

The poet Philip Larkin may have believed he was out of the literary scene by spending a good part of his life acting as a librarian in the provincial city of Hull. But he spoke and complained and wrote letters that achieved his own damnation by way of deeply unpleasant opinions promiscuously expressed. These utterances of ideas and prejudices appear in the recent biography by his sincere admirer, Andrew Motion. Larkin's contemptuous disapproval of blacks, wogs, foreigners, and so on bleakly enshroud the dour melancholy of his witty, beautiful poems—for the moment.

There have been outstanding biographies in our time, works of unremitting scholarly labor that add to our knowledge, elucidate the texts, and are composed with a refinement of style and judgment that honor the subject and give pleasure to the reader. Although these large undertakings are admirable in documentation and many other qualities, English literature is also enriched by odd, personal, less than definitive, glories—De Quincey's exhilarating memories of the Lake Poets, Henry James on Hawthorne, and a forgotten book, a quirky biography of Stephen Crane by the poet John Berryman.

"But they are wrong!" biographers in the stacks complain about so many irreplaceable documents of the past. Even Wilson is condescending to the miracle of Boswell's life of Johnson. Wilson promotes, with reservations, a newer work by Joseph Wood Krutch, itself, of course, superseded. To speak of Dr. Johnson: the heartrending, brilliant *Life of Mr. Richard Savage* is etched in falsehoods offered by Savage himself. Johnson's "life" is a sort of unwitting forgery written with genius, alive after the original, the true Richard Savage, has fallen into dust.

Edmund Wilson, were he living now, would be over one hundred years old. Jeffrey Meyers begins his biography with the chapter heading: "Red Bank, 1895–1907." Red Bank, New Jersey, was the scene of Wilson's birth, and for those of a literary inclination he may be said to have put the town on the map. His great-great-grandfather Kimball, on the mother's side, had married a Mather of New England. Meyers's first paragraph opens with this fact or stress:

> Edmund Wilson's ancestors served the altars of learning and committed murders in the name of God. He was descended from Cotton Mather, seventeenth century puritan divine and zealous witch hunter during the Salem trials, and shared many characteristics—intellect, bookishness, linguistic ability, temperament, energy, productivity and multiple marriages—with his eminent forefather. The prodigiously learned Mather, more widely read than any other American of his time, had entered Harvard at the age of twelve and spoke seven languages. Known for his arrogant

manner and aggressiveness in controversy, he overtaxed his nerves by indefatigable industry, poured out more than 450 works on an enormous range of subjects and still managed to acquire three wives.

Except for the demonism that captured the extraordinary mind of Cotton Mather with abominable results, Wilson does share the learning and immense productivity of his ancestor and managed to exceed him in the matter of wives by having four. Perhaps the opening of Meyers's book is not so much to indicate the intellectual brilliance of the two as to alert the reader to a consanguineous "arrogant manner and aggressiveness in controversy."

During his formative years Wilson grew up with a secure place in upper-middle-class society (a position he was unable to maintain for most of his writing career) and became attached to his ancestral home. He was shy and sensitive, interested in flowers and in drama, fantasy and magic, and always absorbed in books. He felt alienated from his parents, developed a difficult, demanding character, and inherited from his father an irritable disposition and a peremptory mode of discourse.

Wilson was not a New Englander of the seventeenth century in temperament or attraction to religion. When the poet Allen Tate became a Roman Catholic, or a sort of Catholic since he subsequently took advantage of the civil law and obtained two divorces, Wilson wrote him in a letter: "I hope that becoming a Catholic will give you peace of mind; though swallowing the New Testament as factual and moral truth seems to me an awful price to pay for it. You are wrong, and have always been wrong, in thinking I am in any sense a Christian. Christianity seems to me the worst imposture of any of the religions I know of. Even aside from the question of faith, the morality of the Gospel seems to me absurd."

Jeffrey Meyers's *Edmund Wilson* is organized in the conventional chronological manner, which serves well here and follows more or less the organization Wilson employs in his autobiographical volume, *A Prelude*, which takes him up to 1919, the date of his release from service in World War I. Wilson was not much like other young men. He was clumsy and bulky, short, five feet six inches, immune to the attraction of competitive sports. And yet, at the Hill School in Pottstown, Pennsylvania, he made interesting friendships, learned to admire certain of his teachers, studied among other subjects Latin, Greek, and French without, as Meyers tells us, making especially good grades but nevertheless building the foundation of his interest in languages. He went on to Princeton, an important part of his life, and there wrote and studied, made friends, notably Scott Fitzgerald and the scholar Christian Gauss.

Princeton social life lay in the eating clubs: "These clubs are remarkably uninteresting," he wrote, and added: "Since I did not play billiards or bridge, there was nothing to occupy me except to sit, as I sometimes did in winter, in front of our big open fireplace and read the papers and magazines." Odd as Wilson might have been, it does not appear that he felt himself so or in any way suffered from shame or anxiety about his nature or how he might appear to others.

Wilson grew up an only child, but he had a very well-populated family of connections. On his first trip to Europe when he was thirteen years old, the party was large: his parents, uncles, aunts, and cousins, each of whose character and fate he describes. The diary of this thirteen-year-old is printed in *A Prelude*. "I do not recommend for its interest the 1908 diary of my first trip to Europe, but I am printing it for the sake of completeness, and because it provides me with a pretext for explaining certain family matters."

The existence of the diary is the interesting consideration here. The keeping of diaries and, in Wilson's case a lifelong journal, are marks of confidence and self-esteem, an early sense of vocation. What one experiences is important to record, even when events are trivial, because the diarist is present. Still, the confidence, the being comfortable with his body and mind, are perhaps clues to the daunting and, in a way, unexpected inclusion in later years of precise, he believed, details of sexual adventures. Wilson's diaries were not published until after his death, and then they were edited and arranged by decades such as *The Twenties, The Thirties,* and so on up to *The Sixties.* They are a remarkable exercise of creative, intellectual, and physical energy produced as if under some self-appointed duty by one who was forever publishing reviews, extended essays, complex books, and undertaking exhausting journeys all over the world. The diaries are casual, perhaps, but they show a workman's sense of care, craft, and also thrift. Some of the recordings therein, such as those on Scott Fitzgerald and Edna Millay appear intact or, expanded, in book collections.

Throughout his life, here and abroad, Wilson was acquainted with a great number of distinguished and interesting people, and many became attached to him for his charm, his knowledge, his vivid conversation—indeed, the specially high quality of his work and of himself. But there is a latitudinarianism in Wilson, an open spirit, not disclaimed by a certain gruffness at times. As he writes about his daily life, he will give many pages to, for instance, an old farming family, the Munns, to their daily affairs, the various members of the family. The diaries, as we have them, are not different in style from his professional work. The collections of literary articles, written for *The New Yorker* and other magazines, found in *Classics and Commercials* and in *The Shores of Light* and *The Bit Between My Teeth,* are not diminished by thinking of them as the diaries of a professional man at his desk, with the texts to be examined, the author's life to be wondered about, in much the same way as he approaches the vast army of real persons who have passed his way.

In Meyers's biography of Wilson, wives and other ladies, "mistresses" and fumbles, have their place and their more than considerable number of pages. The publications of books are mingled with the calendar of life events and critical judgment is supplied by the reviews lying about in the attic of magazines and newspapers. The "fight" with the IRS over unpaid taxes owes its details to Wilson's book on the subject. More interesting for literary history and personal display is the "quarrel" with Vladimir Nabokov. The combats with the IRS and Nabokov were comedies, however painful each might have been for the participants.

About the IRS: There was Wilson, a gentleman always broke and with expenses not unwarranted, if often uncovered. He worked more diligently and with more conspicuous concentration than a president in the Oval Office. Wilson must have felt that as an independent, self-employed producer of strange small-business goods he was somehow not a wage earner required to give his deputed allotment with a burdensome regularity. The use of the nation's taxes for the Cold War and other misappropriations, as he viewed them, probably entered his mind later, although his distaste for militarism, weapons, and so on was sincere and marked by vehemence. The fact probably was that he simply didn't want to pay his taxes and this led to a pleasing amnesia as the time rolled around and led in the end to grimly calculated penalties and much harassment. Still, the affair was a comedy in the operatic sense, with the distracted, tousled hero and the rogues looking for gold under the bed.

Nabokov's translation with commentaries of Pushkin's *Eugene Onegin* was a folly of such earnest magnitude that it might have been conceived in *Bouvard and Pécuchet*. It was attacked by Slavicists for its wild, peculiar vocabulary in English and for its "original" dissertations on matters of prosody. Wilson was critically dismayed and moved without hesitation to say as much. He felt himself competent in the Russian language and certainly knowledgeable about Pushkin, to whom he had devoted an essay in *The Triple Thinkers*. Indeed, in that volume he translated "The Bronze Horseman" into "prose with an iambic base." The translation is a gift to those who wish to receive it. It is instructive and agreeable to read, much in the helpful spirit of the prose translations at the bottom of the page in the Penguin series of poetry in German, Spanish, and other languages. Wilson had embarked on a formidable accomplishment in his study of Russian, which he followed with his astounding assault on Hebrew. In his mid-sixties, we find him in a state of excitation about Hungarian. About this late effort, he was heard to say that he felt like "an old character in Balzac, huffing and puffing to his last liaison."

Wilson did not show any special modesty or hesitation in his contentious review of Nabokov's *Eugene Onegin;* however, the scholar Clarence Brown found Wilson guilty of the "unbelievable *hubris* of reading Nabokov's petulant little lessons about Russian grammar and vocabulary, himself blundering all the while." The pages of literary magazines were stuffed to grogginess with Wilson and Nabokov eloquently engaged about the properties of Russian and English pronunciation, metrical traditions in both languages, personal and literary qualities. John Updike's review of *The Nabokov-Wilson Letters* takes its title, "The Cuckoo and the Rooster," from an Ivan Krylov fable. In the midst of the battle, Nabokov wrote with his characteristic left-handedness, "I have always been grateful to him [Wilson] for the tact he has showed in not reviewing any of my novels while constantly saying flattering things about me in the so-called literary circles where I seldom revolve."

Wilson reviewed Nabokov's book on Gogol with a generous degree of plus and a scattering of minus. His reservations are the clue to an irreconcilable difference in the practice of the two writers: the style of composition. Nabokov's Gogol book is one of the most exhilarating, engaging, and original works ever written by one writer about another. Wilson acknowledges its uniqueness, but he finds himself annoyed by Nabokov's "poses, perversities and vanities." These "perversities" are the glory of Nabokov's writing, and they are the grandiloquent, imaginative cascade of images and diversions Wilson could not normally accept. He dismissed *Lolita:* "I like it less than anything of yours I have read." After *The Real Life of Sebastian Knight,* Nabokov's first novel in English, Wilson was more or less "disappointed."

In *Patriotic Gore,* a dazzling monument in the national literature, Wilson has a chapter on "American Prose." It is his idea that American writing abandoned the cultivated standards of the eighteenth century and in the first half of the nineteenth century fell into deplorable exaggeration, rhetorical display, fanciful diversions more or less arising out of the models of the sermon and public addresses. Therein, he writes a shocking appraisal that suggests the impossibility of his finding pleasure and beauty in Nabokov:

> There is nothing in the fiction of Hawthorne to carry the reader along: in the narrative proper of *The Scarlet Letter,* the paragraphs and the sentences, so deliberately and fastidiously written, are as sluggish as the introduction with its description of the old custom house. The voyage of the *Pequod* in *Moby Dick,* for all its variety of incident and its progression to a dramatic end, is a construction of close-knit blocks which have to be surmounted one by one; the huge units of *Billy Budd,* even more clottedly dense, make it one of the most inappropriate works for reading in bed at night, since it is easy to lose consciousness in the middle of one.

The chapter on Charles Dickens in *The Wound and the Bow* is one of Wilson's glowing achievements. It is rich in complexity, original in ideas, moves around the challenge of the novels and of the life of Dickens with a speculative and interrogating ease that is altogether remarkable. The essay is also a perfect example of Wilson's method as a critic. The title of the collection is suggested by Sophocles' play *Philoctetes,* and the theme is that the sufferings and traumas in the lives of artists have a deep connection with the release of creativity.

In the case of Dickens, the "wound" is well known: The family fell on hard times, and the boy was taken out of school and sent to work in a blacking factory, a cruel, degrading, and forever damaging fate. At the end of the day, the boy would visit his family, now residing in Marshalsea Prison due to the father's debts. Even when the elder Dickens received a legacy, the family did not immediately take the boy out of the factory and return him to school, a lapse he could never forgive. This wound in his youth has naturally been seen as the base for Dickens's hatred of cruelty to children, his exposure of hypocrisy throughout society, his contempt for knavery, social and intellectual pretense, money grubbing, lying—all embodied in a host of characters, an army invading London. These smarmy characters have their opposites in good, long-suffering, generous little people and sometimes good big people.

It is Wilson's idea that the bad people/good people duality arose from Dickens's inability to create characters of mixed motives and believably warring inclinations. He feels the author was approaching this in the unfinished novel, *Edwin Drood,* which is examined in great detail. Scholarship, recounted by Wilson, has shown that there were other humiliations in Dickens's past: His grandparents had worked as domestic servants in the household of Lord Crewe; the father of Dickens's mother was found guilty of embezzlement and fled. The facts about Dickens's past were hidden by Dickens himself. One of the most interesting stories is told by his son; not long before the author's death, the family was playing a word game and Dickens came up with: Warren's Blacking, 30 Strand. No one present understood what he was talking about. So there is a feeling, as the essay maintains, in Dickens himself of a kind of inauthenticity. By an argument too dense and detailed to examine here, the number of murders in the novels, the obsession with the murders indicate in the end that Dickens had murdered himself, a psychological element in Wilson's study.

So there is the "wound," but what about the "bow"—Dickens's style? The breathless flow of adjectives, metaphors, and similes, the description of clothes, houses, streets, alleys, and occupations, the skewered visual genius of one who describes the knobs on an impostor's head as "looking like the crust of a plum pie." The perpetual motion of Dickens's outrageous imagination seems wearisome for Wilson.

Nabokov's lectures at Cornell on *Bleak House* seize the novel when it is flying off the page, seize it with delight. The listeners are invited to note the lamplighter as he goes about his rounds, "like an executioner to a despotic king, strikes off the little heads of fire" or the Jellyby children "tumbled about, and notched memoranda of their accidents on their legs, which were perfect little calendars of distress." On and on the lecturer goes, remarking on names, alliteration, and assonance.

In his essay on American prose, Wilson explains his own preference in literary style. He sees the tragedy of the Civil War as breaking the fabric of romantic exaggeration, embroidery, false eloquence. His models are the stories of Ambrose Bierce and Lincoln's Gettysburg Address, among other examples. Sobriety, terseness, lucidity, and precision—and, indeed, his own compositions are wonderful in clarity, balance, movement, language, always at hand to express the large capacity of his mind and experience, whether current fiction, the Russian Revolution, or the Dead Sea Scrolls.

And yet Wilson, for all the practicality of his method, could be unpredictable and never more so than in his embrace of Joyce's *Finnegans Wake,* another language to learn, as it were. "In conception as well as in execution, one of the boldest books ever written," he remarks in the essay devoted to the novel in *The Wound and the Bow.* The essay is somewhat parental in approach as he guides the reader through whatever factual information might be useful, such as the age, occupation, marriage, and children of Earwicker. There are some rebukes, typical of Wilson's household rules: "And the more daring Joyce's subjects become, the more he tends to swathe them about with the fancywork of his literary virtuosity." Still, he brings to *Finnegans Wake* a beaming affection and solicitude.

Sex, Mary McCarthy, *Memoirs of Hecate County,* and so on. Mary McCarthy has written in her memoirs of her detestation of Wilson's body and soul, information provided by her decision to become his wife. She has disguised him in satirical portraits in her fiction, a disguise on the order of sunglasses. They were divorced after a span of seven years during which she bore a son by Wilson and after which she lived, wrote, and added two more husbands. A marriage, however successfully escaped, rankles more in the memory than an old, ferocious bout of the flu, but no matter, her preoccupation is extreme. She had much in common with Wilson, especially in the need to instruct. Some persons are not content to have a deep aversion to another but feel the command to have others share the documented distaste. This is different from jealousy of, for instance, Wilson's subsequent marriage to the attractive, cosmopolitan, domestically gifted, and loyal Elena Mumm Thornton. It would appear that McCarthy wanted to instruct Elena in the true nature of her husband, instruct Elena and everyone else. Otherwise consider the oddity of the amount of repetitive energy put into denunciation of the past by one so pleasantly situated in life, so rich in experience, friendships, new loves, handsome surroundings—all of that.

What was Wilson thinking of in descriptions in his diaries of his swaying home after an "encounter," only to awaken the next day and put it all down? He was, of course, thinking of himself, the principal actor in the drama, the "I." The "I" in a partnership on the bed or couch, or whatever, will, if he is in a mood to leave a record, need to move into the sensations of the "she." About Marie, a pickup, "Her cunt, however, seemed small. She would not, the first time, respond very heartily, but, the second, would wet herself and bite my tongue, and when I had finished, I could feel her vagina throbbing powerfully."

Memoirs of Hecate County, a fiction, more or less, with the real-life persons serving in the short and the longer story run down by the biographer, like a policeman tracking suspects. The book was banned, but it has survived and is probably still read because of its interesting reputation for salaciousness and the genuine interest of the book. It was a bizarre composition to add to the stately list of literary and cultural studies already long and commanding when it was published in 1946. "The Princess with the Golden Hair," the principal, most arresting tale, became the occasion for a good number of amusing, unfavorable reviews. The "princess," a remote and withholding beauty of the pre-Raphaelite sort for whom the narrator longs, did not arouse a like yearning in many readers. Interest, if not quite yearning, arrives when the princess-frustrated, first-person narrator, an art critic, takes a diversionary spin down to Fourteenth Street and a dance hall called the Tango Casino. There he meets Anna, a "hostess." She is poor, has spent time in an orphanage, has a brutal husband and a little girl and much misery and deprivation in her life. This background is finely done by Wilson as it flows in and out of the "couplings." Anna is a "relief"—not much more, if a lot of relief. Her lower-class "hard protruding little thigh bones" seem inadequate when at last the "luxurious" princess is brought to bed. "Her little bud was so deeply imbedded that it was hardly involved in the play, and she made me arrest my movement while she did something special and gentle that did not, however, press on this point, rubbing herself somehow against me—and then came, with a self-excited tremor."

"Clinical" was applied to the sex writing in the diaries and in the fiction. Cyril Connolly thought the fornications had "a kind of monotony," and John Updike found the writing "leaden and saturnine"; Raymond Chandler said Wilson managed to make "fornication as dull as a railroad timetable."

Jeffrey Meyers has produced a long book, 483 pages. There is a lot of Wilson to be sifted, and so there is a lot of Meyers. We might think the biographer has brought together the immense flow of Wilson's life and work, both of which are scattered in the many publications and collections. Meyers has certainly not made of the object of his labors the worst one could imagine—drinking, vanity, and so on—nor has he been able to create the brilliant, irreplaceable mind and spirit. Too many facts, of whatever laudatory or

Norman Mailer:
The Teller and the Tape

~ ~ ~

The "oral tradition," if that is a suitable slot in which to deposit the large number of books arising from the taped interview, is a labor-saving curiosity in which our country leads the world. We have here a "literature" of remarks, a fast-moving confounding of Gertrude Stein's confident assertion that "remarks are not literature." The exuberant exploitation of the possibilities of this "vampire capital" are just beginning and, indeed, the whole enterprise has about it a limitlessness in all its aspects.

"The transcript totaled twenty thousand pages" (*Mailer: His Life and Times,* by Peter Manso). "A major biography."

"For the third time, Cathy Zmuda transcribed hundreds of thousands of spoken words—perhaps millions in this instance" (*Working,* by Studs Terkel).

"It is safe to say that the collected transcript of every last recorded bit of talk would approach fifteen thousand pages" (*The Executioner's Song,* by Norman Mailer, a novel).

Quite a lot taken down, but why not more? What is to deter? The spoken "pages" each of us produces in a lifetime would outpace all the libraries of the ancient and modern world. First-person narration, this stratospheric memory bank floating freely in the universe, idling there, waiting for the button and the circling tape, is of a simplicity quite beautiful in shape. Like a bank account under a prescription, it can be "attached" by the collector, in print known as the author, and drawn upon in circumstances of great variety and for purposes strange or banal or merely useful. To ponder the field, scan the prospect of effortless remembering and remarking, opens up a prodigiousness on the loose, a monumentality of retailed playback.

Give voice to the voiceless, remember the neglected and the isolated. Sometimes the starting point is an awareness of the impending ending; we are always at a point where time is running out for those who have lived through this or that, significant or insignificant. Slave narratives, old soldiers, superannuated craftsmen, Indians, Appalachian folk, immigrants, blacksmiths—a bond of mutuality arises between the instrument and the voice, the sophisticated person's research plan and the honoring of the survivor by the very gesture of seeking out, taking down. What is said, details, turns of speech, life rhythms, bygone social patterns might be interesting in themselves and useful for the historian down the way. Of course, the historian's scrutiny will have a somewhat diminishing effect upon the unexamined flow because of the limits of spoken memories as documentation and the limits of each of us as a representation of historical events.

The modesty of the philanthropic intention commends it to us. The tapes and transcripts resting in the eternal peace of the libraries are a sort of gravestone for vanished persons who lived their days among a group not fully articulated. If nothing much is done with it, there is a charitable satisfaction in knowing that it exists. Liberalism, egalitarianism, a form of reverence, sent the WPA researchers to the Okies and tenant farmers, to field hands and prisoners with their songs and stories.

As documents, the innocent tapes bear a resemblance to the letters and diaries of obscure persons who happened to live in a time of upheaval or who by mere placement in the scheme of things were led to thoughts beyond the weather and family greetings. But these solitary compositors worked under the conventions of literacy, of writing, and the restraining self-consciousness of their written documents is different from the restraints, selections, and omissions of speech. It is often the task of the historian and the imaginative writer to discover the silences behind speech, the silences that produced the romantic text of James Agee's *Let Us Now Praise Famous Men.*

Listening in.

The tape-recorded books of today are not a gift to the cemetery of history. Instead, what we have here is a sort of decomposed creativity, a recycling similar to that of the obsolete ragman who turned old clothes into paper. Propagation is the intention, and storage is failure. Thus, confrontation enters between the asker and the asked, and the relation is more insinuating, less sentimental, more modern, you might say, and certainly more efficient.

The books are various indeed. Appeal is to the point, appeal of the subjects, the root idea. Except in a few cases, appeal can be said to be the only measure of quality. Taped books are roughly to be divided into the active solicitation of the words of the unknown and the active solicitation of the remarks of the known, or remarks about the known, the celebrated—or if not celebrated, notorious.

Mono.

The simplest method is to give each person his time and move on to the next. The sequential interviewer is likely to reign over the text in the benevolent and more or less disinterested manner of the anthropologist or social worker. The "composition" is fluid, open, carefree. Exploitation is circumvented by the general air of affirmation. The worth of the recorded person is what is being affirmed rather than the singularity of the voice, the words.

Studs Terkel, for instance, appears in a manner surely much like that of the scouts in the WPA days. He is updated by the large extent of his own packaged and distributed tapes, but still old-fashioned, the sympathetic, thoughtful leftist, true to the proletariat and the dispossessed and ignored. His task is clever and concrete, even if he must travel hither and yon and come back burdened with a trunk full of *oh* and *well, you know* and *I mean* and *let's see here.*

Working: People Talk About What They Do All Day and How They Feel About What They Do* is almost six hundred pages of small, crowded type, some 135 occupations, among them doorman, airline stewardess, farmer, miner, model, cabdriver, spot welder, hooker, and a few names such as Pauline Kael, Eddie Arroyo, Bud Freeman—that is, critic, jockey, jazz musician. About all this Terkel briefly sets the scene or briefly interrupts here and there. ("He's the doorman at a huge apartment building on Manhattan's Upper West Side.... The walls could stand a paint job.... He wears his uniform.")

The pages turn, the workers flow by as if coming out of the mill at the end of the day shift. Not one makes an impression, can be remembered—many they are and many another they might be. Just who is the hairstylist or the cabdriver? Or, rather, what are they? They do not have clothes, tics, parents, houses, fantasies. These persons are not metaphors, not a composite, and none has the weight of a line of statistics on position, social status, religion, training, whatever. The most striking thing is that few have vocal particularity. There is seldom an ear in the talking pages, hardly an echo of the fractured expressiveness heard around us.

Cabdriver: "I hate to admit that driving a cab is no longer the novelty to me that it once was. It has its moments, but it's not the most ideal job in the world as far as determining one's attitude is concerned."

*New York: Pantheon, 1984.

Sanitation worker: "You get just like the milkman's horse, you get used to it. If you remember the milkman's horse, all he had to do was whistle and whooshhh!"

The sanitized diction brings to mind *60 Minutes,* and this is not necessarily a prudent pruning for publication. The current stranger and his tape recorder, whether wishing it or not, find the subjects living in the atmosphere of television with its neat dispersal of the claims of the individual person, its condensations and programmings, its inattention and formalized forgetting, its dehydrated vocables ready for the freezer.

Tape recording without an interpretive intelligence is a primitive technology for history. It offers a moment of publicity in an undermining void. The protocol of the meeting and the docile instrument steadily transmitting pages are an orthodoxy, promoting a cheerful but rigid disengagement. The spuriousness of the encounter is ordained by the one-sidedness of advantage, all of it accruing to the "author."

To understand the meaning of attention to the unknown and unrecorded, one can go back to the great Victorian masterpiece, Henry Mayhew's *London Labour and the London Poor.* Or in our own time to Ronald Blythe's *Akenfield: Portrait of an English Village* (1969). Here the old bell ringer talks and is "taken down" by some method. But his presence moves the listener, Blythe, to reflections: "Lost in an art-pastime-worship based on blocks of circulating figures which look like one of those numismatic keys to the Great Pyramid secret, the ringing men are out on their own in a crashing sphere of golden decibels."

Polyphonic.

Taped books about persons of established interest are now designed to make a more sophisticated use of the gathered material. A person, or rather a personality, is the center, replacing an abstraction of theme or place. Slabs of recollection, one after another, would dilute the attention to the central subject; the "authors" of interview books are now allowed to slice up the interviews and disperse the remarks through-out the pages, to bring them in at appropriate points, to create some-thing like a conversation in a crowded room. There is no intention to reproduce dialogue; each recollector is on his own, but his or her hold-ing forth is subject to judicious interruption in the interest of narrative. The speakers are witnesses, coins in a box, offerings, gratuities. They are the base metals to be transmuted into gold—that is, into pages.

In *Mailer: His Life and Times*, by Peter Manso, "more than two hundred people were interviewed over a period of forty months, some interviews filling more than ten hours." Transcript close to 20,000 pages, offered as a "major biography" of Mailer, and itself a "major literary event"; gigantism is something of a phenomenon in written books and on the fairgrounds, but for the taper the world is a hippodrome of garrulity.

All contemporary biographers rely upon the interview as one of many sources, including the biographer's vision, necessary for the construction of a life. In Manso's biography, the interview is the only source, except for a few snippets from reviews and letters, and thus it seems to offer a fresh aesthetic of sorts: You, and in this case your times, are what people have to say about you. The high inter-est of the unfolding of this proposition, the assertiveness of the speakers, has to do with the large proportions of Mailer himself, his confidence and intrepidity, his florid pattern of experience, his disasters met with an almost erotic energy of adaptation. This promiscuity, the volume of precipitous encounters from which he has emerged like a knight from the forest, seems to have encour-aged an elevation of indiscretion among the contributing friends, a situation much in the interest of the pages. Manso tells us the right of review was sometimes requested but "in most, not."

The drastic distances between gossip, the libertine loquacity of the dinner table, and print dissolves, as we would expect since the enterprise is committed to print only as a vessel of the waters of orality. Wives are snubbed, well-known people are maliciously hooked by a phrase and flounder about like so many fish trapped in a net. Mailer himself enters briefly here and there, but of course his presence, his invulnerable presence, is in every line.

The absence of an author, the lack of a signature of responsibility, the conception of ideas as shadows of comment, vague and undefended, in a like way absorbs the activity of the commentator, the critic. What can be said about more than six hundred pages of anecdote? Description is possible and recapitulation of lively asides, but that involves a measure of culpability, the passing on of gossip. Yet any reader will think some of these books are more appealing than others, and *Mailer: His Life and Times* might be judged to score—to score more or less, since an equation of judgment rests merely on the availability of consenting voices.

Perhaps one can judge Mailer to be a "good" idea. He is a spectacular mound of images and, like such self-creations, mystifying and impersonal, and thereby a structure of anecdote corresponds in some way to his own accumulated articulations. His writings, the frame of the structure, are to be incorporated only glancingly or studied in the anecdotal pile, but then the work, the sharp intrusion, is the knife in the heart of most biographers.

We see that the writer had a youth, a formidable, adoring mother somewhat along the lines Freud thought friendly to a son's success. The family is smart—cousin, sister, and Mailer himself making their way from Brooklyn to Harvard. Constant writing from the beginning, *The Naked and the Dead,* a splendid success, the army, marriage, political complexity increased by friendship and "reality," second wife, "violent and orgiastic period" (his words), self-advertisement, stabbing of wife, antiwar activity, prisoner of sex, children, more marriages, Marilyn Monroe, Jack Abbott, Gary Gilmore, further marriages and children, impressive alimony, and with a new wife and child a mellow middle age. And, of course, books at every point.

Total recall adds much to the outline, even if Mailer's public has its own storehouse of dramatic recollection. Since little has been hidden along the way, Mailer is then a subject to be discussed rather than discovered. Revelation is scarcely to be wished about the living, but this premature interment is something of a finale. What we have here is a tomb of pharaonic memorabilia, brick upon brick in the sand.

The compositional blur of Mailer's *The Executioner's Song* is once more engaged by the frenzied entrance of the promoter Lawrence Schiller into the life and time of N.M. Schiller claimed his space in the "real-life novel" and received the recognition of the results of his relentless encroachments in the formation of that spectacular publication. Schiller's memory is composed of dollars, deals, contracts, and every kind of worry in the motel room and on the telephone. Crisis is his overcoat, and he sweats from one threatened crash to another, crashes such as Gilmore's "cop-out" suicide attempt or, worse, his refusing to, as they say, die with dignity rather than accept, if it came, a reprieve to a life sentence.

Schiller is a most interesting gladiator in combat with reluctant witnesses, negotiations, speed, and deadlines. In the canniness of his inquisitions he often exceeds himself, but he is a professional and brings to mind the shock of method. (Solzhenitsyn experienced the shock of the West in an encounter with two hopeful biographers. Withdrawing, he said, "The collection of 'information' in this way is not different from police spying.")

Preparation for *The Executioner's Song* is detailed once more in Manso's compilation. Schiller: "By then [May 1977] I'd given him about 9,000 pages of what eventually was over 16,000 pages of interview transcript." The interviews are put together and come out quite un-Mailerish, as was noted. We find the author in a bit of staging such as, "In the mountains, the snow was iron gray and purple in the hollows, and glowed like gold on every slope that faced the sun." Just a bit of that here and there, nothing much when compared with Truman Capote's *In Cold Blood,* another killer book of great interest and of another kind.

Capote's research, acquaintance with the cast of characters, the reputed dialogue and landscape are presented in the authorial manner throughout, incorporated into a text. About one of the killers, we read that he had a face "halved like an apple, then put together a fraction off center.... The left eye being truly serpentine, with a venomous, sickly-blue squint that although it was involuntarily acquired, seemed nevertheless to warn of bitter sediment at the bottom of his nature." This could not be *said* by anyone.

Mailer had his tapes in abundance; having them, he came forth, to the astonishment of a few, with a text remarkable for its plainness, its anonymity. He *shaped,* as it were, *The Executioner's Song.*

Arthur Kretchmer, editor of *Playboy:* "You've got the fucking plains in your text. It's right there." Earlier Mailer said: "I picked it up from Norris. If the book has any feeling of small-town life, I guess I picked it up from Norris." Norris Church, his wife, grew up in Atkins, Oklahoma, population 1,391.

Schiller, about *The Executioner's Song* and the possibility of its winning the Pulitzer Prize (it did, for fiction): "Because the detailing is there, the flatness, and Mailer doesn't exist in the book. They have to give him the award." This bit of literary criticism is engaging. Schiller seems to fear that *The Executioner's Song* would be written—like Mailer's *Marilyn,* perhaps. At the worst in the thick, resonant diction, the demonic, original clutter of Mailer's high style, which would impugn the gray-hide, elephantine mass of the record and its extraordinary, deathly appeal.

It's true that Mailer "doesn't exist in the book"—or largely true. And has he created the voice, the plains, the flatness, the Westness of it? Aren't the voices and landscape those of Vern and Brenda, Nicole and Garry and Bessie, accurately taped, recounting the scenery of their life with Gilmore, filling in for Schiller or whoever, appearing on every page against the dental drill of the pursuit?

The invisible hand.

A bit of neatening, of course, and punctuation, the period, the comma. The taped text is always a great, gluey blob, and what is needed are sentences dry and separate as kernels of corn. A close reading of taped books suggests that the invisible hand is less busy than might be imagined. Punctuation, laying it out, pasting it up. The real labor of the books returns to the source, the wretched bulk of the testimony, the horror of its vast, stuttering scale. The collector is much impressed, and perhaps depressed, by the challenging magnitude. He has lifted it, sorted it, had secretaries hard at work to contain the monstrousness of what his machine has brought into being.

We notice the invariable publicity given to numbers: the thousands of pages, the millions of words, the long, long hours of interviewing, the large cast tracked down. The insistence upon number indicates that it is a validation. But a validation of what, of whom?

Tapes are what they are, no more and no less than themselves. They are the property of the speaker, even if he has freely surrendered his rights; surrendered or not, nothing belongs to the author. Excision, deletion, yes, and placement, the packaging of the property. It is accepted that the gibberish must be shaped up and, thereby, allowed to become itself, the speaker's words made legible.

Additions are a moral problem. The author can receive his book as a liberal, in all senses, gift, but he cannot reciprocate, cannot in good faith add decorative phrasing and color as an advancement of the verbal interest and appeal of his given text. For the imaginative writer, wit and a pleasing intervention of adjective and image might be a natural temptation. But here the prohibition seems clear. The author's own words in the mouth of an interviewed subject are artificial, illicit, a reverse and most peculiar form of plagiarism. There is little evidence that the compiler of talk feels this as a constraint. What is needed from time to time is the practical matter of emphasis, keeping the attention of the reader.

The Executioner's Song is the apotheosis of our flourishing "oral literature" thus far. (To see it as Mailer's best book, as many have done, is much too fast. Mailer is a river of words, ornamental, evocative words, and cascading notions and designs. There is no plainness, flatness in him, but there is, was, a lot, in the tapes.)

He—and Capote also in his different construction—had a plot and, through none of their devising, an adjunct in the death penalty.

This publicly ordained ending from which there was no escape might have prompted Mailer to his most genuine contribution to the tale of Gary Gilmore. Mailer's mark on the book is an accentual one. By accent, placement, and distribution, and finally insistence, no matter what a contrary cynicism about reality might have suggested, he created a romance. From Schiller's pit, we can say that Mailer has excavated a *Liebestod,* possibly proposing it as a redemption of the squalor of this long, long death trip so arresting to the voyeur in most of us.

We can imagine a fraudulent tape-recorded production offered by a shy recluse as his own thousand pages of unheard sound. No, that would mean writing—and the tape recorder is first and last a labor-saving instrument.

(*1985*)

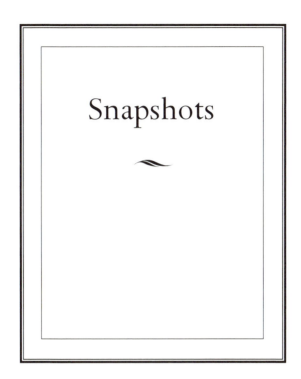

Snapshots

Mary McCarthy
in New York

~ ~ ~

Intellectual Memoirs: New York 1936–1938. I look at the title of these vivid pages and calculate that Mary McCarthy was only twenty-four years old when the events of this period began. The pages are a continuation of the first volume, to which she gave the title *How I Grew.* Sometimes with a sigh she would refer to the years ahead in her autobiography as "I seem to be embarked on how I grew and grew and grew." I am not certain how many volumes she planned, but I had the idea she meant to go right down the line, inspecting the troops you might say, noting the slouches and the good soldiers, and, of course, inspecting herself living in her time.

Here she is at the age of twenty-four, visiting the memory of it, but she was in her seventies when the actual writing was accomplished. The arithmetic at both ends is astonishing. First, her electrifying ("to excite intensely or suddenly as if by shock") descent upon New York City just after her graduation from Vassar College; and then after more than twenty works of fiction, essays, cultural and political commentary, the defiant perseverance at the end when she was struck by an unfair series of illnesses, one after another. She bore these afflictions with a gallantry that was almost a disbelief, her disbelief, bore them with a high measure of hopefulness, that sometime companion in adversity that came not only from the treasure of consciousness, but also from an acute love of being there to witness the bizarre motions of history and the also, often, bizarre intellectual responses to them.

Intellectual responses are known as opinions, and Mary had them and had them. Still, she was so little of an ideologue as to be sometimes unsettling in her refusal of tribal reaction—left or right, male or female, that sort of thing. She was doggedly personal, and often this meant being so aslant that there was, in this determined rationalist, an endearing crankiness, very American and homespun somehow. This was true especially in domestic matters, which held a high place in her life. There she is grinding the coffee beans of a morning in a wonderful wooden-and-iron contraption that seemed to me designed for muscle building—a workout it was. In her acceptance speech upon receiving the MacDowell Colony Medal for Literature, she said that she did not believe in labor-saving devices. And thus she kept on year after year, up to her last days, clacking away on her old green Hermes nonelectric typewriter, with a feeling that this effort and the others were akin to the genuine in the arts—to the handmade.

I did not meet Mary McCarthy until a decade or so after the years she writes about in this part of her autobiographical calendar. But I did come to know her well and to know most of the "characters," if that is the right word for the friends, lovers, husbands, and colleagues who made up her cast after divorce from her first husband and the diversion of the second, John, last name Porter, whom she did not marry. I also lived through much of the cultural and political background of the time, although I can understand the question asked, shyly, by a younger woman writing a biography of Mary: "Just what is a Trotskyite?" *Trotskyite* and *Stalinist*—part of one's descriptive vocabulary, like *blue-eyed*. Trotsky, exiled by Stalin and assassinated in Mexico in 1940, attracted leftists, many of them with socialist leanings, in opposition to the Stalin of the Moscow Trials, beginning in 1936, which ended in the execution of most of the original Bolsheviks and the terror that followed.

The preoccupation with the Soviet Union, which lasted, with violent mutations of emphasis, until just about yesterday, was a cultural and philosophical battleground in the years of Mary McCarthy's "debut" and in the founding, or refounding, of the *Partisan Review*. In that circle, the Soviet Union, the Civil War in Spain, Hitler, and Mussolini were what you might call real life, but not in the magazine's pages more real, more apposite, than T. S. Eliot, Henry James, Kafka, and Dostoevsky.

Her memoir is partly "ideas" and very much an account of those institutional rites that used to be recorded in the family Bible: marriage, children, divorce, and so on. Mary had only one child, her son Reuel Wilson, but she had quite a lot of the other rites: four marriages, interspersed with love affairs of some seriousness and others of none. Far from taking the autobiographer's right to be selective about waking up in this bed or that, she tempts one to say that she remembers more than scrupulosity demands—demands on the rest of us at least as we look back on the insupportable surrenders and dim our recollection with the aid of the merciful censor.

On the other hand, what often seems to be at stake in Mary's writing and in her way of looking at things is a somewhat obsessional concern for the integrity of sheer fact in matters both trivial and striking. "The world of fact, of figures even, of statistics ... the empirical element in life ... the fetishism of fact" are phrases taken from her essay "The Fact in Fiction" (1960). The facts of the matter are the truth, as in a court case that tries to circumvent vague feelings and intuitions. If one would sometimes take the liberty of suggesting caution to her, advising prudence or mere practicality, she would look puzzled and answer: But it's the truth. I do not think she would have agreed it was only her truth—instead she often said she looked upon her writing as a mirror.

And thus, she will write about her life under the command to put it all down. Even the name of the real Man in the Brooks Brothers Shirt in the fiction of the same name, but scarcely thought by anyone to be a fiction. So at last, and for the first time, she says, he becomes a fact named George Black, who lived in a suburb of Pittsburgh and belonged to the Duquesne Club. As in the story, he appeared again and wanted to rescue her from New York bohemian life, but inevitably he was an embarrassment. As such recapitulations are likely to be: Dickens with horror meeting the model for Dora of *David Copperfield:* "What a form she had, what a face she had, what a graceful, variable, enchanting manner!" Of course, the man in the Brooks Brothers shirt did not occasion such affirmative adjectives but was examined throughout with a skeptical and subversive eye. About the young woman, the author herself more or less, more rather than less, she would write among many other thoughts: "It was not difficult, after all, to be the prettiest girl at a party for the sharecroppers."

The early stories in *The Company She Keeps* could rightly be called a sensation: They were indeed a sensation for candor, for the brilliant, lightning flashes of wit, for the bravado, the confidence, and the splendor of the prose style. They are often about the clash of theory and practice, taste and ideology. Rich as they are in period details, they transcend the issues, the brand names, the intellectual fads. In "The Portrait of the Intellectual as a Yale Man," we have the conflict between abstract ideas and self-advancement, between probity and the wish to embrace the new and fashionable. About a young couple, she writes: "Every social assertion Nancy and Jim made carried its own negation with it, like an Hegelian thesis. Thus it was always being said by Nancy that someone was a Communist but a terribly nice man, while Jim was remarking that someone else worked for Young and Rubicam but was astonishingly liberal."

In the memoir, we learn that we can thank Edmund Wilson for turning the young Mary away from writing reviews to undertaking fiction and thereby producing these dazzling stories. We also learn that she thanks him for little else. A good deal of the pages left at her death tell about her affair with Philip Rahv and *analyze* the break, in fact a desertion, from him and her marriage to Wilson. I must say that much of this drama was new to me. I was not in New York at the time. I met Mary for the first time in the middle 1940s when I was invited to Philip Rahv's apartment. She was with a young man who was to be her next husband after the "escape" from Wilson—that is, she was with Bowden Broadwater. Philip was married to Nathalie Swan, Mary's good friend from Vassar.... A lot of water had flowed by.

The picture of Mary and Philip Rahv living in a borrowed apartment on East End Avenue, a fashionable street over by the wrong river, since Philip was very much a downtown figure, rambling round the streets of Greenwich Village with a proprietary glance here and there for the tousled heads of Sidney Hook or Meyer Schapiro and a few others whom he called *Luftmenschen.* The memory, no matter the inevitable strains of difference between them, has an idyllic accent, and she appears to have discovered in the writing, decades later, that she loved Rahv—a discovery I will call amusing for want of a better word. There was to be an expulsion from the garden when Edmund Wilson meets Mary, pursues her, and finally, a not very long "finally," gets her to marry him.

The account of her moral struggles is a most curious and interesting one, an entangled conflict between inclination and obligation; the inclination to stay with Rahv and the obligation to herself, her principles, incurred when she got drunk and slept with Wilson and therefore had to marry him. The most engaging part of this struggle is not its credibility or inner consistency but the fact that Mary believed it to be the truth. There was a scent of the seminarian in Mary's moral life, which for me was part of her originality and also one of the baffling charms of her presence. Very little was offhand: Habits, prejudices, moments, even fleeting ones, had to be accounted for, looked at, and written in the ledger. I sometimes thought she felt the command to prepare and serve a first course at dinner ought to be put in the Bill of Rights.

I remember telling her about some offensive behavior to me on the part of people who were not her friends, but mere acquaintances, if that. When she saw them on the street up in Maine she would faithfully "cut them"—a phrase she sometimes used—while I, when her back was turned, would be waving from the car. Yet it must be said that Mary was usually concerned to make up with those she had offended in fiction, where they were amusingly trapped in their peculiarities, recognizable, in their little ways, not to mention their large ways. Among these were Philip and Nathalie Rahv, whom she had wounded, painfully for them, in a novella, *The Oasis.* They, too, made up, after a time, after a time.

Details, details: Consider the concreteness of the apartments, the clothes, the inquisitive, entranced observing that had something in it of the Goncourt Brothers putting it all down in the Paris of the second half of the nineteenth century. They will write: "On today's bill of fare in the restaurants we have authentic buffalo, antelope, and kangaroo." There it is, if not quite so arresting as Flaubert making love in a brothel with his hat on. Mary remembers from the long-flown years that they on a certain occasion drank "Singapore Slingers." And the minutiae of her first apartment in New York: "We had bought ourselves a 'modernistic' Russel Wright cocktail shaker made of aluminum with a wood top, a chromium hors d'oeuvres tray with glass dishes (using industrial materials was the idea), and six old-fashioned spoons with a simulated cherry on one end and the bottom of the spoon flat for crushing sugar and Angostura." The cocktail age, how menacing and beguiling to the sweet tooth, a sort of liquid mugger.

Unlike the Goncourts' rather mad nocturnal stenography to fill their incomparable pages, I don't think Mary kept a diary. At least, I never heard mention of one or felt the chill on rash spontaneity that such an activity from this shrewdly observing friend would cast upon an evening. From these pages and from the previous volume, it appears that she must have kept clippings, letters certainly, playbills, school albums, and made use of minor research to get it right—to be sure the young man in Seattle played on the football team. In these years of her life, she treasured who was in such and such a play seen in an exact theater. On the whole, though, I believe the scene setting, the action, the dialogue came from memory. These memories, pleasing and interesting to me at every turn, are a bit of history of the times—going to *Pins and Needles,* the Federal Theatre's tribute to the Ladies Garment Workers Union, a plain little musical with fewer of the contemporary theater's special effects than a performance of the church choir.

The pages of this memoir represent the beginning of Mary McCarthy's literary life. She was a prodigy from the first. I remember coming across an early review when I was doing some work in the New York Public Library. It was dazzling, a wonderfully accomplished composition, written soon after she left college. As she began, so she continued, and in the years ahead I don't think she changed very much. There was a large circle of friends in France, England, and Italy, as well as here at home, but Mary was too eccentric in her tastes to be called snobbish, and I did not find her an especially worldly person. She was not fashionable so much as discriminating: But beyond it all there was the sentimental and romantic streak in her nature that cast a sort of girlish glow over private and public arrangements.

Year in and year out, she made fantastical demands on her time and her budget for birthdays, Christmas, presents, banquets, bouquets, surprises, a whole salmon for the Fourth of July, traditional offering. I remember Natasha Nabokov, the mother of Ivan Nabokov, a publisher in Paris, telling me of a Thanksgiving in Paris where Mary found an approximation of the American turkey and brought forth "two dressings, one chestnut and one oyster." Keeping the faith it was. I often thought the holiday calendar was a command like the liturgical season with its dates and observances. Perhaps it was being an orphan, both of her parents having died in the flu epidemic of 1918, that led her to put such unusual stress on the reproduction of "family" gatherings.

Here she speaks of her "patrician" background, a word I never heard her use about herself. It was true that she came from the upper-middle class, lawyers and so on, but all of it had been lived so far away in Minnesota and the state of Washington that one never thought of her as Middle Western or Western but instead as American as one can be without any particularity of region or class. In any case, she created, even in small, unpromising apartments, a sort of miniature *haut bourgeois* scenery, without being imitative. And she would arrive in New York with Mark Cross leather luggage, a burdensome weight even when empty, pairs of white leather gloves, a rolled umbrella, all of it reminding of ladies of a previous generation, and no thought of convenience. Of course, she didn't believe in convenience.

Wide friendships and hospitality, yes, but there were, in my view, only two persons, outside the family circle, for whom she felt a kind of reverence: The two were Hannah Arendt and Nicola Chiaromonte, both Europeans. Chiaromonte, a beautiful man with dark curls and brown, I think, eyes, was a curiosity in the *Partisan* circle because of his great modesty and the moderation of his voice in discussion, a gentle word for what was usually a cacophony of argument. An evening at the Rahvs' was to enter a ring of bullies, each one bullying the other. In that way it was different from the boarding school accounts of the type, since no one was in ascendance. Instead there was an equality of vehemence that exhausted itself and the wicked bottles of Four Roses whiskey around midnight—until the next time. Chiaromonte, with his peaceable, anarchist inclinations, was outclassed here.

I suppose he could be called a refugee, this Italian cultural and social critic and antifascist. Here, he published essays but did not create a literary presence equal to his important career when he returned to Italy in the late 1940s. After his death, Mary wrote a long, interesting essay in order to introduce an American edition of his writings on the theater. I remember an anecdote she told me about

Chiaromonte, and it alone is sufficient to show why she so greatly admired him. The story went as follows: stopped at border, trying to escape the Nazi drive across Europe, Nicola was asked for his passport, and he replied, Do you want the real one or the false one?

Hannah Arendt, of course, was or became an international figure with *The Origins of Totalitarianism, Eichmann in Jerusalem,* and other works. I can remember Mary at Hannah's apartment on Riverside Drive, a setting that was candidly practical, a neat place, tending toward a mute shade of beige in appointments. For an occasional gathering, there would be drinks and coffee and, German-style it seemed to us, cakes and chocolates and nuts bought in abundance at the bakeries on Broadway. Mary was, quite literally, enchanted by Hannah's mind, her scholarship, her industry, and the complexities of her views. As for Hannah, I think perhaps she saw Mary as a golden American friend, perhaps the best the country could produce, with a bit of our western states in her, a bit of the Roman Catholic, a Latin student, a sort of New World, bluestocking *salonière* like Rahel Varnhagen, about whom Hannah had, in her early years, written a stunning, unexpected book. The friendship of these two women was very moving to observe in its purity of respect and affection. After Hannah's death, Mary's extraordinary efforts to see her friend's unfinished work on questions of traditional philosophy brought to publication, the added labor of estate executor, could only be called sacrificial.

I gave the address at the MacDowell Colony when Mary received the medal, and there I said that if she was, in her writing, sometimes a scourge, a Savonarola, she was a very cheerful one, lighthearted and even optimistic. I could not find in her work a trace of despair or alienation; instead, she had a dreamy expectation that persons and nations should do their best. Perhaps it would be unlikely that a nature of such exceptional energy could act out alienation, with its temptation to sloth. Indeed, it seemed to me that Mary did not understand even the practical usefulness of an occasional resort to the devious. Her indiscretions were always open and forthright, and in many ways one could say she was like an open book. Of course, everything interesting depends upon which book is open.

Among the many charms and interests of her unfinished memoir are the accounts of the volatility of her relations with the men in her life. She will say that she doesn't know why she left her first husband, backed out on John Porter, and deserted Philip Rahv. That is, she doesn't know *exactly* but can only speculate. What, perhaps, might be asked nowadays is why the gifted and beautiful young woman was so greatly attracted to marriage in the first place, why she married at twenty-one. She seemed swiftly to overlook the considerable difficulties of unmarried couples "living together" at the time: the subterfuge about staying overnight, facing the elevator man, hiding the impugning clothes when certain people appeared, keeping the mate off the phone lest there be a call from home—unimaginable strategies in present-day cities. There were many things Mary didn't believe in, but she certainly believed in marriage, or rather in being married. She had no talent at all for the single life, or even for waiting after a divorce, a break. However, once married, she made a strikingly independent wife, an abbess within the cloister, so to speak.

In her foreword to the paperback edition of *Memories of a Catholic Girlhood*, she speaks of the treasures gained from her education in Catholic convent and boarding schools, even finding a benefit in the bias of Catholic history as taught.

To care for the quarrels of the past, to identify oneself with a cause that became, politically speaking, a losing cause with the birth of the modern world, is to experience a kind of straining against reality, a rebellious non-conformity that, again, is rare in America, where children are instructed in the virtues of the system they live under, as though history had achieved a happy ending in American civics.

Nonconformity can be a tiresome eccentricity or arise from genuine skepticism about the arrangements of society. Think of the headache of rejecting charge cards, the universal plastic that created a commercial world in which trying to use a personal check would bring one under suspicion. Going along with fidelity to old-fangledness, Mary and her husband declined the cards and had to carry about large sums of money, rolls of bills that reminded me of nothing so much as men in fedoras in gangster movies. Still they did it and I think with some amusement in a trendy restaurant or Madison Avenue shop.

So, we meet her here, in 1936, marching in a Communist May Day parade, marching along with John Porter, a new man who looked like Fred MacMurray. The conjunction of romance and the events of the day is characteristic of Mary at all points in her life. At the end of her memoir, two years have passed, and she has covered a lot of ground: divorce, a new marriage, unhappy, one that lasted seven years, "though it never recovered." Never recovered from Wilson's mistakes and shortcomings as she saw them.

I would have liked Mary to live on and on, irreplaceable spirit and friend that she was, even though I must express some relief that her memoirs did not proceed to me and my life to be looked at with her smiling precision and daunting determination on accuracy. She had her say, but I never knew anyone who gave so much pleasure to those around her. Her wit, great learning, her gardening, her blueberry pancakes, beautiful houses—none of that would be of more than passing interest if it were not that she worked as a master of the art of writing every day of her life. How it was done, I do not know.

(*1992*)

The Magical Prose of Poets:
Elizabeth Bishop

~ ~ ~

Over the years, Elizabeth Bishop, the poet, wrote a number of short stories, several portraits (one of Marianne Moore and another of a primitive painter living in Key West), several descriptive pieces set in Brazil, and an introduction to her translation from the Portuguese of *The Diary of Helena Morley*. All are now in *The Collected Prose*, edited and introduced by her publisher, Robert Giroux. Herein one will find Elizabeth Bishop's mastery of a moderate tone, even in the most searing fictions based upon painful recollections of her early life. One will note the characteristic curiosity, in her case often a curiosity about the curious, and it will be muted, as in her poems, by a respect and tolerance for what the curiosity discovers. There is also, here and there, the unusual visual sharpness that prompts her to challenge, as in a duel, the expected adjectives of description. She finds the words to make her victory convincing.

I remember when "In Prison" appeared in *Partisan Review* in 1938. This story, or prose reflection, was immediately famous, if such a claim is possible for a single short work appearing in a small magazine. But those were smaller times, the skyline was not so tall, and fame did not demand the most intensive exploitation of available space. So you were not likely to forget "In Prison" and the chain-gang men sometimes at home for the weekend and *their striped trousers hanging on the wash line.*

Poets can, of course, write prose. They can write it as well as or ill as they write verse, although I think certain slothful and not very intelligent poets are more daring in mediocrity when they write prose, the prose of a review for instance. Sometimes these items on the passing scene show a distraction about word and idea more suitable to the shooing away of the family dog than to a compositional task. Still, when the habit of poetry exists, it will usually invade the poet's prose with a natural suffusion of its peculiar ways. Some have the two talents in a sort of separation. D. H. Lawrence and Thomas Hardy write novels, it seems to me, as novelists—that is, not as poets. Their great production, their themes and ideas, their stories chosen to dramatize a particular history and at the same time to speak of the general fate of human beings: All of this attests to a primary gift for fiction, a conquest of the form so abundant as to seem predestined. They could not refuse to be fiction writers any more than they could refuse to be poets. In their novels we will notice that the thorn of a rose will draw blood at the moment of first love, that the howl of a vicious, virile rabbit will ignite the emotions of a man and woman hesitating in the field. The metaphorical concentrations of poetry quietly seep into the rush and flow of the narration. And yet, neither Hardy nor Lawrence lingered long enough to summon the vast "poetic effects" of Joyce and Proust.

Nothing is more striking to me than the casual prose of poets, with its quick and dashing informality, its mastery of the sudden and offhand, the free and thrown away. "The wretched, fishing jealousies of Leontes." *Fishing?* Yes. That is Coleridge. Corbière's "mild waterfront sensuality"—the words are Laforgue's. Thinking about Mayakovsky's working-class dress, Pasternak saw it not as an affront to the respectable but as a warning to the "black velvet" of Mayakovsky's talent. Protesting the Russian Symbolist's use of images and sets of images as if they were so many handy kitchen utensils, Mandelstam cried out (or so it seems on the page) that an image was inappropriate for everyday use, "just as an icon lamp would be inappropriate for lighting a cigarette."

Elizabeth Bishop's prose, as we read it collected and whole, gives me the idea that she set about the writing as an enterprise, something she would do from time to time with the prose part of her mind. It was the same mind that wrote the poems, but that does not alter the fact that certain of her stories were composed in the generally acceptable manner of the time. I think particularly of "The Baptism," "The Farmer's Children," "Gwendolyn," and "The Housekeeper." I notice that each appeared in due course in such places as *Harper's Bazaar* and *The New Yorker,* and were reprinted in the "Best" collections of the year.

These stories are a skillful blending of the parts; they know how to give information, how to dramatize a scene, and how to reach the popular drift of "epiphany" at the end. (Perhaps only a poet could have loved Gwendolyn for her beautiful name: "Its dactyl trisyllables could have gone on forever so far as I was concerned.") The stories are genuine. You learn from them, and your emotions are solicited by the fate of the characters and the construction of the scene. They are fine examples of the kind of fiction still offered weekly and monthly by the more thoughtful magazines and indicate to me that Elizabeth Bishop certainly could have been a fiction writer had she wished it.

Little in that to amaze. What is startling, on the other hand, is that her best prose fictions ("The Sea and Its Shore," "In Prison," "In the Village") are aesthetically radical, rich, and new in conception and tone. They are "experimental," as we used to say. In the late 1930s, the fiction in the little magazines often struggled with the challenge of Kafka. It was possible to come up with an abstract and fixed situation of interest, but to uncover the mobility of the abstract is a rare gift. The static must move the mind, the invention, in a swirl of significance both intellectual and emotional. Much must happen from the point of stasis, otherwise there is a nullity, and with so much stripped away there is boredom.

"The Sea and Its Shore" is a magical instance of creative invention. A man, with no biography, is hired to keep the beach free of paper. For this purpose, he is given a stick with a nail set in the end, a wire basket in which to burn the day's trash, and a little house, a primitive beach shelter. Gradually, he begins to read the scraps of paper, to be knowledgeable about what the different kinds look like, the quality of the sheets wet and dry and, of course, the garbled messages on the crumpled sheets. He watches the paper blown about by the wind: "The papers had no discernible goal, no brain, no feeling of race or group. They soared up, fell down, could not decide, hesitated, subsided." As he read the "insect armies of type," everything seemed to become print, the whole world. A sandpiper, rushing here and there, looked like a "point of punctuation." Finally, everything must be burned since "burning paper was his occupation." This little treatise and speculation on floating print, wind-tossed paper, fragments of literature, printed letters, nonsense, mysterious truncations, arrives from the wonderfully resonant center of the given idea. The contemplation of the prodigality and expendability of print by way of the man on the beach and his stick with the nail in it is a pure and serene fiction exemplifying what we mean by inspiration.

Two stories are of great autobiographical interest and one, "In the Village," is a brilliant modern short story. The first, "The Country Mouse," was left unpublished, although it is a finished work. It is not more revealing and heartbreaking than the other; one might wonder why it was withheld.

Elizabeth Bishop was born in 1911 in Worcester, Massachusetts. Her father died less than a year after her birth. Her mother, from Nova Scotia, suffered a mental collapse, which finally became permanent when the child was only five years old. From the death of her father up until the age of seven, Elizabeth Bishop lived with her mother's family in Nova Scotia. At the age of seven, she was suddenly removed to Worcester, to the father's family, taken from a simple farm and small maritime village to the well-to-do manufacturing Bishops of Massachusetts.

"The Country Mouse" tells of this removal. "I had been brought back unconsulted and against my wishes to the house my father had been born in, to be saved from a life of poverty and provincialism, bare feet, suet puddings, unsanitary school slates." In her new home, she was miserable and felt much like the nervous, troublesome family dog, Beppo. The last paragraph of the story underlines the year 1918, the recognition that she at seven years was doomed to her identity, to her "I, I, I," as a poem has it. The story ends: "Why was I a human being?"

"In the Village" tells of the mother's return from the mental hospital when the girl is five years old. A seamstress is brought in to make a new dress that will signify the end of the black-and-white mourning clothes. In the midst of the fitting, the mother screams, the scream of a new collapse and the destruction of hope. "A scream, the echo of a scream, hangs over that Nova Scotian village. No one hears it; it hangs there forever, a slight stain in those pure blue skies."

The story then becomes something else, a brilliant rendering and ordering of certain fresh fictional possibilities. It becomes a sort of sonata of sounds filled with emotions for the child. The scream is balanced by the sound of Nate, the blacksmith, at his anvil. "*Clang.* The pure note: pure and angelic." Another sound enters like a patch of color on a canvas. *Whack.* The little girl is taking the family cow through the village to a grazing space. *Whack* goes the child's directing stick when the cow meanders about and must be gently brought into line.

The child passes by the village houses, one of them the house of Mr. McLean. (I note that is the name of the Boston hospital where the mother of "the scream" is confined until her death, but no significance attaches since Mr. McLean is a wholesome figure in the village scene.) His old dog, Jock, is, in italics, *deaf as a post*. The sweet sounds of a pastoral life and the sound of lost hope in the scream are elements smoothly woven into an original fictional tapestry. The degree of composition is great—the pauses, the contrasts, the simplicity of it so very complicated. The story is true, but it cannot be accurate because of the artfulness.

"The Country Mouse" is finely written but written in a spirit much closer to the documentary, to the statement. "My mother was not dead. She was in a sanitorium, in another prolonged 'nervous breakdown.'" And "I had been brought back unconsulted." For a sensitive and reserved nature, autobiographical accuracy is a greater deterrence to publication than the deeper and more disturbing transformations of experience by art. So "The Country Mouse" lay in the drawer, and "In the Village" was published.

The portrait of Marianne Moore was also found unpublished and somewhat unsettled among the poet's papers. As we have it now, it is one of the best of its kind in our literature, a literature more barren than most in significant memoirs. It is kindly, even adoring. The Moore household in Brooklyn, the cadence of the speech, the remembered odd scene, the visit to the circus are treasures of eccentricity and authenticity. Above all, the portrait is illuminated by the equity that prevails between the remembered Marianne Moore and the remembering Elizabeth Bishop. Still, I think perhaps it was withheld not from dissatisfaction but because of a squeamishness about the process of documentation, a hesitation about imposition, about *using*.

Reading over the portrait of Marianne Moore, it occurs to me that Elizabeth Bishop appears to us to have been more like the older poet than she was in life. The friendship leaves things somewhat askew. Both were discreet, brilliant, original, unmarried, quirky, and refined in taste and manners. But Elizabeth Bishop's life was far more complicated—or showed more stress and volatility, since we never know about the inner life. She was less spectacular in wholeness of being, more contemporary indeed as a soul living out the years.

Many things—her orphanage only one of them—weighed on her spirit. She knew also the weight of drinking and the weight of the years of not drinking. She had asthma attacks, allergies, and love affairs that did not always end happily, far from it. She was as open to experience in space as Marianne Moore was pleased to be confined. She went far out to sea in both the literal and metaphorical sense. Like some figure in Thomas Mann, the cold north and the treacherous passions of the south met in her nature. She loved houses and objects, and she had an eye for them, for shells and feathered necklaces made by the Indians of Brazil, for treasures carefully chosen and looked after. And for larger acquisitions also: handsome pieces of furniture, chests and bureaus made from Brazilian woods in various shades and decorated with the diamond patterns of Minas. There was the modern house in Petrópolis, in the hills where the emperor used to have his summer palace. The house was thoughtful and careful, set near a waterfall, and everything in it was standing in its place, arranged just so. There was the ancient house in hard-to-get-to, historic, beautiful Ouro Prêto, a folly perhaps, but who could travel to Ouro Prêto and not put a hand to a fine, falling-down treasure of bygone days in a Brazil nearly out of its mind with love for modernity?

As I remember, there was very little money. What had passed on to Elizabeth came from one of those faded family businesses and from investments that seemed to wither in the box. To go here and there, to have the things and the houses, required an awful prudence and watchfulness, and yet the span was daring and profligate. She *would* go up to the Amazon, even if she was quite uncomfortable doing so. Strange things happened in her presence, emanations, a sudden efflorescence that might have come from the rubbing of a lamp. Once, we were in a museum in Rio where there were many Indian artifacts, when Elizabeth suddenly stopped and said, "Look." We turned around, and there was a group of naked Indians looking at Indian artifacts.

And then she left Brazil after so many years and returned home to take up the life of our kind in order to make a living. That is, she began to teach, even though for such a long time she had been afraid or shy of it, even shy about giving readings. Her last post was at Harvard. There she found an apartment, not in Cambridge or on Beacon Hill but down on the waterfront, as a sort of pioneer in the development of that part of the city, a modern and very handsome development but a bit out of the way.

Many look forward to the publication of Elizabeth Bishop's letters, look forward to knowing in full the incomparable glow, the luster of the thoughts and sights written in her small, curling, rather crooked script. Someone is weeding the garden, another has just come up the road in the inconvenient tropics.

Elizabeth Bishop was indeed a perfectionist. She was also a natural writer with an unusual patience; nothing appears to have been excavated with visible sweat and aching muscle. And yet perhaps it was that the great natural gifts seemed too easy, and she must wait to make everything absolutely right in tone and rhythm, without insistence. She didn't want to leave too much paper on the beach.

(1984)

Tru Confessions

~ ~ ~

Chatty, gossipy remembrances of the deplorable history of Truman Capote's last years may be read, in some instances, as revenge or payment-due for the dead author's assaultive portraits of friends and enemies, although few of the interlocutors can command Capote's talent for the vicious, villainous, vituperative adjective. George Plimpton has spent some years tracking down and taking down the remarks of those who crossed Truman's journey to literary fame and to his unique crocodilian celebrity. The remarks are deftly arranged to avoid lumps of monologue piling up one after another like wood stacked for the winter. Instead the voices having their say about the charms and deficits of the absent one find Plimpton at the console professionally mixing the sound, as it were. His phrase for the effect is the unrehearsed, companionable exchange at a cocktail party. This is a large accommodation to raw opinion, to mincing literary judgments of hapless inappropriateness, to character analysis sweet as peaches or impugning as a jailhouse witness for the prosecution. It must be said that method and result have a suitability to the subject, since Capote himself, when not writing, was party-going, forever receiving and producing banter about feckless stumblings and torrid indiscretions.

He was born in 1924 in New Orleans and spent his early years in Monroeville, Alabama. His mother, Lillie Mae Faulk, married at seventeen a man named Arch Persons by whom she had the child, Truman. He was left in the care of relatives, maiden ladies of an eccentric turn useful to the Southern literature of Capote's period. After a time his mother divorced and the son was brought to New York and to Connecticut, where Lillie Mae, name now changed to Nina, married Joseph Capote, who adopted the child under the name of Truman Garcia Capote. *Other Voices, Other Rooms* was published when Truman was twenty-four years old, and this happy beginning of his creative life was in pitiable contrast to his family life. His mother committed suicide five years later, and two years after that Mr. Capote was sent to Sing Sing prison for forgery and grand larceny.

So Truman was on his own and on his way. He was an early master of camp flamboyance and defiance. He was short, effeminate, with a very noticeable, high-pitched, whining voice. And pretty enough, if never quite as fetching as the photograph that enhanced the cover of *Other Voices, Other Rooms*. It appears that with his curious voice, his ways, he decided to brazen it out, to be himself with an ornamental courage and an impressive conceit. He was a figure, what old ladies used to call a "sketch," and smart and amusing, ambitious as a writer and as a society darling, a coquette of wit at the great tables, on the yachts, in the splendid houses in Italy, France and Mexico. Southern accent, cascades of anecdote, boy genius, as all including himself conceded, and productive in the hours of the afternoon when the hostess was napping.

Other Voices, Other Rooms: the best of his down-home fictions, confidently written, picturing a small-town world in the South. Motheaten grandeur, garrulous ne'er-do-wells, colored-folk exchanges in the kitchen with the only souls who lift a hand and here named Missouri, called Zoo, and her Papadaddy, Jesus Fever, and others who enter the action with drag-queen names like Miss Wisteria and the hermit, Little Sunshine. It is a coming-of-age story for young Joel Knox, as the fictions of his closest Southern contemporaries are likely to be: Carson McCullers's *The Heart Is a Lonely Hunter* and *The Member of the Wedding;* Harper Lee's *To Kill a Mockingbird.* We might note that in these books the girls are as tomboyish as Capote's Joel is girlish. Reading over these writers brings to mind the triumph of their contemporary Flannery O'Connor, painting a similar landscape and filling it not with cute hunchbacks and dwarfs but with predatory swamp rats, literally God-forsaken Bible salesmen intoning their handy lies in magical speech rhythms, all transcending the fictional clichés in the dramaturgy of the generation after Faulkner.

In Capote's novel, Joel Knox, age twelve, has been left in the care of his relations after the death of his mother and the flight of his father. At last he is summoned by the father, now married to Miss Amy, to join him at Skully's Landing, a run-down estate that will have no modern plumbing facilities or electricity, but the boy will discover that once in the parlor there were gold draperies, a gilded sofa of lilac velvet, and so on—all now covered with dust. Both the present decay and the parlor trumpery of a more glamorous past are not unexpected when the domestic scenery is to be assembled for a place called Skully's Landing and in a Southern state.

The father does not appear, nor is information given about him until later in the novel, and then we learn that he is upstairs, paralyzed, and communicating his needs by throwing tennis balls down the stairs. The plot is complicated by ghostly appearances, crazy down-South ways of passing the time, but we can find it held together by the sweetness of the boy's nature and a lyrical generosity about the follies of grown-ups. And by the kindness of the black cook, Zoo, a sort of kissing cousin to Ethel Waters in the staging of *The Member of the Wedding.*

The most interesting of the "characters" living in Skully's Landing is Cousin Randolph, a connection of the stepmother, Miss Amy.

Randolph, a painter and sherry-drinking idler, has a history; he's been around, studied abroad, and while in Madrid copying the old masters in the Prado he meets Dolores, a cold but somehow overwhelming beauty, and they become lovers. The two of them abandon Europe and land in Florida, where Dolores takes up with Pepe, an impressively muscled boxer, mean, handsome, potent and violent. Randolph, in a ferocious epiphany, discovers himself in love with Pepe and filled with a devastating longing.

> I could not endure to see him suffer; it was agony to watch him
> fight ... I gave him money, brought him cream-colored hats,
> gold bracelets (which he adored, and wore like a woman),
> shoes in bright Negro colors, candy silk shirts ...

The end of it was Pepe, drunk, destroying Randolph's paintings, calling him "terrible names" and breaking his nose. And then Pepe is off with Dolores, off no one knows where, but Randolph sends letters to random post offices here and there. "Oh, I know that I shall never have an answer. But it gives me something to believe in. And that is peace."

Randolph is a nice, rather lachrymose fellow, a well-born "queer" of some cultivation and too many afternoon sips from the bottle, altogether a configuration at home in the little towns, and no doubt still there. Joel, the boy, is moved by Randolph's confession and also moved to an awakening of his own nature. In a final scene they go to an old abandoned hotel, once a brothel, and in a somewhat murky rendering spend the night together.

Plimpton has printed a review of *Other Voices, Other Rooms* by the majorful Diana Trilling, which was published in *The Nation,* January 31, 1948. Despite the "claptrap" she praises the compositional virtuosity of the novel and finds that such skill in one so young "represents a kind of genius." However, she is morally distressed about Cousin Randolph, "a middle-aged degenerate aesthete," and more dismayed by what she reads as the *lesson* of the plot.

At the end of the book the young Joel turns to homosexual love offered him by Randolph, and we realize that in his slow piling up of nightmare details Mr. Capote has been attempting to recreate the emotional background to sexual inversion. What his book is saying is that a boy becomes a homosexual when the circumstances of his life deny him the other, more normal gratifications of his need for affection.

The devil made me do it. A shirking of moral responsibility, as she sees it, and in no way faithful to the text and to Joel's relation with Randolph. One thing you can say about Capote is that the "closet" was never, never anything to him except a place to find bits of silver cloth, old faded snapshots, love letters and trinkets.

The Grass Harp is blown about by the winds of whimsy, here, rocking the cradle in the treetop. The narrator, again a young boy once more sent to live with relations, two unmarried ladies who are sisters. They and others spend a good deal of time picnicking and chatting in a house high up in a chinaberry tree. The tree house was fifteen or twenty years old, "spacious, sturdy, a model of a tree house, it was like a raft floating in a sea of leaves ... to sail along the cloudy coastline of every dream." Up in the tree you can hear the grass harp "always telling a story—it knows the stories of all the people on the hill, of all the people who have ever lived, and when we are dead it will tell ours, too." The novel was composed while Capote was living in an "absolutely marvelous" villa in Sicily, named La Fontana Vecchia. It was, astonishingly, turned into a grandiose Broadway production, music by Virgil Thomson and sets by Cecil Beaton. Thomson describes the debacle:

The set which Cecil designed, particularly the one with the big tree, was so large and heavy that nobody ever saw it until the opening in Boston. There was no point in setting it up in New York for rehearsals ... On the Sunday afternoon before we left for Boston, there was a professional matinee...Everybody wept buckets. Then we moved up to Boston, and once we got into the set, nobody out there in the seats ever wept anymore. The set was too large and complicated—very grand, something for the Metropolitan Opera.

Well, no matter. Such was Capote's celebrity that "House of Flowers," a scrawny short story set in Haiti, was mounted as a Broadway musical with music by Harold Arlen, set by Oliver Messel, choreography by George Balanchine and direction by Peter Brook. The A list for little Tru.

The South, the days of youth gone by, the downtown with its shops and taverns and their funny names, the collection of harmlessly deranged kinfolk, were there to be called on by the writer as a sort of *spécialité*, like Key lime pie and conch fritters, to be exploited again and again in holiday postcards such as *A Christmas Memory, One Christmas,* and *The Thanksgiving Visitor.*

Cousin Randolph, the tree house, and the rest of it will serve the muse for a time, and then Capote will bring his fiction to New York City, that place Marianne Moore, in a poem, found "starred with tepees of ermine and peopled with foxes." In his portmanteau, Capote will be carrying, like some revivifying patent medicine, a very useful stimulant in the composition of the successful *Breakfast at Tiffany's,* that is, Christopher Isherwood's *Goodbye to Berlin.*

Into Plimpton's time capsule we have the wish of several young, or once young, ladies to be the inspiration for the beguiling Holly Golightly, the center of *Breakfast at Tiffany's.* Doris Lilly, identified as a gossip columnist and author, is as insistent as if she were the claimant in an inheritance battle.

There is an awful lot of me in Holly Golightly. There's much more of me than there is of Carol Marcus (who is now Carol Marcus Matthau) and a girl called Bee Dabney, a painter. More of me than either of these two ladies. I know.

Primogeniture does not adhere to any of the pals circling around the house in New York. Fortunately for the attractiveness of *Breakfast at Tiffany's* (1958), the model is the "Sally Bowles" section in Isherwood's book of 1938. In both novellas, the first-person narrator is a young writer who finds himself living next door to an interesting young woman, Sally Bowles in a Berlin pension and Holly Golightly in a shabby New York town house broken up into small apartments.

Both girls are beautiful, each afloat and searching for a place to land with a man if not rich at least giving evidence of being in touch with money. They attach themselves to one after another, only to find themselves abruptly dropped, an annoyance from which they bounce back in a way that reminds one of professional boxers, on the mat one minute and up the next, a little unsteady, but with fist in a salute. Among the many correspondences between Isherwood and Capote we have the fleeing man's tendency to leave a letter.

Klaus to Sally Bowles:

My dear little girl, you have adored me too much.... You must be brave, Sally, my poor darling child.... I was invited a few nights ago to a party at the house of Lady Klein, a leader of the British aristocracy. I met there a beautiful and intelligent young English girl named Miss Gore-Eckersley....

And so it goes.

José, a Brazilian diplomat making his escape from Holly Golightly's radar:

My dearest little girl, I have loved you knowing that you were not as others. But conceive of my despair upon discovering ... how very different you are from the manner of woman a man of my faith and career could hope to make his wife ... I am gone home.

Sally Bowles gives herself a *faux* "country" background in a very amusing imitation:

> Daddy's a terrible snob, although he pretends not to be.... He's the most marvellous business man. And about once a month he gets absolutely dead tight and horrifies all Mummy's smart friends.

Holly Golightly, from Tulip, Texas, real name Lulamae Barnes, was a runaway starving orphan picked up by a country horse doctor whom she married at age fourteen, and ran away from to New York. The horse doctor turns up in New York hoping to reclaim his wife and providing one of Capote's most inventive comic interludes. However, Tulip, Texas, does not always inhabit Holly Golightly's conversational style—the rhythms of Sally Bowles perhaps overwhelming national boundaries. (There is a mention of French lessons given to smother Holly's Texas defect in preparation for a film career.) Nevertheless here she is in a typical locution: "But, after all, he *knows* I'm preggers. Well, I am, darling. Six weeks gone. I don't see why that should surprise you. It didn't me. Not *un peu* bit." At times her diction crosses to the Rhine. "I suppose I'll sleep until Saturday, really get a good *schluffen.*"

The two stories come to an end on a postcard. Sally Bowles, off on her amorous journey, sends a card from Paris, another from Rome with no address.

> That was six years ago. So now I am writing her. When you read this, Sally, if you ever do—please accept it as a tribute, the sincerest I can pay, to yourself, and to our friendship. And send me another postcard.

Holly in a postcard goodbye from South America: *"Brazil was beastly but Buenos Aires the best. Not Tiffany's, but almost ... Will let you know address when I know it myself.*" And the narrator reflects: "But the address, if it ever existed, never was sent, which made me sad, there was so much I wanted to write her."

Breakfast at Tiffany's has its own charms, and if the astute Capote has done a transatlantic rearrangement perhaps we can think of it in musical terms: Variations on a Theme by Haydn. Something like that.

Christopher Isherwood, resident of Los Angeles, was present at Capote's funeral, and Plimpton publishes what the novelist John Gregory Dunne remembered about the moment. "And Chris did the most graceful thing of all. He said, 'There was one wonderful thing about Truman. He always made me laugh.' He started to laugh, turned around, and sat down. Perfectly graceful and gracious." And then Carol Marcus Matthau, who in Doris Lilly's deposition is definitely *not* the model for Holly Golightly, has some unpleasant things to say about Isherwood. (Unpleasantness about persons not the object of the enterprise in "oral biography" is a treacherous fallout of the indiscriminate form.) Truman Capote in his fiction never achieved anything as rich and beautiful as the stories in *Goodbye to Berlin*, of which "Sally Bowles" is only one, or as brilliant as *Mr. Norris Changes Trains* and *Prater Violet*. Not to the point here, since with a few exceptions, it appears that the only "brilliant writer" and "genius" the assembly is aware of is Truman Capote. No, mournful as it is to remember, there is another writer mentioned again and again in Plimpton's pages, a writer who, like Capote, knew a lot of rich people and who wrote something herein called "Proustian."

In November 1966 Capote gave in the Plaza Hotel in New York what you might call his "in-cold-blood party" for five hundred guests. As a sort of provenance for the fête, the calendar moves backward. The murder of the Clutter family, husband and wife and two teenage children, occurred in November 1959, in the town of Holcomb, Kansas. After reading an account in the press, Capote soon took off for the site of the crime. Two young men were arrested a month later and in March 1960 convicted of the crime and sentenced to death. On April 14, 1965, Perry Smith and Dick Hickock, the convicted murderers of the Clutter family, were hanged in the Kansas State Penitentiary for Men in Lansing, Kansas. Six years had passed after the conviction, by way of legal appeals and stays of execution, before the author, Truman Capote, could write *finis* to *In Cold Blood*, his account of the killers, the detectives, the town, the trial. Six months after the hanging, the serialization in *The New Yorker* began, and publication in book form soon followed.

At last it was Carnival time, with beads, masks, spikes of feathers in voodoo headdresses, bunny fur, witch wigs and a band playing show tunes. The party at the Plaza acquired the fame of a coronation for the very successful book, still a work of riveting interest for its portrait of the misshapen bodies, language, highway felonies and idiotic plans and dreams of two savage, talkative, rawhide murderers, Perry Smith and Dick Hickock.

After the publication of the book, Capote spends a good deal of his time and thought on nomenclature, that is, his naming of the work a "nonfiction novel" and claiming to be the only begetter of the form. Sometimes in the discussion one might be reading about an eagle-eyed blind man, but that would have a greater philosophical interest. In most works of any length about crimes there is much that is not mere documentation; there is the setting of the scene: the neat little trailer before the blood-splattered walls, the dog at the garbage can with an arm in it, the handsome house, usually called a mansion, where the deceased was just putting night cream on her face when ... There are scenes in Capote that appear to be "fiction"; one early chapter has Nancy Clutter, the daughter, at home on the day of her death, chatting on the phone about a lesson in pie-baking or about her boyfriend, Bobby. This is followed by Mrs. Clutter in a conversation with Jolene, the thirteen-year-old for whom Nancy was to give the lesson in pie-baking. The Clutters are dead, and the reader supposes the quite banal chapter to be what the author would imagine to be the actions of a "normal" family living out their last hours in Kansas farm country. Not easy to enliven since the family is denied the bizarrerie of Alabama homesteads. However, in an interview, Capote seems to disclaim imagination and to place the origin of everything in the testimony of the living who overheard or took part in the conversations.

Perry Smith, thirty-one years old, and Dick Hickock, twenty-eight years old, are on parole from prison and, at the beginning of the composition, are making their journey to commit a robbery and kill whoever will frustrate their plan. They made their way to the house in Kansas and in the interest of "leaving no witnesses" slaughtered the four family members. The case was solved when the police were told by a cellmate who had once worked for Mr. Clutter that he had given information about a safe in the house containing ten thousand dollars—given the information to Smith and Hickock as they gathered their meager belongings and abilities and were set free. There was no safe in the house, and the cons came away with forty dollars, a radio and a pair of binoculars.

On the way from birth to death, as it were, there is an appallingly rich lode of archival gold for Capote to shape and polish and send to market, all of which he does with a skillful hand. The detectives on their way to pawnshops and motels and the very striking confession of the killers about their wanderings before and after, their description of their gruesome destruction of each single Clutter; accounts of the early life of the killers by their relatives and their own summations given at the request of a court psychiatrist; Capote's interviews, his visit to the holding cells where the two awaited execution, his claim of having corresponded with each twice a week for the five years between conviction and execution.

While both the condemned and the author were waiting out the stays, Capote made no secret of his *qué sera, sera* impatience to get it over with. Quite a few remembered this curious bit of literary oral history. When the book was published, it did occasion jokes and some serious memories which the pugnacious and vindictive Capote did not find amusing. On a TV show, William Buckley, Jr., said, "Well, we've only had a certain number of executions in the last few years—whatever it was—and two of them were for the personal convenience of Truman Capote." The composer Ned Rorem at a party heard Truman say about his book, "But it can't be published until they're executed, so I can hardly wait." Rorem, when the book came out, sent a letter to be published in a magazine, which said, among other things: "Capote got two million and his heroes got the rope." (Needless to say, Rorem got *his* in Capote's later book *Answered Prayers*.)

Party-going with its temptation to social misdemeanors was also the ground of a confrontation between Capote and the English critic Kenneth Tynan. After hearing that the execution date had been irrevocably set, Capote, according to Tynan's wife's interview with Plimpton, said: "I'm beside myself! Beside myself! Beside myself with joy!" Tynan reviewed *In Cold Blood* for *The Observer* in London:

> For the first time, an influential writer of the front rank has been placed in a position of privileged intimacy with criminals about to die and, in my view, done less than he might have to save them … No piece of prose, however deathless, is worth a human life.

Truman, in his reply to the paper, wrote that Tynan had "the morals of a baboon and the guts of a butterfly."

Capote never showed an interest in political or moral debate, and perhaps that was prudent since ideas, to some degree, may define one's social life and could just be excess baggage he didn't need to bring aboard; and, worse, boring, like the ruins and works of art he declined to get off the yacht to see. In any case, he could not have "saved" Smith and Hickock, who had confessed; the appeals rested upon legal matters such as the competence of the state-appointed defense attorneys, whose summation took only ninety minutes—the jury before returning the death sentence "deliberated" only forty minutes.

Still, one might reflect about the book and wonder what a sentence of life without possibility of parole might have been for the execution of the nonfiction novel. Two alive central characters with plenty of time to become jailhouse lawyers would not have been useful to the author, publisher or movie-maker. These are troublesome men. And then there is the actual hanging in the dreadful Kansas shed, "a cavernous storage room, where on the warmest day the air is moist and chilly"; and: "The hangman coughed—impatiently lifted his cowboy hat and settled it again, a gesture somehow reminiscent of a turkey buzzard huffing, then smoothing its neck feathers—and Hickock, nudged by an attendant, mounted the scaffold steps." Wouldn't that have been missed?

There is a moment in *In Cold Blood* when Perry Smith says to his partner in the murders: "I just don't believe anyone could get away with a thing like that." In *Answered Prayers,* the unfinished nonfiction novel, using the actual names of a transcontinental cast of mostly well-known persons or, if disguised by a fictitious name, carefully designed to be identifiable, Capote made his own shackled step to the social gallows. The first of the scatalogical offenses to be published was "La Côte Basque," a story or something, taking place in the fashionable restaurant of the same name. It is lunchtime and the proprietor is seating or not seating according to the heraldic rankings of the metropolitan scene. Capote, under his *nom de plume* of P. B. Jones, or "Jonesy," is lunching with "Lady Coolbirth" in the absence of the Duchess of Windsor, she having canceled because of a bout of hives.

Champagne is ordered, which somehow promotes a scurrilous bit of anecdote about the composer Cole Porter. On and on to the supposedly overheard conversation of two identified nymphs about town. Across the way in the restaurant, dining with a priest, is the wife who in a *famous* court case was acquitted of having shot her well-born, rich husband. But she is not to escape the dossier proposed by Jonesy and Lady Coolbirth detailing her rise from a "country-slum" in West Virginia, real trash with a pretty face, who went on to a whirl on the continental carousel where she was known as "Madame Marmalade—her favorite *petit déjeuner* being hot cock butter with Dundee's best." The woman in fact committed suicide a few days before "La Côte" appeared in *Esquire* magazine. Whether she knew the unveiling in store for her is not certain, but at least she was out of the way.

Others were still around to meet themselves in degrading tableaux, sometimes performing under an alias which was a pasted-on Woolworth's mustache that failed to fool any tots in the playground. The chitchat proceeds: "Why would an educated, dynamic, very rich and well-hung Jew go bonkers for a cretinous Protestant size forty who wears low-heeled shoes and lavender water?" It seems the "porcine sow" was the governor's wife, and in a grotesque seduction on the Pierre Hotel sheets the gentleman was proving something, avenging the old days when even the most established Jews weren't welcome in WASP country clubs, boarding schools, and so on. The gentleman in this unaccountably destructive and self-destructive portrait was everywhere quickly identified as the husband of the most elegant woman in the city. From what we read she had been for some years a true friend, the most valuable and perhaps most surprising trophy, solid silver, Truman had won, scored in the field.

Capote had, like a leper with a bell announcing his presence, horrified those he most treasured, and with many he was marked with the leper's visible deformities, a creature arousing fear of infection. There is much ado about this in Plimpton: calls unanswered, intervention by friends unavailing. "Unspoiled Monsters," another section of *Answered Prayers,* concerns itself with the chic homosexual world and what used to be called the stars of stage, screen, and radio. P. B. Jones is again the narrator, about thirty-five, a writer, sponger, and wit: "Starting at an early age, seven or eight or thereabouts, I'd run the gamut with many an older boy and several priests and also a handsome Negro gardener. In fact, I was a kind of Hershey Bar whore—"

Jonesy gets around, to a room in the YMCA, "work" as a prostitute masseur, and off to every grand spot in Europe. It's not quite clear just how a back rub could get the little charmer from the Y to the Ritz in Paris, Harry's Bar in Venice, everywhere. But he must move about in order to reveal all the habits, hang-ups, perversions, fears, unpaid bills of the slit-savoring bitches, muff-divers, whining masochists, drug addicts, patrons of Father Flanagan's Nigger Queen Kosher Cafe. Woe to all who passed his way, with Capote toting their names, occupations, contorted faces, the passports of their public identities, material that makes *Answered Prayers* resemble the files of J. Edgar Hoover.

What was Capote thinking of? At times one is led to imagine him afflicted with Tourette's syndrome, a disease described in recent years with much sympathy by Oliver Sacks. It brings on facial tics, not unusual in other physical misfortunes; the true peculiarity of the symptoms is echolalia, endless talking characterized by an uncontrollable flow of obscenities. Still, Capote knew all there was to know about gossip and understood that in a gifted form it will not be about imagined persons but about real people, not about John Doe but about Cecil Beaton, to name one of his many punitive divertissements.

In his own love life, about which he never wrote, the record seems to ally Truman with Cousin Randolph and his sudden devasting passion for the boxer Pepe. First, the man who came to fix the air conditioner and was snatched away from his wife and children, spiffed up with new clothes, dental rehabilitation, and taken along to the great palazzos in Venice, to the yachts sailing in blue summer waters. The poor fellow gets very bad reviews at every port and perhaps to his credit returned them by taking off, leaving Truman "devastated," in a "big collapse."

And there was John O'Shea, a sort of financial adviser, with wife and four children, and ready to abandon all for a luxe life with Truman. Vodka, gunplay, theft and disappearance of O'Shea; heart-break and atonement by Truman, who helped the O'Shea family and brought the attractive, honest daughter to stay in the flat in New York.

Capote himself wasn't a pleasant vision in his last years of drugs and drink, but he collected new friends who cared for him up until his death in Los Angeles, out West where new life, if you can hang on, begins. An unexpected fact from his last will and testament: In honor of Newton Arvin, a critic and professor of literature and an early friend of Truman and his writing, Capote endowed two handsome yearly prizes, one for fifty thousand dollars and the other for one hundred thousand dollars. They were to be given to writers of imaginative criticism.

(*1998*)

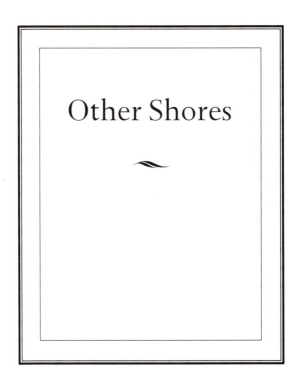

Other Shores

Something Out There:
Nadine Gordimer

～～～

Something Out There" is the title story of Nadine Gordimer's new collection. Eighty-five pages of fictional mastery. Those who know this unsurpassed talent might say, Once more, and not surprising. Note the way the author opens the plot, arranges the magical correspondences, finds the fixed points, and sets them in a broad open space where many drifting, always to the point, things can wander.

Something is out there. *It*, a large mysterious shadow, is photographed by a young man with his new bar-mitzvah camera. A Persian tabby and an old dachshund are found mauled, and the newspapers speak of "wild animals in the plush Johannesburg suburbs." The excitement is a "nice change from the usual sort of news, these days." The usual sort is not a puzzle since this is South Africa.

Meanwhile, a few paragraphs on, something else is out there. Mr. Klopper, an Afrikaner rental agent, is closing a deal with a young English-speaking couple who seem to want a few months of rundown privacy and will settle for a decayed farm that has been on the agent's books for three years. The vague young couple meets with

Mr. Klopper and his wife in the Kloppers' house, a plausible if self-conscious new place filled with modern appliances and crocheted slings for hanging plants and a minibar with stools covered in the skins of an impala—and, for all that, a suburban house retaining the gloom of the "long, gaunt passages" of the farmhouses of Klopper's youth "when the Boers were a rural people." The dark hallways in the anxious hopefulness of the house design return the Kloppers to history, give them a sort of genetic weight, a shading of melancholy generations behind the split-level lounge and the dried-flower-and-shell pictures.

Something out there is making a noise in the trees on the golf course where four doctors are looking for a lost ball; an illicit couple in a borrowed house hears a scruffling sound outside the window next to the bed. (A spy sent by his wife, or is it her husband ruining the afternoon?) Out there on the rented farm, the couple is joined by two young black men dropped off by a van. The men give the proper signal and settle in with due accommodation to apartheid. (They will, if seen, pretend to be newly hired farmhands.) The four, saboteurs, begin their preparations by bricking up a shed to hold rifles, ammunition, detonators, and timing devices with which they will blow up a power station.

The shadow, the noise in the trees will turn out to be a lost baboon, which will at last be found dead, although by that time its celebrity will have begun to fade because "some of the suburbs the creature had made uneasy were without electricity for eighteen hours" because of the explosion. "No one has ever found out who let the baboon loose" and "nobody knows who the saboteurs, dead or alive, really are."

Thus the plot, the skeleton of a bold work imagined in layers of episode, some like a cloud briefly overhead and others like a collision on the highway, all blundering intrusions and fortuities binding the larger world to the baboon and the bombing preparations. A black man, tending a corn patch left over from his days with the previous owner, disturbs the terrorists with his timid, uncertain goings and comings; from the back of the house of Sergeant Chapman, a police interrogator, a leg of venison disappears into the jaws of *it*, and the sergeant learns the news of it while he is having a snack with his fellow policeman at a Chinese takeout; Eddie, one of the black terrorists, makes an imprudent visit to Johannesburg to look at the things in the supermarket and clothing stores, just to see once more what the old streets are like. The unblinking Mrs. Klopper turns her car into the farm's driveway to give the nice young couple a tin of her homemade biscuits.

The baboon is nothing special, just the native species, the old stock. The terrorists are strayed native species also. The person and the animal in disorientation appear on the landscape and disappear into its vastness, leaving gnawed bones and a hole in the ground near the power station where, filled with ammunition, Mrs. Klopper's biscuits tin will be found. Everything falls into place, connects, flashes forth with a naturalness so very artful—the winged contrivances of reality if there is a gift for them.

Pale freckled eggs. These words begin the masterpiece, the novel *The Conservationist* (1975). "Eleven pale freckled eggs. A whole clutch of guinea fowl eggs." Mehring, a man from the city, has bought a large farm for a weekend retreat—only twenty-five miles from town. He thinks of it as a tax deduction, a good investment, a means of impressing his girlfriend and also—this with a rather subdued, businesslike lyricism—a way to get in touch with the pastures and fields that are South Africa. Mehring is annoyed that the children should be playing a game with the eggs that they have found in the field, and he is thinking about this nuisance while his black herdsman, Jacobus, is trying to get his attention. Jacobus is trying to tell the weekend farmer something: "Something happen, something happen." What he has to tell is that the body of a dead black man, a stranger, has been found on the place.

The dead body of a black man, *one of them* as they say, lies on the farm, a little earth, a bit of canvas covering it—a corruption. Mehring, a prosperous businessman "in pigiron," an *uitlander*, German, from way back, lies down on his land one afternoon and nods off, to awaken "staring into the eye of the earth with earth at his mouth." In this curious moment, he is merely a body, a stranger seeping into the earth like that other one whose rotting face and shreds of clothing are still there even after a flood of monstrous violence almost destroys the farm. As the waters receded

> a pair of shoes appeared. They held still the shapes of feet, like the ones put out to dry up at the compound. They held more than the shape; they were attached still to a larger object, a kind of long bundle of rags and mud and some other tattered substance more fibrous, less formless than mud, something that suggested shreds, despite its sodden state and its near-fusion with mud and rotted cloth—something that differed, even in this advanced state of decay, from any other substance, as a wafer of what was once fine silk retains unmistakably its particular weave and quality, its persistent durability in frailty, even when it is hardly more than an impress of cross-woven strands, a fossil imprint against the earth that has buried it.

The rotting body is the twin of Mehring's indifferent occupation of the land, his assumption, a whim in fact, of the crops and cattle and black families hovering about, working and trying to get through on the phone to the city to tell him *something happen.*

Mehring's last action in the novel also takes place on the ground—a powerful, appalling nightmare in which, on his way to town, almost there, he gives a lift to a girl stranded in the rain, and somehow, because he finds her hand on his thigh, he consents to turn off into a filthy, ashy mine dump, a menacing bit of city wasteland. The girl is a prostitute, perhaps colored, and has set him up to be robbed, disgraced, discovered, ruined. Scenes from the farm and from his life float through his mind. "Come. Come and look, they're all saying. What is it? Who is it? It's Mehring. It's Mehring, down there."

The Conservationist? The title does not quite prepare for the creative ferocity of this spectacular novel. True, Mehring likes to say that the point of owning acres is to make them pay, get them in shape. But the land is not pigiron shares on the market; it is a phantasmagoria of fickle realities: alfalfa, a cow "borned Friday," a river, swamps, weed-choked beauty, fires, floods, broken pumps, a mile of willow trees, and black Jacobus and Izak and Solomon and all the others. "A typical Transvaal landscape, that you either find dull and low-keyed or prefer to all others (they said)." It is the Indians selling things in their store down the road and the Afrikaner family making a Sunday visit, it is the very poor house, scarcely furnished, not suitable for ambitious assignations—and the body of the dead man which the authorities will not bother to remove. Four hundred acres of veld and fields, the ownership of which for those in industry can be "a sign of having remained fully human and capable of enjoying the simple things of life that poorer men can no longer afford."

Simple things? You drive the Mercedes up for a weekend, and there has been a fire. "The whole farm stinks like an ashtray.... A rat with head intact and eyes open is laid out.... Up into some of the older trees fire has thrust a surgeon's red-gloved hand, cauterizing through a vaginal gap or knot-hole."

And then: "The weather came from the Moçambique Channel." It leaves a drowned, nauseating landscape—"obscene whiskered balloons of a dead barbel were turned up to iridescent-backed flies in the steamy sun. The crystal neck of a bottle stuck out in the mud; pappy lumps of sodden fur with rat's tails" and the remains of the dead man.

Fire and flood are not calamities to punish Mehring, the nervous city man. They are merely what he will find along with the alfalfa and willows. (The knowledge of reed and gulley, planted field, rat and bird and tenant is of such completeness one has to acknowledge the great attachment that has instructed the author's eye with an unabating stream of images.) It is a landscape of squalor, disability, and beauty.

Mehring is distracted, shallow, and sensual. On an airplane, returning from a business trip, he seduces a speechless Portuguese
girl *by hand*, perhaps the phrase is; and all very tiring indeed with
no reciprocating touch from the girl. Yet one does not think of
Mehring as meant to be identified by his genital studiousness. He is
a bit swinish, more than a bit, somewhat heavy with his lugubrious
sexuality, a weight of maleness that seems as much a part of Nadine
Gordimer's white South Africa as the mercurial veld, the chained
dogs, the locations where the blacks are herded, the rubbish dumps.

See Mr. De Beer, an Afrikaner papa making a visit with his wife
and children and his son's wife. (Mehring's thought: "To go into
those women must be like using the fleshy succulent plants men in
the Foreign Legion have to resort to.") Old De Beer, "his clothes
filled drum-tight with his body.... The retaining wall of belly and
bunch of balls part the thighs majestically. Oh to wear your man-
hood, fatherhood like that, eh, stud and authority." So, Mehring
also is a not-so-confident man, with nothing much on his mind except sex and business and brief, baffled attentions to his son, who
likes to speak of Namibia and has books on homosexuality in his
knapsack.

Mehring's qualities do not make him a sympathetic, even sneak-
ingly sympathetic, center of the novel. But he is a center who can
attract about him incident and folk and nuisances and gestures,
catastrophes, asides, and demonic conjunctions of meaning. He
lives by way of the cascading art of the structure, the perfection of
language, the oddity and convincingness of the way dialogue and
idea flow and flow and circle back to catch the eddies of things not
quite said.

The farm is large. He can go off anywhere. (Quite frankly, I can't
wait to get away to my old plaas.—There is a mica-glitter of
malice in the polite refusal of weekend invitations. He is still in
demand; he's needed at table. What a pity, and I had such a
charming woman for you.)

He escapes the prostitute's trap, the ashy dump of social annihilation. And out on the farm the blacks bury the scanty flood-scourged remains of the dead stranger. "He took possession of the earth; theirs; one of them." Pale freckled eggs and the naked nose of one of them—a kind of conservation.

—

"Among the people waiting at the fortress was a school girl in a brown and yellow uniform holding a green eiderdown quilt and, by the loop of its neck, a red hot-water bottle." *Burger's Daughter* (1979): Rosa on a visit to her Communist mother in prison. And some years later, Rosa, after an escape to Europe, will make her way back to South Africa and "a woman carrying fruit boxes and flowers" will be at the door on behalf of Rosa herself, detained after Soweto under the Terrorism Act.

That is the frame, the way Nadine Gordimer likes to set things up, as if on an easel. And then the rectangle dissolves, to become only a memory of containment, formal and yet lifelike in the almost infinite repetitions of form in South Africa, itself a four-sided containment, on guard at the corners, pushing all the squirming, anarchic outgrowth back inside.

Now you are free: the true subject of this resonant, unsettling political novel. Free. Rosa's mother has died of an illness, her brother has drowned in the swimming pool, her father, Lionel Burger, died in prison in the third year of a life sentence ("And here life is life").

The blood ties are broken. Rosa is young, reflective, able to attract the reader's full attention, and thus the old word "heroine" does not seem astray. She is a daughter, daughter of the political impossibility of South Africa, reared in the stockade of the ideas and actions of resistance. The narration is a winding road of past and present, the pages put together by a very contemporary sensibility and almost effortlessly controlled by a remarkable, traditional narrative gift. The writer needs a sort of musicality to manage the breaks and shifts and alternating speeds of this kind of composition, and here the conducting spirit is confident indeed.

Rosa's parents married during the black miners' strike in 1946 and were arrested under the Riotous Assemblies Act; the first Afrikaner nationalist government took office the month and the year she was born; she was twelve when Sharpeville occurred and the black protesters were shot in the back. "Imprisonment was part of the responsibilities of grown-up life, like visiting patients [her father]" or, like her mother, banned as a trade unionist, going off each morning to a cooperative run for blacks and coloreds.

Lionel Burger was famous, a celebrity of antiapartheid, an early member of the South African Communist Party. A biographer is ready with pencil as the hearse turns into the cemetery gates, a Swede has made a documentary film, and when Rosa meets the man in Europe who is to become her lover, he remembers signing an Amnesty International petition against the imprisonment of her ailing father. Burger is a doctor, one of those idealists serving black and white, rich and poor, born into a landowning Afrikaner family, educated in Cape Town and Edinburgh. In his final trial, he explains the pity for suffering aroused by his medical studies and his gradual determination against the suffering of his black countrymen. In Marxism he found oppression analyzed as "forces in conflict with economic laws." He joins the white South African army when the Party goes on "promising the blacks liberation through Communism" after Stalin, the Hungarian and Czechoslovakian uprisings, and all the rest.

The life in the novel is a vivacious family chronicle of relatives, comrades and their children, a little black boy named Baasie raised as a member of the family, picnics, swimming lessons, celebrations for the one let out and plannings for the ones taken in. It is a suburban scene of the educated, white middle class with a servant, a swimming pool, the lovable patriarch doctor who visits the sick and responds to the many occasions for martyrdom the society provides. It is the changing country itself, the ANC, the strikes, liberal whites coming into fashion, visits from foreign journalists, black athletes in the news, petitions, protests, propaganda, some exploitation for the cause. For Rosa, a certain naturalness—school days, growing up, first love—survives despite the intense political character of the private life.

Now you are free. Lionel Burger is dead, the mother and brother also. The family house is sold, the doctor's sign on the front removed. Rosa is a "named" person with many restrictions and no passport. She wishes to go to Europe, and the obtaining of a passport is the circumstance for one of the most revealing bits of portraiture in the book.

She solicits the help of Brandt Vermeulen, one of the "New Afrikaners," member of an old and distinguished family who has been to Leyden and Princeton and New York and Paris and has returned to play a complicated role with certain fresh accents. "He and his kind were the first to be sophisticated enough to laugh at the ... Immorality Act," to be bored by the Reform Church and its denunciation of sport and cinema on Sunday. Vermeulen does not shrink from open contact with blacks and proposes a future not of power sharing but a sort of peaceful "co-existence through hard bargaining." It is said of Vermeulen, *"Man!—he won't scruple to invoke Kierkegaard's Either/Or against Hegel's dialectic to demonstrate the justice of segregated lavatories."* He receives Rosa amid his Kandinsky and Georgia O'Keeffe prints, a poster from an African herbalist shop, his beloved servant Mina and her famous ginger cake, his swimming pool, his memories of Lionel Burger. "Your father was marvellous, we talked rugby—of course he'd been a first team fullback in his medical school days—I decided, what did they mean about this red business!"

When Rosa asks about the passport, Vermeulen says self-mockingly, "I don't just whisper in the Prime Minister's ear." But he lays out the terms on which he will make an effort. No meetings with exiles, no "apartheid victim's daughter visits Tower of London, you know the style of thing." He will try, yes. She doesn't have to be kept prisoner like the "Russians do to their dissident families from generation to generation." A year passes, and she is given a passport and, without saying good-bye to anyone, leaves for Europe. At the airport "surveillance watched her go...."

The second part of the book takes place in France. Her father's first wife, now a Madame Bagnelli, takes Rosa to the south of France, and the landscape is another kind of liberation, worldly bohemianism, "a whole world" outside of what Lionel Burger lived for, as the first wife, herself a Communist in youth, puts it. The conversation here is of the Baader-Meinhof gang, of Cohn-Bendit, the Gulag, the new philosophers, Foucault, and food and clothes and lovers. Rosa has an affair with an academic, French, married; one of those memorable and *triste* unions spent very happily—on the time off. In London, she has an unexpected meeting with Baasie, he who had once been the little black boy who lived in her house as a brother and who now repudiates, insults, her father:

> Everyone in the world must be told what a great hero he was and how much he suffered for the blacks. Everyone must cry over him and show his life on television and write in the papers.... Killed in prison. It's nothing. I know plenty blacks like Burger. It's nothing, it's us, we must be used to it.

Rosa returns to South Africa—because of her father and because even her lover, "the one I could talk to," couldn't quite imagine South Africa: *This place, all of us here.* This place, all of us here: the achievement of *Burger's Daughter.*

July's People (1981) is based upon a device, the presumption of a revolution, an immense uprising in South Africa, riots, arson, the whites fleeing the cities. The Smales family—wife, three children, husband, an architect—are offered the chance to make their way to the remote village of their servant, July. They arrive, and once there the claim of the novel is not the revolution in the cities but the presentation of the black village, the horror of the Smales family's sudden adaptation to nothing—the mysteriousness, you might call it, of the actual facts of ancient deprivation, how and where they live. "July's home was not a village but a habitation of mud houses occupied only by members of his extended family."

The opening line of the novel is July's: "—You like to have some cup of tea?" A black (*sic*) comedy beginning? Yes, perhaps, and more prevailing, the comedy, than the author might have intended. July is in his hut, and they, the whites, are there with him. This domestic uprooting is designed to probe the murky gaps in the reasonably liberal souls of the Smales couple by placing them with the black city servant in his unimaginable habitat back there, among the family members who have themselves scarcely traveled more than a few kilometers.

The bodies of the white family are degraded by dirt and countless malicious lacks and, of course, psychological distortions, all so devastating that in the end the wife hears an airplane in the distance and runs toward it, abandoning her family "like a solitary animal at the season when animals neither seek a mate nor take care of the young." *She runs.* That's it. The last line in the book. Between the tone of "You like to have some cup of tea?" and that of "She runs" lies the aesthetic dilemma of the conception.

The Smaleses, the parents at least, are overwhelmed by the vicious deficiencies of the village, and no detail of smell or nonexistent lavatory is spared. On the other hand, the life of the compound is greatly enlivened by the new circumstance, especially by the father's gun and their vehicle, a yellow truck of the kind used for recreational journeys, for camping or hunting. Since the family is not there, at least not in history as we have had it, their sufferings, their reduction, and their many remaining reflexes of authority mingle somewhat uncomfortably with the devices of classical comedy; the maladaptations, misunderstandings, reversal of roles, the low shall be made high and so on.

There is a visit to the tribal chief, a potentate of a lowly kingdom of nothing. His mood gives pause even to the unhappy white "refugees." The chief has no thought of wishing liberation by the black revolutionaries who will dethrone him. Instead, he dreams of guns to counterattack.

> Those people from Soweto. They come here with Russians, those other one from Moçambique, they all want take this county of my nation. Eh? They not our nation. AmaZulu, amaXhosa, ba-Sotho.... I don't know. They were already there by the mine, coming near here. If they coming, the government it's going give me guns.

July appropriates the truck and is learning to drive. "You know I'm turning round already? I'm know how to go back, everything. My friend he's teaching me very nice."

Many scenes are stunning, the physicality of the deprivation is fiercely imagined. The encounters between Maureen Smales and July are viewed with a cold eye. Still, a certain affective dimension is undermined by the situation, the moral fantasy of its terms. A presentness is assumed for an imaginary future, and the village is vivid as an instruction to the whites as they slip into the destitute pit of black life. Their degradation—is it deserved?—is one thing, and yet one is drawn helplessly toward the magnet of the grotesque amusement their presence in the village represents. They watch a gathering they do not understand. July: "Is not a wedding. —And at the idea of a meeting, he merely laughed. —Sometime we have a party." The extremity of the Smaleses is no match for that.

The riots and disorders in the cities, perhaps a successful over-throw of the white government, are a possibility, one often pre-dicted and feared, and thus the situation does not quite have the distance of desert-island literature. Nor is it meant to. The cities could burn and the whites could flee in their nightclothes, yes. But it is this political immediacy that troubles. It is possible and not yet arrived. The punishment of the Smaleses might be more severe, but in any case there is a question of what we should feel. Their plight is to share the conditions of millions of black people. Are we to feel contempt for faulty adaptation? Or should we not worry too much about the lesson and imagine them just now, at this time, in reality back home with their bedrooms and bathrooms, as July is playing king, as he gloriously plows the gears of the yellow car into a crunching reverse. Something is askew in the vehemence of the moral rebuke to the Smaleses, husband and wife, but nothing, nothing is missing in the brilliance of the imagined detail of their struggle against diminishment.

It might be thought a felicity for a fiction writer to be born in South Africa, that place somewhat colonial and boring and yet, in Nadine Gordimer's writings, so alive with internalized drama that one cannot pass the time of day without meaning something deep and interesting and just there at hand. The warlike alertness in every encounter, the Balkan unsteadiness of Indian, black, Afrikaner, English, European. The psychodrama in the kitchen. But, of course, she has created this world on the pages of her eight novels and seven collections of short stories, and it is one of the major artistic achievements of our time. She meets the challenges of literature, the challenges of language, form, and of an endlessly restless and acute imagination and also the challenge of a great ambition. If these confront South Africa, she has created that too.

There is always the knowledge—how things grow and are harvested, what it is to be a hotel-keeper, how, exactly, a power station is blown up, what the Indian shops and the bars are like, every passage in the city and the country, what it means to be a daughter of the shift-boss at the mine, a soldier, a black girl discovered with a white man. And sex, for this is an eroticized world.

Nadine Gordimer is a liberal intellectual, and you will find the accents and ironies that mind will produce when it re-creates dialogues and shifts of perception and crannies of fear and withdrawal. And nature and the land, the gorgeousness of the description, not necessarily to be united with such great sophistication. Sometimes she seems to find everything is tragically occupied and violated and that even the great animals, the baboon and the lion, are displaced. "A Lion on the Freeway" is only four pages. The sound of the creature: "Roar is not the word." She imagines the lion, "that groan straining, the rut of freedom bending the bars of the cage, he's delivered himself of it, it's as close as if he's out on the freeway now, bewildered, finding his way, turning his splendid head at last to claim what he's never seen, the country where he's king." What he's never seen, the country where he's king.

At the end of "Something Out There":

> The mine-working where Eddie and Vusi [the saboteurs] hid, that Charles identified as belonging to the turn of the 19th century, is in fact far, far older.... Because before the gold rush prospectors of the 1890s, centuries before time was measured, here, in such units, there was an ancient mine-working out there, and metals precious to men were discovered, dug and smelted, for themselves, by black men.

Nadine Gordimer's work is a vast discourse on everything the vast scene provides, the scene itself a landscape created by a majestic imagination.

(1984)

ABOUT THE AUTHOR

ELIZABETH HARDWICK is the author of three previous collections of literary essays, *Bartleby in Manhattan, A View of My Own,* and *Seduction and Betrayal,* which was nominated for the National Book Award. Her novels are *The Ghostly Lover, The Simple Truth,* and *Sleepless Nights,* which was nominated for the National Book Critics Circle Award. Among her honors are the Gold Medal for Belles-Lettres and Criticism awarded by the American Academy of Arts and Letters and a Citation for Lifetime Achievement awarded by the National Book Critics Circle.

ABOUT THE TYPE

The text of this book was set in Janson, a misnamed typeface designed in about 1690 by Nicholas Kis, a Hungarian in Amsterdam. In 1919 the matrices became the property of the Stempel Foundry in Frankfurt. It is an old-style book face of excellent clarity and sharpness. Janson serifs are concave and splayed; the contrast between thick and thin strokes is marked.